MUSINGS

of a

HISTORY TEACHER

*Where America came from
and where it is going*

KEN GROSSMAN

D1468981

ISBN: 979-8-68036-999-9

DEDICATION

*Thanks to my wife, Joan, for her constant love and support,
and to my very talented grandchildren, Julia and Sammy, for helping
to navigate this process.*

PRAISE

Ken Grossman's 'Musings of a History Teacher' is based on his comprehensive study of the important modern literature on the past and future of American Democracy. He has synthesized his studies for teaching courses on the subject in a way that is sprightly written and fascinating. It can be read with great profit and enjoyment by readers of all ages.

Jack B. Weinstein, Professor of Law, Columbia Law School and elsewhere. Author of treatises, articles and books on litigation and history of American law.

PREFACE

The purpose of this book is to view the events of today through the lens of history and to seek out comparable moments in our past that give a sense of continuity. Or conversely, identify events that have no antecedents and therefore require further exploration.

Will today's events become the stories of tomorrow and be part of a long history that charts a particular course? Or will events of today be seen as outliers...stories that chart a different course, whether temporary or permanent.

That deviance is not necessarily a bad thing. A different course may prove to be the right direction for the future. Chances are, however, that a vastly different course, with little in common with our past, may well represent an aberrant moment from which we will hopefully recover and continue our journey toward a 'more perfect Union'.

As I tell my students, events may change over time, but human nature remains the same...to stamp these events with the hallmarks of either our better or lesser angels.

Which aspects of our character will be imposed on these events is in large measure determined by the leaders we have placed in office (hopefully, with our votes). Naturally, there will be opposition on both sides of various issues that will come to the fore. The battle may be tough, even mean spirited on occasion, as each side fights for what is perceives to be the 'soul of America'.

That gets us back to the premise of this book. If we know our past history, and when we have been in similar situations, we can perhaps make a more informed decision as to where our future lies.

The greatest danger to our democracy is not those false gods who seek to lure us into making bad decisions. It is our lack of understanding and appreciation for our best moments that will inspire us toward a brighter and more hopeful future.

Yes, knowledge is power! And in a democracy, it is not the knowledge that the privileged may possess. It is the knowledge that any of us can access if we take the time to read, to listen and to reason, rather than rely on sound bites that seek to distort and prey on ignorance.

I have divided these essays according to various themes that have played a part in our history. Hopefully, these musings will help to explain those moments of success or of failure, especially when placed in the context of specific times and midst all the unique qualities that define the American character.

TABLE OF CONTENTS

CONSTITUTIONAL ISSUES

Much of the content throughout these 'musings' involve the American Constitution, a unique document in the history of all mankind.

While it may not be as visual as the Statue of Liberty for those coming to our shores, it will be even more impactful on their lives.... as it is on ours.

But this document's words are not necessarily a given. They are only brought to fruition through the actions of our government officials, our legislature, our courts... and, yes, 'We the People'... those opening words of this exalted Constitution.

For this is a living document. Its beating heart requires constant attention and nurturing by all these various parties. We may from time to time breach its norms and ignore various telling phrases, with the hope that these 'slights' will be remedied.

But if these omissions continue and are left unattended, we may be at risk of losing it. The loss may not be noticed at first. But slowly it will dawn on us that the constitutional norms we have taken for granted are no longer there. And we are suddenly living in a different universe... with our liberties in jeopardy. If so, it may well be too late to restore its luster, unless through another American Revolution.

George Washington

PRELUDE TO THE CONSTITUTION

INTRODUCTION

The story leading up to the Constitution Convention in 1787, is in itself one of surprises and high drama. There were other founding documents that preceded it, some of which have continued to be revered, and others dismissed.

Those were the times when a few men lit the flame and began a conversation that would lead to the American Revolution. They were all well read and aware of the promise of the so-called Enlightenment...a philosophical movement that believed in man's ability to govern himself and tame his baser instincts.

It was also a time when many still accepted the taxes being levied by the British to pay for their investments in the colonies, including men like Benjamin Franklin and George Washington.

For breaking with the British was no easy task. There were many who doubted the wisdom of this, often from well-to-do families. They were known as Tories, and would eventually set sail for England in great numbers during the war.

This included Benjamin Franklin's son, William, as well as the famous Benedict Arnold, who felt under-appreciated by Washington and others for his daunting military skills.

ENTER JOHN ADAMS

By contrast, there were others, more far-sighted, who saw early on the need to separate from the Mother Country. They included a Harvard-educated Boston attorney from a well-to-do Puritan family named John Adams.

He, practically single handedly, encouraged others to see the need for separation with stirring words that no one else seemed able to speak so eloquently. For that reason, he was to be known as the 'Atlas of the American Revolution', an appellation that has since been replaced by the image of a fairly lackluster President.

It was Adams who suggested writing some sort of document to bind the colonies together, if and when they faced the wrath of the British.

Benjamin Franklin was the first to suggest a unified front, even if we remained under British control. He even put a cartoon of sorts in his Philadelphia newspaper, showing a snake cut into pieces with the caption, 'Unite or die!'.

The document that finally emerged from that first Continental Congress in 1774 was known as the Articles of Confederation. It reflected many of the rivalries among the colonies, none of which wanted to give up its autonomy to some dubious alliance.

Fortunately, however, these colonies agreed to name Robert Morris as the Superintendent of Finance under the Articles. He certainly had the qualifications as the richest man in the colonies, someone who speculated in huge swaths of real estate and had cornered the market in selling cotton to France.

Morris was also the only man with enough money to lend to a bankrupt government at several critical moments during the Revolution, thanks to his deep friendship with Washington, whom he revered.

THE SECOND CONTINENTAL CONGRESS

By the time the Second Continental Congress met in Philadelphia, the situation with the British had deteriorated further, making it considerably easier for John Adams to gain allies for his more aggressive point of view.

It was suggested that he put his obvious gifts to good use and write a document listing all the ills perpetrated on the colonies by the British. But Adams thought he had better things to do. And so he assigned that task to the tall, soft-spoken Virginian who'd arrived in a green phaeton along with his slave, Jupiter. After all, the soft-spoken Tom Jefferson seemed to have little enough to do; and he did have a reputation as a fluid writer, based on the documents he had written for the Virginia legislature.

Jefferson took the task seriously, writing and editing over the next two weeks, before submitting what he felt was a finished document. Although a slaveholder, he still had mixed feelings about his region's economic system. He therefore chose his words carefully, substituting the word 'happiness' for 'property' in one particular clause, not wanting slaveholders to feel further emboldened. It now

5

read as granting 'life, liberty and the pursuit of happiness' to all citizens.

Adams and his committee reviewed Jefferson's handiwork, which was to be labeled 'The Declaration of Independence'. They were pleased with much of it, recognizing many phrases that echoed the noble words of the philosophers of the Enlightenment. But they felt that Jefferson had gone on far too long in his accusations of a multitude of wrongs perpetrated by the British ... particularly the King of England, whom Jefferson now blamed for bringing slavery to our shores.

Most of these words were eliminated from the Declaration, and Jefferson was seen licking his wounds for several days. Nevertheless, he seemed pleased when it was formally adopted on July 6, 1776. And with that, the break with England was complete.

By then, George Washington had been unanimously selected, again with Adam's blessing, as Commander-in-Chief to lead us into battle. It was a role he had been destined to play from his earliest days. He alone had earned a fine reputation from the time of the French and Indian Wars, where he had displayed great valor.

Now, he would depart for Boston to take charge of the American forces gathered there from all the various states.

HAMILTON AND MADISON

After a gratifying victory at Dorchester Heights, the battle moved to New York, where a British armada was poised to launch a major attack and end the rebellion.

American troops were already manning the barricades down at the Battery in lower Manhattan. They included a young man from Columbia College, leading a brigade of fellow students and taking control of British cannons. A local general took note of his actions and was impressed, recommending that he join Washington's staff.

And with that, young Alexander Hamilton entered the annals of American history. He quickly became an indispensable aide-de-camp to Washington, drafting many of his orders and constantly writing to the Continental Congress for additional funds to pursue the war.

He even wrote a thirty-one page memorandum to Superintendent Morris, suggesting the ways in which a financially sound government should be structured. (It is on the basis of this paper that Morris later insisted that Hamilton be our first Secretary of the Treasury.)

Eventually, Hamilton, still longing for military glory, finally got a chance to play a major role in the victory at Yorktown. With the war finally at an end, he was selected to attend meetings of the Continental Congress, where he worked with young James Madison, another well-to-do Virginian who had served with distinction in his state's legislature.

Both Hamilton and Madison met again at a conference in Annapolis to review riparian rights and other issues currently impeding trade among the various states. They shared their increasing frustrations regarding the current system of government and its inability to effectively knit the country together.

With this in mind, they put together a plan to call for a meeting in Philadelphia the following year to address the defects in the Articles of Confederation.

ENTER WASHINGTON

However, both knew that such an improvement could only be successful if they enlisted the support of the most esteemed individual in the country, General Washington...who had retired to Mount Vernon to tend to the needs of his plantation. While Washington readily agreed with the need to create an effective, functioning government, he expressed his reluctance to attend this meeting and risk his prestige.

With that, Madison and Hamilton got to work to gain Washington's confidence. Both soon realized that revising the Articles of Confederation would not do the job properly. Instead, a new document would be required to lay out the architecture for a completely new form of government.

WRITING THE OUTLINE FOR A CONSTITUTION

For the moment, they shared this viewpoint only with Washington, who had complete confidence in their guiding the process. Nevertheless, both men had no illusions when it came to dealing with the concerns of those highly competent delegates who held a host of contrary views.

Madison, slight in stature but fiercely determined, worked day and night at his family home in Montpelier. He and Hamilton envisioned a government composed of three co-equal branches, working to balance each other like a finely tuned instrument.

Madison consulted with his fellow Virginian, Thomas Jefferson, who was currently serving as our Ambassador to France. Jefferson, also possessed of a voracious intellect, expressed his concerns with a large federal government colluding with bankers to deny the rights of a southern plantation economy.

And Adams, another important voice currently abroad in search of funds to keep the government running, stressed the need to guard against those baser instincts of man and his tendency to allow passion to rule their judgment.

Madison and Hamilton as well had differing points of view. Hamilton was admiring of the British form of government, including the workings of Parliament. Even the role of a King and his lifetime tenure impressed him. On the other hand, Madison was more of a republican, admiring those governments of the Greek city-states of ancient times.

A DAUNTING TASK

But both men knew that, even if this Convention, now planned to begin in the summer of 1787, were successful in hammering out an agreement, it would still require the approval of at least three-quarters of the states.

Hamilton was already contemplating a series of essays that he and Madison would be required to write in order to get the document ratified. These will have to lay out in great detail the reasoning behind the various phrases to be drafted into this new Constitution.

Both knew that only this would satisfy the needs of those attending the ratifying conventions, as well as those reviewing this document in future generations. (His judgment has since been redeemed in the eyes of history. Those essays, known as the Federalist Papers, have been cited frequently by the Supreme Court.)

By the Spring of 1787, fifty-five representatives from all the various states had accepted the invitation to meet in Philadelphia to amend the Articles of Confederation. Washington as well had agreed to preside over this conference and lend his prestige. And now, Doctor Franklin had accepted an invitation, having recently returned from Europe.

Both he and Washington would be sitting together on a dais, presiding over the convention without participating in the daily discussions. However, the clever Doctor Franklin had agreed to have Washington and a select few, including Madison and Hamilton, to his home to discuss the day's events and chart their next moves.

Still, Washington had his doubts that this convention would succeed, particularly when the delegates learned that they will be crafting an entirely new Constitution. He accordingly accepted an invitation from the Order of Cincinnatus that will be holding a meeting in Philadelphia around the same time. If this attempt at writing a Constitution were to fail, he would salvage his reputation and plan for another conference. For he knew that without this document, there could be no lasting democracy.

Frederick Douglass

CONCEIVED IN RACISM

CONFLICTED FROM THE START

There were many issues that required compromise to prevent the Constitution Convention ending in failure. Those leaving Philadelphia in the autumn of 1787 knew well that the document was flawed in many ways, with issues to be dealt with by future generations as new problems arose.

Some might require an amendment to clarify a particular point. But others would have to be confronted directly if we were to work toward a 'more perfect Union'. Paramount would be righting the wrongs of a tortured past on the issue of race.

From our earliest days, there were few who doubted the evils of slavery.

Jefferson preferred to blame the King of England for foisting it on the colonies and continued to rail against it in the Virginia House of Burgesses. Many thought (and hoped) it would simply die out as an inefficient economic system. But then the cotton gin made it more profitable and the Louisiana Purchase added the rich soil of those states adjacent to the Mississippi delta, perfect for planting cotton.

The question of how to end slavery became more difficult when the economy of the South was booming and King Cotton was our crop most desired by the rest of the world.

Many of our most revered founding fathers were certainly conflicted on the subject, continually dealing with it in both their public and private lives. None ever thought it would be possible to have the races intermingle or even live side by side. It was assumed that intellectual inferiority and a different chemical make up would doom the chances of that. Many thought it would be far more compassionate to give those Negroes a place of their own outside the country to live out their lives in peace.

But the solution remained for some day in the distant future. What came to be called that 'peculiar institution' was for now simply an accepted way of life for both master and slave.

FOUNDING FATHERS

Ironically, those from the South attending the Constitutional Convention were often accompanied by those favored house slaves, who served as much more than a simple valet.

John Marshall brought along his friend and constant companion, Robin Spurlock, a gift from the time he married Polly Ambler, the daughter of a prominent Virginian. Spurlock was already noted among his community as the best dressed and most literate among them, thanks to the fine role model that Marshall provided.

When Marshall's wife's fragile health deteriorated, Spurlock took over running the household and tending to the Marshall's strapping young boys. There were very few family secrets that escaped the ears and eyes of Robin Spurlock. For that matter, he probably knew Marshall's thoughts better than most when it came to the politics of the day.

Washington as well treated his house slave, Billy Lee, as more of a companion when he attended the Convention in Philadelphia. Lee had been by his side throughout the war, including those dark days at Valley Forge. An excellent horseman, he was also his master's favorite riding companion at Mount Vernon.

Washington was perhaps the most enlightened of those founding fathers. Even when Billy Lee was crippled, the result of too many falls when inebriated, Washington included him in his staff in New York when he assumed the presidency.

In December of 1799, Washington, already retired for the past three years, developed a throat infection after riding in a sudden snowstorm. A simple tracheotomy would have saved his life, but the doctor decided to bleed him far too many times instead. Billy Lee was holding his hand when he died. And upon his death, Washington was the only founding father to arrange for the freeing of his slaves.

These relationships were not unusual for many from the South attending the Convention. Still, when it came to writing the Constitution, it was not difficult for any of these delegates to consider slaves as three-fifths of a person.

THE SCHISM BEGINS

The battle between North and South over slavery begins to harden in the 1830's, when slave rebellions caused a sense of panic in the South, blaming them on those troublesome abolitionists in the North. Many in the North agree with this point of view. Young Abe Lincoln makes his debut on the national stage, criticizing northern men in Illinois for killing a man simply for printing his abolitionist views in his newspaper in Alton.

There are many who are less interested in freeing the slaves than working out some sort of compromise. That includes members of the Whig Party, who finally agreed to empower the federal government to enforce the Fugitive Slave Act, an obligation again written into the Constitution by those conflicted founding fathers.

This Act already protects the institution mandated in the three-fifths clause. But now, it is turned into a more draconian measure ... having northern government officials empowered to help hunt down those runaway slaves and return them to southern slaveholders, without including the right to defend themselves in court.

The schism between North and South grows wider. The South still controls Congress, thanks to the three-fifth clause inflating its representation in the House. It uses that power to pass the 'gag rule', outlawing any debate in Congress when it came to slavery. John Quincy Adams, the only President to launch a second career as a congressman, challenges the South relentlessly, even facing censure for his dramatic words. Nevertheless, he stands firm in his assault on that 'peculiar institution' until the gag rule is finally reversed in 1844.

While the Democrats remain the party of white supremacy and southern sympathies, the Whigs fracture into two wings of the party ... the Conscience Whigs and the Cotton Whigs. The former are adamantly anti-slavery, but the latter is more pragmatic, needing the South's cotton to feed those New England mills weaving it into the cloth that clothed the nation. Still, the art of compromise is inappropriate for the growing number who views slavery as immoral, thanks to the words of men like Abraham Lincoln.

ENTER LINCOLN

The Whig Party disintegrates as a result, ultimately replaced in 1856 by the anti-slavery Republican Party. And in 1860, the Party takes a chance on Lincoln, a simple country lawyer from the plains of Illinois. Not at all well known in the East, he impresses the men of influence with his debut in New York at Cooper Union, where he is uncommonly informed and articulate on the issue of slavery without sounding mean-spirited.

Yet, Lincoln too is willing to make compromises, accepting the given wisdom as to the Negroes' inability to live with the white community. He also believes that colonization is the preferred solution, perhaps somewhere in the Caribbean or on the west coast of Africa.

If not for the South's feeling besieged and provoking war with cannons firing on Fort Sumter, it is hard to say if Lincoln's views would have evolved on slavery.

Fortunately Lincoln has the capacity to grow. He listens to men like Frederick Douglass who convince him that colonization is not the answer for his people. When the South continues to 'out-general' the North, Lincoln cleverly uses his powers as commander-in-chief to strip the South of that vital asset that kept their economy humming, namely slavery.

Still, he and Douglass realize this is just the start, since he has used his wartime powers to write the Emancipation Proclamation and these would expire once the war is over.

RECONSTRUCTION

Douglass, the most elevated of men in the black community, is watching Lincoln carefully as the war drew to a close. He has already published several best selling versions of his autobiography and gained fame among the intellectuals of the white community.

He speaks at Cooper Union where Lincoln won over the leaders of the Republican Party by adeptly explaining that most of those attending the Constitutional Convention did not favor the expansion of slavery.

Douglass now speaks boldly for permanent freedom for his people, saying, 'No war but an abolition war ... no peace but an abolition peace ... liberty for all, chains for none.' He and Lincoln would only have two conversations before the assassination at Ford's Theater, the last one after Lincoln's second inaugural, urging the nation to bind up its wounds and ascribing guilt to both sides.

Shortly before Lincoln's death, Congress creates the Freedman's Bureau. Douglass, a proud man, sees this as an engine for progress, but yearns to see his people standing on their own, saying, 'The Negro needs justice more than pity, liberty more than old clothes'.

He forgets that others of his race may not possess his special gifts when he spurns Christian charity as patronizing, saying, 'Give us equality before the law and special associations for our benefit may cease' ... as well as, 'With charity we shall be crippled.'

JOHNSON'S BETRAYAL

Now after the death of Lincoln, it will be up to Andrew Johnson to lead the way... with Congress expecting a pliant president, based on his prior words and actions. But instead, he shows himself to be sympathetic to the old regime, returning confiscated land to the planter class. The South now feels emboldened to restore law and order their way.

A disappointed Frederick Douglass launches a crusade to get the black man the right to vote. He says, 'They gave us the bullet to save themselves. They will yet give the ballot to save themselves.' He visits the White House to persuade the President, reminding him of the obligation. 'Lincoln called on the black man to save the

Union...and now they should be given the vote with which to save ourselves.'

He continues to try to appeal to Johnson's sympathies, knowing that he too was once poor man in a rich men's South. He says, 'If poor whites and poor blacks were given the vote, they would unite to achieve the justice denied by the rich.' Johnson is unmoved. He has now thrown his lot in with the planter class.

The South enacts Black Codes, defining 'employment guidelines' for one-sided labor contracts, a new form of indentured servitude enforced by confederate officers roaming the countryside. The Ku Klux Klan is formed by veterans in Tennessee to assume this role and quickly launches additional chapters in all states in the South, garnering great local support from all levels of society.

Sharecropping becomes the economic way of life for a black family, sharing the profits for a particular crop or season. Even when this is challenged, with blacks barred from serving in juries, there is little chance of a fair verdict.

CONGRESS FIGHTS BACK

Feeling betrayed by the President, Congress fights back, angered by the realization that the South has just gained a huge electoral advantage with emancipation, without changing to a free labor system.

Nevertheless, blacks begin to make progress as Federal officials join with the Freedman's Bureau to prosecute violations of a Civil Rights Bill that takes on the Black Codes. It defines all citizens as entitled to 'the full and equal benefit of all laws regarding person and property.' This is followed by the 14th Amendment, which codifies these rights.

The Republicans in the Senate impose military rule over the South, allowing the North to prosecute violations in federal court. A Final Reconstruction Act divides the South's eleven states into five military districts under commanders selected by Grant from his military team, and empowered to protect life and property.

A Second Reconstruction Act expands district commanders' authority over election procedures to register blacks, with Johnson again fighting back.

The Radicals tire of Johnson's intransigence and commence impeachment proceedings that fail to pass by one vote.

Republican coalitions, including local blacks and carpetbaggers from the North, are now large enough to hold state conventions and adopt platforms for sweeping change. These include integrated schools, universal access to public facilities, tax policies to break up planter monopolies in landholding ... as well as abolishing discriminatory laws regarding corporal punishment, imprisonment for debt and seizing homesteads to pay off debt.

For the moment, blacks make additional gains, holding positions on city councils and minor political office, enabling them to distribute patronage to their brethren.

THE SOUTH FIGHTS BACK

Democrats are already emboldened and feeling besieged. They vow to fight back and destroy those fraudulent state constitutions once Northern bayonets are removed. Taxpayer Conventions are organized to challenge reckless spending and higher taxes imposed by a landless class. They demand that men of property be restored to positions of power.

With the northern economy already booming, some Republicans are now willing to limit access to land for blacks, knowing that northern investment to rebuild the economy will be jeopardized without guaranteeing the sanctity of property for the planter class. Southern States pass 'railroad aid bills' to attract northern capital as Democrats initiate what is called the 'New Departure'. This includes controlling the press and appealing to white supremacists as well as enacting a poll tax and residency requirements to limit voting rights.

KKK chapters are already spreading throughout the South, acting as an arm of the Democratic Party in every state. Attacks on blacks turn into bloodbaths, called a 'negro chase'. The Colfax Massacre in Louisiana on Easter Sunday leaves almost three hundred dead. Although the numbers are still in their favor to continue governing, Republican governors in the South are already intimidated and reluctant to call out state militias, fearing an interracial war.

GRANT AS PRESIDENT

Grant is elected president in 1868. He pushes to redeem the Lincoln legacy, calling for ratification of the 15th Amendment to ensure the vote to blacks in his inaugural address. But northern industry needs the coal and iron ore from the South for its steel mills.

Even Frederick Douglass is used for purposes that do not benefit his people when he is selected as president of the Freedman's Bank in Washington. By then, the bank has been mismanaged and is already insolvent. When an economic downturn hits the country and the bank fails, Douglass is made to look like another example of the black man's inability to make it in a white man's world.

For that matter, many now question whether blacks can take control of their own destiny. Even the Supreme Court seeks to limit the scope if the 14th Amendment, citing a distinction between rights granted by the state versus 'attributes of national citizenship' granted by the federal government. This includes jurisdictional questions over crimes against blacks, overturning sentences and giving the KKK the green light to continue acts of terror.

The same distinction eviscerates the Civil Rights Bill, giving states and property owners the right to discriminate in public accommodations. Reconstruction continues to lose support when regional commanders overreact with military intervention in Louisiana. From now on, Republicans will only 'wave the bloody shirt' and show concern for blacks at election time.

THE END OF RECONSTRUCTION

By 1874, we have entered the Gilded Age where business controls the national agenda. The North is weary of conflict as the South regains control of two-thirds of the state governments. The process accelerates in 1876 when Rutherford B. Hays loses the popular vote, but wins in the Electoral College thanks to a political deal with several southern states. In the process, northern business interests press Hayes to agree to leave southern 'Redeemers' free to impose Home Rule. Once again, Frederick Douglass is offered another position, this time in government as marshal of the District of Columbia, to keep him loyal to the Republican Party.

President Hayes now honors that bargain and orders federal troops surrounding state houses to return to their barracks, allowing white supremacists to take over. The activist state is dismantled and blacks are stripped of even minimal property rights. Sharecropping turns them into laborers rather than a partner with property rights.

With his goals reduced as well as his vision for a better future, Douglass blames his people for their lack of progress, saying, 'We must not talk of equality until we can do what the white peoples can do.... If twenty years from now the colored race has not advanced beyond the point where it was when emancipated, it is a doomed race.' Still, he tries to make the best of the situation, saying 'Suffering and hardships made the Saxons strong and suffering and hardship will make the Anglo/African strong.'

Instead of integrating with whites as he had hoped, blacks will now withdraw from southern life and form communities of their own. Over the next decades, Frederick Douglass will receive other appointments for remaining loyal to the Republican Party and tolerating its back-sliding on black rights. This will include his appointment as Minister to Haiti. But again, he gets caught in a web of internal party discord and submits his resignation, with the press saying that a black man cannot fairly represent a black country.

Still, he sees the irony of the black man's plight, including his, when he says, 'The Negro meets no resistance on a downward course.

It is only when he rises in wealth, intelligence and manly character that he brings upon himself the heavy hand of persecution.

THE GREAT MIGRATION

The only alternative for many is to flee the South and seek a new life in the North, a movement that would be known as The Great Migration. Even then Negroes face northern unions, fearful of blacks working for lower wages and taking jobs. Segregation is replaced with overt discrimination in the North in housing, schooling and the right to vote.

The courts mirror the times. The Supreme Court's decision in the Cruickshank Case finds that under the Fourteenth Amendment, the owner of a public accommodation can restrict admission under his property rights and that redress can only be sought in a State Court. The case of Plessy v. Ferguson will follow fifteen years later, approving segregated facilities and schools, as long as they meet the standard of 'separate but equal'.

Shortly before his death, a disappointed Douglass says, 'The Supreme Court has surrendered and converted the Republican Party into one of money rather than a party of morals.'

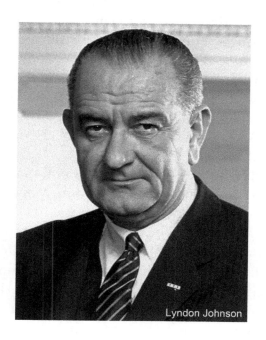

Lyndon Johnson

AN ERA OF REDEMPITION

The Great Depression of 1928 forces the nation to reconsider the underpinnings of a collapsing economy. Like the election of Lincoln at a time of crisis, the election of Franklin Delano Roosevelt in 1932 is a watershed event. FDR discards old economic theories as his Administration creates work opportunities through a host of government programs. Thanks to the constant efforts of his far-sighted wife, Eleanor, this includes opportunities for black workers, despite the pushback from various vested interests.

Eleanor supports fair housing and workers' rights, thanks to her relationship with important labor leaders like the UAW's Walter Reuther. This effort continues under Harry Truman, a man from Missouri who overcomes his native bias and insists that all branches of the military integrate. Still, the 14th Amendment mandating 'equal protection under the law' is in large part disregarded in daily life and by the courts. That is, until the fortuitous appointment of Earl Warren as Chief Justice of the Supreme Court in 1953.

President Dwight D. Eisenhower, the man who launched the Normandy invasion and defeated the Nazis, is the first Republican to reach the presidency in twenty years. A confirmed centrist, he believes in gradual rather than precipitous change in society, as well as in court decisions.

He owes Warren, formerly the Governor of California, a favor for helping him win the Republican nomination. Warren insists on an appointment to the Supreme Court upon the first vacancy. It is his good fortune, and ours, that the first vacancy is that of Chief Justice.

Warren follows the path of John Marshall, building a close relationship with all the other justices and slowly persuading them to join him in a series of groundbreaking unanimous decisions. This includes Brown v. Board of Education, rejecting the doctrine of 'separate but equal' and integrating public schools across the nation, especially those in the South.

Eisenhower does not favor this decision, but he feels duty bound to enforce it and uphold the law of the land. When the South threatens to rebel, he sends federal troops to Little Rock to confront state actions to the contrary.

CIVIL RIGHTS LEGISLATION AT LAST

In 1960, John F. Kennedy is elected president, the first to be born in the Twentieth Century. By now, new leadership has emerged in a black community sensing that the door has been opened for change. This includes Martin Luther King Jr. He had already come to prominence as the head of the Montgomery Bus Boycott, triggered by the refusal of Rosa Parks to give up her seat to a white man. That battle had been won, but there was more to do.

King is a new prophet for the black community. He follows in the footsteps of his father as well as the foremost civil rights activist of another day, CL Franklin, the most influential African American preacher through the '40's and '50's. His message of non-violence stresses that freedom comes with responsibility and liberation with self-restraint. This is also the twin message of America, the American Revolution that leads to the discipline of following the strictures of the Constitution.

In August of 1963 the March on Washington, the largest gathering to date, presses for Civil Rights legislation in Congress. The highlight is King's late afternoon address, when he says that America is a broken promised land, defaulting on those promises. President Kennedy has already reached out to Dr. King to discuss a legislative agenda before he is assassinated in Dallas on November 22, 1963. The mantle of the presidency falls on the shoulders of Vice President, Lyndon Baines Johnson, a Texan with a progressive record, beginning in the era of FDR and the New Deal.

Johnson stands before a joint session of Congress and honors the fallen JFK, saying, 'All I have, I would have given gladly not to be standing here today'.

As a son of the South, he knows only too well the history of racism that has kept blacks from realizing rights, written but never realized in the Thirteenth, Fourteenth and Fifteen Amendments. Now as President and representing all the people, something deep inside this political genius tells him that his legacy requires bold action, even if it is calculated to lose the South as a Democratic stronghold.

He goes to work, knowing he will need at least fifty Republicans to join Democrats to attain cloture and avoid the usual filibuster, a tactic that Southern politicians have used for decades to close down an uncomfortable conversation.

He gets Minority Leader, Everett Dirksen, on board by appealing to his idealism as a man from Illinois, the land of Lincoln, even if this requires a few additional political favors. When the cloture vote is due, he even has a terminally ill Senator from California wheeled in to assure its passage.

On February 20, 1964, less than three months after the assassination, the House passes the strongest Civil Rights Bill since Reconstruction. He signs the bill at the White House on July 2, 1964, and he gives the first signing pen to Dirksen.

FDR had the New Deal and now LBJ is building what will be called, 'The Great Society', an extension of the Bill of Rights, giving every American the ability to reach his full potential. With the momentum and the votes in place to finish the work and seal his legacy, Lyndon Johnson adds legislation that builds on the work of FDR, including:

1. A war on poverty, concentrating on inner cities and overlooked rural areas.

2. Medicare for the elderly, the only government mandated health care up to that date.

3. A job training act, including public works for distressed communities.

4. A Voting Rights Act to eliminate all exclusionary and punitive tests imposed primarily on African Americans to suppress rights granted under the Fifteenth Amendment.

With his popularity at an all-time high, Johnson goes before Congress to deliver a televised message. His words are prophetic. 'There is no Negro problem. There is no southern problem. There is only an American problem. It is all of us who must overcome the crippling legacy of bigotry.'

To galvanize the nation and build support, Martin Luther King and other civil rights leaders stage a march from Selma to Montgomery, Alabama. The South remains adamant that their way of life will survive this assault by the Party they have supported since the days of Jackson. When marchers reach the Edmund Pettus Bridge, they are assaulted by state troopers and attack dogs, a moment watched in horror on television by millions.

REGRESSING ON CIVIL RIGHTS

But there will be more backsliding, as there was during Reconstruction with political parties valuing votes above a moral reckoning. Between 1972 and 1992, with Republicans controlling the presidency, except for the brief Carter years, little is accomplished in the way of expanding and enforcing civil rights legislation.

The Reagan years celebrate the mastery of the marketplace and 'trickle down' economics...dismissing government programs as intrusive giveaways.

This is instead a time of stagnating wages for the entire middle class and growing income inequity. Programs for the disadvantaged are painted as gifts for unworthy citizens while taxes are cut for the wealthy. The working class, blacks included, are told that scarce government funds require cuts in an already meager safety net.

On balance, the urban black community, where most reside, will be constantly dismissed as a drain on society...an outlook that will eventually pervade the thinking of many, including the police.

AFFIRMATIVE ACTION

Nevertheless, one hopeful note of the times includes the benefits of racial diversity that is accomplished under the Education Amendments to the Civil Rights Act under Title lX. Under the banner of 'affirmative action', this has encouraged business to make a good faith effort to hire women and racial minorities, evolving into a more proactive program that gives preference over similarly qualified candidates.

There is a significant portion of the population that oppose this concept as establishing quotas, rather than being color blind and giving everyone the same rights under the 14th Amendment. Ironically, this includes the one black member of the Supreme Court, Clarence Thomas. In some ways, his belief that such programs imply weakness and inferiority resemble words spoken by Frederick Douglass. For he too saw his own unique life story as somehow typical of what other blacks could achieve on their own.

Yet, under this process, the rate of minority employment in businesses and institutions has grown considerably. Even the National Association of Manufacturers has lobbied to leave it in place for a number of reasons. The military as well has joined in cases arguing its constitutional validity, saying that it is needed to develop capable minority candidates in a military that was increasingly racially diverse.

Its survival seems to depend on a Supreme Court that has moved increasingly to the Right. For the Court has never come up with a workable standard to establish an urgent constitutional need or compelling state interest.

On the contrary, the legal standard is still the <u>Bakke Case</u>, decided in 1978, where the Court was conflicted in striking down an affirmative action program as contradicting the Fourteenth Amendment's 'equal protection' clause. However, at the same time the Court recognized the right of a school to determine who will sit in the classroom and upheld the right of any school of higher learning to have a race-conscious standard.

President Obama, noting that the issue would be a lightening rod for a black president if he were to press the case for higher education, chooses instead to focus on improving K-12 access for minorities ... those formative years that are the foundation for higher education.

But as of now, the signs do not look hopeful for the Court to anchor 'affirmative action' to a discernible constitutional standard.

The Court's recent holding in <u>Shelby v. Holder</u>, scuttling portions of the Voting Rights Act as having outlived its usefulness, indicates a proclivity to chip away at civil rights legislation and thereby hinder its effectiveness. If the legacy of Reconstruction teaches us anything, it is that laws may be written but an enforcement process requires that the intent remains clear. One hundred fifty years ago, an entire race was denied its rights embedded in three vital Amendments to the Constitution. When the Courts lose interest, the people do as well.

If this were the case, once again individualism would triumph over what is best for the collective society, a policy that has already corrupted our economy with egregious income inequality and will now do the same regarding racial justice.

CHOICES TO BE MADE

The Obama presidency awakens the racism buried deep in the American experience, especially of those who see the President as representing the onset of the multicultural society they most fear.

The Trump presidency, which follows, is in large part a result of those fears, as blue-collar workers in the Rust Belt abandon their Democratic roots. A President who winks at racism and gives a nod to white supremacists turns back the clock on progress in race relations. Thriving in the chaos he creates, rather than offering viable solutions, he seeks to shred belief in our institutions and Constitutional norms. And most at risk are the most vulnerable, who see blacks as enemies rather than allies in trying to restore democratic norms.

How this will end is still a story yet to unfold. But it may be that society has been evolving, under the radar, so to speak. The Obama years may have changed perceptions as to what constitutes a brighter future, especially when compared with the venality and gross incompetence of the Trump presidency.

Suddenly, issues like expanding gay rights have the support of a majority of Americans. As does national outrage at the excessive use of force by police within black communities, often leading to needless deaths. Movements like 'Black Lives Matter', once perceived as extremist, have the support of average Americans. Is this to be a passing phase or could competence and decency seem more important than the party affiliations that have torn us apart for far too long?

We may once again be working toward a more perfect and inclusive Union in finally correcting that fatal flaw in our Constitution.

John Marshall

VITAL PHRASES IN THE CONSTITUTION

OVERVIEW

The Constitution is the work of those fifty-five delegates who attended that convention in Philadelphia in the summer of 1787. However, it was John Marshall, our most revered Chief Justice, who gave it life through three decades of landmark decisions.

The words of the Constitution must never be taken for granted or easily glossed over. They are prophetic in their meaning, intended to be definitive in some respects and ambiguous in others. For this was seen as an ever-evolving document, written at a time when the nation was barely out of the 'womb'. It was based on the philosophy of The Enlightenment, a time of a hopefulness and belief in man's ability to govern himself, despite those baser instincts that might surface at any given moment.

In analyzing the precise language of the Constitution, we should start with the opening line.

'We the People of the United States, in order to form a more perfect Union.'

This phrase alone is monumental in guiding us toward that more perfect Union.

Those who took issue, might have preferred that it read 'We the States'. For this would have elevated the 'states rights' argument that led to the Civil War. But the fact that the People...all the people...have given their blessing in establishing this Constitution says otherwise.

In fact, this very point was argued vociferously in many of the state ratification conventions that followed the writing of the document. That argument would have elevated the rights of individual states as co-equal with, or perhaps even above, that of the Union being created under the Constitution.

But that view would have been preposterous, not only according to the words enshrined in this document, but also as to the history leading up to the writing of the Constitution. For this document was actually intended to replace the ineffective Articles of Confederation, which gave each state far too many rights, including an absolute veto power regarding any legislation.

This flawed document had so stymied enacting proper legislation that men like Washington often blamed it for many of the ills in fighting the Revolution...including the inability to properly clothe, arm and pay the troops.

Another phrase at the opening of the Constitution bears noting.

'To secure the Blessings of Liberty to ourselves and our Posterity'

The question can certainly be raised as to what those 'blessings' included. Were they merely 'freedoms to' enjoy all those rights and privileges so long denied?

Or was it 'freedom from' a life of want and deprivation. This might include the right to live a good and decent life that guaranteed the right to the fruits of one's labor... as well as future benefits such as social security and, yes, even healthcare as a right rather than a privilege!

Those definitions of 'Blessings of Liberty' are all valid considerations. It is only the ethos of the times as to the interpretation one wants to impose on these words.

The first three Articles in the Constitution lay out the powers and duties of the three co-equal branches of government.

ARTICLE I AND THE LEGISLATURE

Article 1 is the longest and most detailed among the three, highlighting the legislative branch's exalted standing in the eyes of the founders...that deliberative body that would carve out the laws to govern a rapidly expanding population and landmass.... a daunting task that no other country had dared to attempt without a king (or some other 'despot') to oversee the process.

Section 1:
This lays out the various hallmarks of a bicameral legislature...meaning, in our case, the House and the Senate.

The House is to apportion its members according to the population of each state. The Senate is to have each state elect two members, regardless of population.

It was widely understood by those fifty-five delegates attending the Constitution Convention in Philadelphia in 1787 that without one body granting equal apportionment, the smaller states would never have ratified this document.

Section 2:
The phrase stating that the 'number of representatives (in the House) shall not exceed one for every thirty thousand' may be telling when it comes to the concept of 'reapportionment' and 'one man one vote'.

These issues have taken on greater meaning in a country with large and growing urban centers versus miles of rural landscape with rapidly diminishing numbers.

And yet, the number of Representatives in the House has been frozen at 435 for decades, despite significant population growth unevenly distributed among the various states.

Another phrase in Section 2 that bears mention, states that...

'The House of Representatives shall choose their Speaker and other Officers; and shall have the sole Power of Impeachment'.

It has not been rare in our history that the Speaker of the House may be the one to challenge presidential authority or what was perceived to be 'overstepping' the bounds of presidential authority.

The most eminent Speaker to do so in prior times was Henry Clay, consistently standing up to President Andrew Jackson's expansive view of the presidency. (Clay was the one to have the President

censured in the Senate back in 1832 for dissolving the constitutionally mandated Bank of the U.S.)

Section 3:
While the House may initiate and vote on the impeachment process,
it is the Senate that has...

**'The sole Power try all Impeachments'...and con-
vict only with the 'Concurrence of two-thirds of the
Members present'.**

This has of course recently played out in the impeachment trial
of Donald Trump for colluding with a foreign power to seek political advantage.... clear grounds for impeachment based on the
founders' fears, noted in the Constitution, of foreign meddling in
our domestic affairs.

The fact that the Republican majority voted almost unanimously
for acquittal is more a sign of 'politics at play' rather than fealty to
the Constitution. (Based on the history of impeachment, this is not
an unusual result.)

Section 8:
Enumerating the powers of Congress. Among the most important
in the eyes of history are...

'The power to lay and collect taxes'

This power was instrumental in asserting federal supremacy over
state courts, another aspect of that ongoing issue of 'states rights'.

In the landmark case of McCullough v. Maryland in 1819, the
Supreme Court denied the state's right to tax a properly mandated
federal institution.

Chief Justice Marshall's words highlight this judicial supremacy:
'The power to tax is the power to destroy'.

'To regulate Commerce…among the several States'

This rather innocuous sounding phrase…. better known as the 'commerce clause'…. has been used numerous times by the Supreme Court to fulfill Alexander Hamilton's vision of an expansive, creditworthy nation.

Our greatest Chief Justice, John Marshall, during his more than three decades on the Court (1801-1836), initiated this process in 1824 in <u>Gibbons v. Ogden</u>, known as 'the emancipation proclamation of commerce'. This case gives free rein to interstate commerce, without the imposition of duties or the deleterious effect of monopolies.

The 'commerce clause' has been widely used in established precedent throughout our history. It is the basis for many Court decisions that have led to the creation of that 'more perfect Union'.

In truth, many of the cases that come before the Court have an effect of one sort or another on interstate commerce. For example, even state legislation to chip away at the right to an abortion, enshrined by the Supreme Court in <u>Roe v. Wade</u>, can affect interstate commerce.

For example, in limiting access to abortion clinics, it forces many women to cross state lines in search of a proper facility…putting an onerous burden on the woman and on the state that affords her that constitutionally mandated right. On those grounds alone, such state laws might well be overturned as inhibiting commerce under the 'commerce clause'.

'To promote the Progress of Science and useful Arts…by securing the exclusive Right to Discoveries'

While this clause is intended to protect proprietary rights, the first six words highlight an interest, enshrined in the Constitution, to 'promote science'.

Perhaps this power should be used today to enact and fund legislation on a host of scientific initiatives that are relevant to our 'national security, including the need to develop 'green technologies' to replace our dependence on fossil fuels and address the challenges of climate change.

In addition, the coronavirus has made us aware of the need for ongoing federally coordinated scientific research to address future pandemics.

'The power to declare War'

This power, granted to Congress, is perhaps the most obvious to have migrated more and more over time to the Chief Executive under his powers as commander-in-chief.

In an age where war can come to our shores instantaneously in a missile attack, there is little if any time for a deliberative body to 'declare war'. Instead, the Congress can only give it a 'rubber stamp' after the fact.

Congress has, from time to time, attempted to reassert its authority, as with the Church Commission in the 1970's. This was initiated to examine obvious wartime failures of judgment ... as in Vietnam or Iraq... and create accountability of various sorts to limit the damage in terms of 'blood and treasure'.

'To provide for calling forth the Militia to execute the Laws of the Union, suppress insurrections and repel Invasions'

The words 'suppress insurrections' are at best a relic from a time when a fragile nation feared disturbances of any sort. Washington as president, personally led troops to suppress what was known as 'The Whisky Rebellion'. History has deemed this an overreaction... something out of character for our first president, always applauded for his good solid judgment.

Today, the word 'insurrection' would need to be something much more significant... something on the scale of a nationwide threat to the safety and security of the Union. The danger lies in the wrong Chief Executive using this vague and poorly defined word to serve his own interests.

'To make all laws which shall be necessary and proper for carrying into Execution the foregoing Powers'

This is known as 'the necessary and proper clause'.... another of those monumental phrases used by our most eminent jurists to fulfill the intrinsic meaning of a Constitution. For this document could only consist of a limited number of words that spoke to the hopefulness of creating that more perfect Union. The 'necessary and proper clause' speaks to the elasticity built into this document to meet the challenges of the future and keep the Constitution relevant to the times.

This clause in effect mandates any legislation or actions by the Chief Executive that are required to fulfill the obligations delegated under the Constitution. Of course, the Supreme Court has the final word as to whether this worthy goal has been accomplished properly.

There is today a judicial pseudo-philosophy called 'originalism' that often seeks to overturn this longstanding judicial precept. In truth, it is nothing more than an attempt to shroud a right wing political movement in a black robe, requiring a jurist to delve into the intentions of those founders at the time of writing the Constitution... and limit the meaning of various phrases. (So much for judicial hubris!)

Section 9:

'No Person holding any Office of Trust... shall accept any...Emolument...of any kind whatever from any foreign state...'

This particular 'emoluments' clause deals with members of Congress. With today's hordes of lobbyists representing vested and powerful interests, it is too bad that the prohibition as to 'accepting gifts' applies only to those from a foreign state. (Perhaps a re-reading behind the intent of this clause is in order.)

Section 10:

No State shall...make any Law...impairing the Obligation of Contracts...'

These words, known as the 'contract clause', were used many times in our earliest years by the Marshall Court to build a vision of a reliable and creditworthy nation.

The decision in <u>Dartmouth v. Woodward</u> in 1819 reaffirms this point. The case involved the state government of New Hampshire's attempt to convert a private college into a state institution. As the college had been established under a corporate charter... and therefore assumed to be a contract of sorts... Chief Justice Marshall denied this state action as a breach of contract law.

He used the case to further explain why a state could not tamper with this contractual obligation, stating that 'corporations are an artificial being and not a state instrument'.

These words, now well-established precedent, should also have been considered by the Court to the recent <u>Citizens United</u> case, focusing on the phrase, 'corporations are an artificial being'.

Instead, the Court elevated the status of corporations to something approaching individuals, deciding that that they were entitled to the right of free speech. This elevation of 'an artificial entity', to be worthy of First Amendment freedoms, represents a gross distortion of our public discourse. It allows faceless corporations free to spend huge sums of money to promote a point of view that is often antithetical to the public good.

And this at a time of declining union membership, when the average working man or woman has no one to give voice to another point of view. One wonders what the Court was thinking...and what John Marshall would have thought.

ARTICLE II AND THE CHIEF EXECUTIVE

Section 1:
This includes many of the particulars that qualify a person to be elected as President of the United States of America. It is the portion noting the 'Oath or Affirmation' before entering this office, that most bears scrutiny.

> **'I do solemnly swear that I will...to the best of my ability preserve, protect and defend the Constitution of the United States.'**

Perhaps the phrase 'to the best of my ability' gives any President a degree of latitude in meeting this standard. However, it should be noted in an amendment of some sort that a pattern of exceeding verifiable constitutional norms should be specifically noted as grounds for impeachment.

This would give greater clarity and more verifiable grounds to a process that is constitutionally mandated under Article l, yet vague enough to allow constitutional malfeasance without a conviction. (The history on impeachments without a guilty verdict further validates the political nature of this process.)

Section 2:

'The president shall be Commander in Chief of the Army and Navy of the United States and of the Militia of the several states.'

This is perhaps the most noteworthy presidential power, enshrining the concept of civilian control over the military.

Those attending the Convention in Philadelphia were comfortable with this delegation of authority, knowing that the exalted Washington would be our first president. However, there is always the concern that those Commander-in-Chief powers may be subject to abuse... particularly by presidents who might be tempted to flex their 'military muscle' to win an election.

Even Lincoln was wont to expand those powers beyond constitutional bounds. The Court ultimately overturned his denial of the right of habeas corpus at the height of the Civil War, fearing that public trials would give voice to those opposing the war.

Section 4:

'The President...shall be removed from Office on Impeachment for, and Conviction of, Treason, Bribery, or other high Crimes and Misdemeanors.'

As noted previously, although there have been numerous grounds, no president has ever been impeached... although Richard Nixon probably would have been if he had not resigned. This tells us that the process is flawed and may need to be rethought.

ARTICLE III AND THE JUDICIARY

Section 1:

This vests judicial power in one Supreme Court and 'such inferior Courts as the Congress may from time to time.... establish'.

It needs to be understood that the Federal Judiciary was by far the weakest and ill-defined branch of government at this point. Its jurisdiction over states was still in question as was its limited appellate role.

Section 2:

Lays out in great detail the various types of cases over whichever judiciary presides.

Section 3:

Establishes the guidelines in determining guilt for Treason.

This section is particularly noteworthy for the Burr Treason Case of 1807. Chief Justice Marshall cites the precise language of the Constitution regarding the need for 'the testimony of two witnesses to the same overt acts' and finds that this has not been accomplished.

He therefore decided for the defendant, despite Aaron Burr's obvious attempt to build an empire within the interior of the country.

But it his using this case to define certain specific norms of presidential behavior that Marshall really shines. For, in this decision, he skewers President Thomas Jefferson, who had initiated this case, for withholding evidence and ignoring court subpoenas and thinking he is 'above the law'.

Marshall thus used this opportunity to exert the Court's moral as well as its judicial authority to set things right. A President has been warned that more may follow if he does not behave according to constitutional norms. (Would we have a Supreme Court today with the mastery to use its standing to set things right!)

Ironically, the most noteworthy power vested in the judiciary is not mentioned at all.

While it was assumed that the Court had the power of 'constitutional review', it was the Marshall Court's unanimous decision in 1803 in the landmark case of <u>Marbury v. Madison</u> that officially enshrines this power within the Court.

Again, this case represents a dazzling display of judicial skill. For, in an era of two-party strife, Marshall cleverly writes a decision that gives something of value to both the prosecution and the defense. There will be no complaints on the verdict. Marshall knows that he is powerless to enforce any other outcome.

But he has given the Court that which it most desires ... the acknowledged right and responsibility to interpret the legislation of Congress and the actions of the Chief Executive as to their constitutionality.

ADDITIONAL ARTICLES
Some others bear scrutiny today and in the future, including:

Article V:

> **'The Congress, whenever two-thirds of both Houses shall deem it necessary, shall propose Amendments to this Constitution'....to be 'ratified by the Legislatures of three-fourths of the several States.'**

It is interesting to note that our first Ten Amendments were written specifically to assure that the Constitution would be ratified by the necessary three-quarters of those thirteen states.

These amendments enshrine specific liberties for every citizen....
mostly guaranteeing the freedom to live a life free from government intrusion.

Actually, Madison was against enumerating specific freedoms, concerned that the omission of others might imply a lack of
importance.

To cover this possibility, the founders added the **Ninth
Amendment.**

> **'The enumeration in the Constitution, of certain
> rights, shall not be construed to deny or disparage
> others retained by the People.'**

It may be time to now enshrine other sorts of liberties in the
Constitution, namely those that represent freedoms that only a government can guarantee.

This might include universal health care for all, the right to
higher education, and the right to a guaranteed minimum income.
In other words, rights that guarantee a life of fulfillment for all
Americans as opposed to those individual rights, currently listed
in the first Ten Amendments that do not address the needs of the
'collective whole' of society.

Considering that we now have political turmoil in Congress...
with parties acting as adversaries rather than collaborators in forging that more perfect Union...these 'gifts of liberty' should not be
subject to politics and continued uncertainty.

ARTICLE VL:

> **'All Senators and Representatives'... 'Shall be bound
> by Oath or Affirmation, to support the Constitution;
> but no religious Test shall ever be required as a**

Qualification to any Office or public Trust under the United States.'

This seemingly innocuous clause is actually extremely telling and should at some point be addressed by the Supreme Court, even by those justices foolish enough to embrace the doctrine of 'originalism'.

For religion has for far too long intruded into the 'public square, where, as this clause indicates, fealty to the Constitution is the only 'religion' of all Americans, regardless of creed, ethnicity or religion. (Would it surprise us to learn that most of our founding fathers were deists... and not formally bound to any form of religious practices?)

THE BILL OF RIGHTS
Nor does the **First Amendment** contradict this premise in saying:

'Congress shall make no law respecting an establishment of religion, or prohibiting the free exercise thereof.'

Government should play no part in the area of religion (or, for that matter, be influenced by those practicing their form of religion.) That remains a part of one's private life ... free to practice one's religious beliefs or free to practice none at all.

With a Republican Party pandering mercilessly to the evangelical community to secure votes ... and encouraging this intrusion of religion in the public square... it is long overdue for the Court to reestablish constitutional norms.

The Second Amendment calls for:

'a well-regulated Militia, being necessary to the security of a free State, the right of the people to keep and bear Arms, shall not be infringed.'

This of course is a major issue to be dealt with today, and only because the Court chose to impose the doctrine of 'originalism' in the Heller decision, written by Justice Scalia. Scalia actually took the liberty of ignoring the first thirteen words of this amendment, which clearly tied the possession of firearms to the collective need for a militia at certain moments, not specifically defined.

With this sleight of hand, Scalia turned the Second Amendment into an individual right without any restraints other than those imposed (or not) by a partisan Congress and well as state and municipal governments.

It is ironic that this so-called 'originalist' invented his own logic that contradicts the plain meaning of the founders...and turned gun ownership into a First Amendment freedom that is the antithesis of serving the 'collective good'. And a majority of the Court was complicit in this judicial folly. The Court would be wise to reverse this decision...as it did with <u>Dred Scott</u> and <u>Plessy v. Ferguson</u>...other decisions that negatively affected large segments of the public just to satisfy the so called individual rights of the few...permanently scarring the judicial landscape.

The Tenth Amendment states that:

'The powers not delegated to the United States by the Constitution, nor prohibited by it to the States, are reserved to the States respectively, or to the People. '

The final phrase, 'or to the people' provides the escape clause for the federal judiciary to limit state jurisdiction, even where the Constitution is silent on this point.

For it is the People who have established the Constitution, not the States. And they would logically be the first beneficiaries of this silence, even if the states were to claim jurisdiction under the doctrine of 'residual powers'.

It was John Marshall who defined this point far more than any other Supreme Court Justice since that time. His decision in 1819 in <u>McCullough v. Maryland</u> restricts state sovereignty with several telling phrases that resound through the ages up to today.

> **'We are a government of the people (i.e., not of the states) giving implied powers to enact.'**

In solidifying the judicial use of both the 'necessary and proper clause' and these 'implied powers' to expand the powers of federal authority, Marshall writes:

> **'Let the end be legitimate, let it be within the scope of the Constitution and all means which are appropriate and consistent with the spirit of the Constitution are constitutional'.**

Although states continued to argue over the scope of so-called 'residual powers' right up to the time of the Civil War, Marshall established federal supremacy as a bedrock principle in constitutional law. The most he would yield on this subject was to say that,

> **'States are members of a great empire, for some purposes sovereign, for some purposes subordinate... and 'states have residual powers, but not if they clash with federal authority.**

The Twelfth Amendment lays out in great detail the election process and elements that the Electoral College in determining the President (and Vice President at that time).

Because it is filled with outdated procedures that are not relevant today, it may be time for the Court to find the proper test case to lay out new rules to govern the selection of a Chief Executive.

As a President has just won in the Electoral College while losing the popular vote, the Court may want to revisit that issue ... as well as the distortion of the concept of 'one man one vote' due to demographic factors never anticipated by the founders.

Certainly the process of updating this Amendment would provide the proper forum for asking these questions.

The Fourteenth Amendment, ratified in the summer of 1868, prior to the election of Grant, represented the hopefulness of many that the legacy of Lincoln could be redeemed after being tarnished by his successor, Andrew Johnson.

Known specifically for its 'equal protection' clause, it places obligations on the states that were to end the discrimination and other heinous acts of slavery.

> **'No state shall make or enforce any law which shall abridge the privileges or immunities of citizens.... nor deny to any person within its jurisdiction the equal protection of the laws.'**

Once federal troops were removed from the region, the South chose to impose a new form of slavery under 'Jim Crow', ignoring the Fourteenth Amendment. It would take another hundred years until the Civil Rights legislation of 1964 redeemed the promise of the Thirteenth, Fourteenth and Fifteenth Amendments.

Nevertheless, the words of the Fourteenth Amendment, never specifically mentioning terms such as 'bondage', 'slavery' or 'indentured servitude', have been used to extend similar rights to other disenfranchised members of society...a testament to the Constitution's ability to constantly reach for that 'more perfect Union'.

The Twenty Fifth Amendment deals with the removal of a President due to disabilities of various sorts, having nothing to do with Impeachment.

This scenario is highly relevant today in particular with Presidents well into their seventies. However, it is interesting to note that this process requires a number of steps, including 'written declaration that the President is unable to discharge the powers and duties of his office'...and 'a two thirds vote by both Houses of Congress'.

Based on these multiple requirements, it might be difficult to execute removal in a timely manner to avoid unforeseen consequences. In this regards, it might be useful to review the situation regarding President Woodrow Wilson. After suffering a severe stroke in 1919, his wife, with a complicit White House staff, performed as an unauthorized 'presidential stand-in' throughout the balance of his term.

CONCLUSION

Many of the points noted above may require the Supreme Court to get involved.

From time to time, the Court has bursts of energy that supply us with groundbreaking decisions. Such was the case with the Marshall Court in the founding era and with the Warren Court in the middle of the Twentieth Century.

We are once again in turbulent times with many long festering issues that need to be addressed to renew the promise of America. Why they have been left unresolved for so long...and how they might be approached...is in large part the purpose of this exercise.

TRUE JUDICIAL ACTIVISM

This phrase has been used in the past, mainly by think tanks and various interest groups on the Right, to criticize jurists and their decisions that seem to expand the words of the Constitution beyond the meaning they alone deem worthy of acceptance.

In effect, their assumptions are 'judicial activism' of another sort, limiting the purview of what the Constitution offers, more for political reasons than those of the law.

The reach of the courts in our daily lives has always been a subject open to a healthy debate...one that our most esteemed legal scholars have constantly dealt with.

Is an issue better dealt with by the legislature or by the people themselves through their right to vote? Certainly, John Marshall, our most prominent justice of the founding era, was sensitive to this question, particularly when he was mandated with the task of making the judiciary a worthy third branch of the government under Article lll.

His masterful decision in <u>Marbury v. Madison</u> was ultimately intended to grant the Court the right and responsibility of constitutional review over the acts and legislation of the other two branches of government. Although this was not specifically mandated under the Constitution, Marshall assumed that it was an implied power in order for the Court to effectively do its job.

To achieve this, he was adept in giving something of value to all parties with an interest in the Marbury decision. One might call this 'playing politics', or 'judicial engineering', or even 'judicial activism'.

Yet it was highly effective in gaining what was needed to fulfill the inherent meaning of Article lll. That was to create an effective third branch of government to counterbalance the rights and privileges of the other two.

So let's for the moment set aside those implications that the term 'judicial activism' is somehow out of the mainstream. Let's admit that all of the Supreme Court's major decisions have in one way or another significant political and social implications.

Can one deny that <u>Citizens United</u> has unleashed a torrent of corporate money in our politics and elevated the 'voice' of a few over the many? Or that the <u>Heller Case</u> of 2008, overlooking a key phrase of the Second Amendment, unleashed a torrent of guns... and senseless killings?

These decisions, applauded on the Right, clearly played politics... and not necessarily for the betterment of society. One could easily call these decisions 'judicial engineering' or 'judicial activism'.

Certainly one could argue that both issues would have been better left to the legislature, rather than permanently embedded in the decisions of the highest Court...particularly as neither followed a preponderance of legal precedent. On the contrary, both forged new (and dangerous) territory, particularly Heller, under a newly invented legal concept of 'originalism'.

Unlike either case, there are, however, many issues that can and should be resolved by the Courts as we attempt to create that 'more perfect Union'.

These might be defined as issues that have festered far too long without being addressed by Congress. Issues that have had a negative effect on a robust democracy...issues that have little prospect of being remedied by our two major parties, acting as opponents rather than collaborators in defining those important benchmarks of a 'more perfect Union'.

It is therefore up to the Supreme Court to take up the mantle as the prime 'definer' of these American values. This is what the times require, as they have been pivotal in our past. Certainly that was the case with the Warren Court of the mid-nineteen fifties, when it redeemed the message of the Fourteenth Amendment's promise of 'equal protection under the law' with <u>Brown v. Board of Education</u> to overcome segregation in schools and elsewhere.

Or in overturning <u>Plessy v. Ferguson</u> and its mandate of 'separate but equal' as an inherent and outdated oxymoron when it came to our educational system in the South.

Post-Brown cases were intended to right the wrongs that Congress was not willing to address, for clearly partisan reasons. At the same time, these cases clearly dealt with issues that had constitutional implications in moving us toward that 'more perfect union'.

Perhaps, using that benchmark as the standard, the Court should be dealing with some of the issues listed below:

Let us admit that Marshall used the still fragile powers of the Court to knit a country together, adeptly using the Constitution's 'implied powers' and 'necessary and proper' clauses...as well as greatly expanding the meaning of the 'commerce clause'. These decisions were in the main unanimously rendered by a Court composed of justices from both parties of the times. Finally, these decisions have stood the test of time, cited continually down through the ages in other cases argued before the Court. If this could be accomplished in the founding era, then surely today's Court can follow this esteemed legacy in knitting this country back together in other meaningful ways.

Below are some of the most important issues to be tackled...issues that are overdue in needing to be addressed. The Court would surely be praised in the annals of history. Some might decide these issues in a definitive manner. Others might simply set the proper guidelines and benchmarks for Congress to address many of them. In either case, these decisions would hopefully lead us toward that more perfect Union...which should be the ultimate benchmark to be attained by any Court decision.

With the taint of partisanship invading the Court as well in recent times, and with liberal and conservative justices voting as a bloc in their decisions, perhaps it is time for another Marshall or Warren to gain unanimity in these decisions. That would further enshrine them as solid precedent...and dismiss once and for all the taint of partisan politics within our judicial system.

The list of issues to be tackled in one way or another should include the following:

- Restoring the meaning of 'one man one vote' ... and eliminating or taming the reach of gerrymandering and the Electoral College.

- Setting benchmarks and equitable enforcement policies for immigration that promote economic benefit for the nation and honor the rights of those seeking a better life.

- Identifying the reasons behind the rise of political movements out of the mainstream and identify certain constitutional standards based on their contributing to that phrase, 'a more perfect union'.

- Restoring the principles behind Madison's Federalist #10 and re-establishing a level playing field of countervailing interests, none of which dominate a national conversation ... making this a constitutional standard.

- Establishing an enforceable standard as to the responsibilities of traditional and social media, while protecting freedom of speech.

- Establishing guidelines for reviving the tradition of two centrist parties that share enough core values to seek common ground in resolving the compelling issues of the day.

- Taking a fresh look at the potential for the Court to use the 'implied powers' and 'necessary and proper' clauses to provide the country with a 'new bill of rights' to amplify the rights of the many versus the privileges of the few.

James Madison

THE CONSTITUTION AND 'CHECKS AND BALANCES'

C hecks and Balances' is a phrase that has echoed down through
the past two centuries when it comes to the Constitution.

It was introduced into our collective vocabulary by James Madison,
the man most responsible (along with Hamilton) for getting the
Constitutional Convention to take place in the hot summer of 1787.
That event, with the 55 signers (plus Franklin and Washington who
sat on a dais above the fray) in Philadelphia from May through

September, was a highly improbable event. The attendees were all expecting to revise the ineffective Articles of Confederation when they were informed of the change in plans.

Madison crafted the outline using many works by the philosophers of the Enlightenment, supplied by Jefferson, who was still in Paris as our lead ambassador. The objective was to create a document that was in balance, with the three branches of government making sure that each respected the powers granted to the other two.

The legislature received the most attention in Article I in terms of delegated powers. As Washington was assumed to be the first to occupy the office of Chief Executive, the specific duties and powers enumerated in Article II were rather brief ... allowing Washington to 'fill in the blanks'.

The Judiciary was the least defined under Article III until John Marshall arrived on the scene in 1801 as the Chief Justice. He reshaped the Judiciary, securing the power of constitutional review regarding state and federal laws and the actions of the Executive Branch.

Now let's look more carefully into the term 'checks and balances' as to the multiple meaning that can and should be applied. The first is to thwart (or check) unconstitutional acts (better known as 'overreach') of a branch of government or department thereof and bring the relationship with the other two branches back into a more harmonious and proper balance.

As the powers of the Executive branch have generally increased since 1787, for a variety of reasons, it should not be surprising that 'overreach' has often been on the part of a sitting president.

The reasons for this are manifold. Some of the most noteworthy are the result of presidential actions that have remained unchallenged as well as the exigencies of history.

These include the following:

1. As Andrew Jackson hypothesized, the President is the only official elected by all the people and therefore occupies an elevated space.

2. A president can have more of an impact on the public consciousness, especially as today's methods of communication have vastly increased that ability.

3. Multiple precedents have defined the President as ' the sole organ' in dealing with foreign affairs...a term first coined by Hamilton in making Congress more of a a 'rubber stamp' in the process.

4. With wars continuing for more than a decade, placing the country on 'high alert', presidential powers as 'commander-in-chief' have virtually exploded without end.

5. Today's president has 'all the facts', courtesy of a multiplicity of sources (the NSA, CIA etc.), giving his decisions an unassailable supremacy vis a vis Congress.

If Madison were to view this situation objectively, and in accord with his concept of 'checks and balances', he would be aghast. In fact, he would be ready to anoint a president as 'King', which Washington in fact turned down in 1789 and again in 1796, when he left office after two terms to 'live under his fig tree and vine'.

FINDING A GREATER MEANING
But, there is another way to evaluate the concept of 'checks and balances' in today's world that Madison might have approved of. Though unspoken, it is at the heart of Constitution.

The Federalist Papers were written by Hamilton, Madison and Jay to explain in greater detail the meaning behind the words and phrases of the final product that would be the Constitution. And no one could undertake this task better than these three, who had been 'present at the creation'.

All of them rightly felt that their words would be vital in the ratification process, when it came to the states debating various points. As it turned out, Hamilton, the most fluid and brilliant among them, wrote the majority of the Federalist Papers, followed by Madison...with only a few written by John Jay.

However, Madison's Federalist #10 is at the heart of the matter when it comes to the issue of 'checks and balances'. In this particular essay, he explained why a republic, which had previously existed only as Greek city-state, should thrive in a much larger venue with a rapidly growing population.

His answer, in a nutshell, was that there would be an abundance of countervailing interests in this larger landscape that would thwart the ability of the few to dominate the conversation. In other words, 'checks and balances' for Madison is at the heart of that conversation among all Americans ... and not just the workings of a tripartite government. It is evident in the invaluable writings of Madison that chronicle the daily conversations at the Constitutional Convention that all those present agreed with his premise.

HONORING THE TRUE MEANING

The next question would therefore be...how do we honor this concept, which appears to be an inherent constitutional mandate, if and when we find that our society is out of balance. Should we permit one or more interest groups to dominate the conversation without requiring compromise to win the day?

Again...let's look to history to supply possible answers.

The Marshall Court (1801-1836) decided cases that related to the most pressing issue of the day... knitting together a country that had hitherto looked at a state's interests as dominant over those of the nation. In other words, the Court was trying to realize the aspirations and ideals that underlay the writing of the Constitution...e pluribus unim, 'out of many... one!'

In the process, Chief Justice John Marshall gave us almost 450 unanimous decisions, many of which addressed that particular point, providing:

1. The growing supremacy of federal law over state law, except where otherwise permissible.

2. Decisions in commercial cases that favored the greatest number and did not favor those citizens of a particular state.

3. A balanced approach to assigning powers to both the Legislative and Executive branches ... through fealty to the words of the Constitution and the use of the 'implied' and 'necessary and proper' clauses.

Today, the courts would be performing the same vital service for the nation as the Marshall Court, if they were to view cases through the lens of advancing the precepts of 'checks and balances', the most important precept underlying the words and spirit of the Constitution.

Rather than being strictly partisan and favoring one group or ideology over another, this would also give these decisions the bipartisan luster of 'constitutionality' that realize the true meaning underlying the Constitution.

This might include:

1. Deciding cases to limit gross income inequality on the basis of 'checking' the ability of any group to have an excessive voice in our national dialogue.

2. Endorsing tax policies that favor the same objective under the same mandate of 'check and balances'.

3. Limiting the funds to be used in politics to restore 'checks and balances'...and neutering decisions like <u>Citizens United</u> as 'unconstitutional' by inviting the dominance of the few over the many.

4. Deciding cases that involve gerrymandering and voter suppression and perhaps even the viability of the Electoral College through the lens of 'checks and balances' to eliminate the interests of various groups over the will of the many.

PAST PRESIDENTS

There is nothing more important today in that ongoing challenge to work toward that 'more perfect Union' than to honor the Madisonian dictum of 'checks and balance' and fight against unwanted influence of the few against the many.

Our history has shown that great presidents set the stage for restoring that balance mandated by the Constitution. Examples include:

1. Jackson's mission to open the political dialogue to other sections of the country and include the common man.

2. Lincoln's message that we are entitled to a level playing field of opportunity for all men regardless of their color.

3. Teddy Roosevelt's determination to tame the influence of big business and act as the arbiter to limit their excesses vis a vis both the government and the working person.

4. FDR's expanding his powers as commander-in-chief to apply to a domestic crisis (that is the equivalent of war) in order to give dignity in the workplace and in retirement for every man.

5. LBJ's civil rights legislation vindicating the staggering toll of the Civil War by finally honoring Lincoln's words that all are entitled to life, liberty and the pursuit of happiness'.

FUTURE PRESIDENTS

A future president, to deserve the honor of 'presidential greatness', would have to propose legislation to restore a society that is 'in balance' when it comes to promoting the meaning under the Constitution. If this legislation were challenged in the courts as to its constitutionality, the first line of defense would be in promoting the very goals enumerated in crafting our most famous founding document...that is, to create a level playing field so that no special interest should have a clear path to overwhelming a national dialogue and restoring the proper balance prophesied by Madison.

THE SAVING GRACE
OF LIBERALISM

SIMPLE VERSUS COMPLEX SOLUTIONS

Today, Liberalism seems to be under attack here in the United States and in Europe as well, with more autocratic or nationalist alternatives being offered. Nor is this the first time this has occurred, particularly at times of great economic distress or international turmoil.

For It is always easier for vested interests to propose a simple solution to complex problems, rather than deal with the reasoned and often painstaking debate that liberalism encourages.

Both World Wars had us retreating into a predictable cocoon of isolationism (i.e., nationalism) and blaming other nations for the world's problems before we were ready to understand the reality of the situation and send our men to Europe to finally win both wars.

A HISTORY LESSON

Based on human nature, the public will always be tempted to choose the easy answer. Liberalism initially loses out to the quick fix in the early stages of great stress, social or economic.

Such was the case leading up to the Civil War, when men like Stephen Douglas, Henry Clay and John Calhoun, all very capable and nimble politicians, grabbed the public's attention with words that sounded reassuring.

But moral hollowness of their solutions was made plain by a man named Abraham Lincoln, who emerged with words that slowly but surely elevayed the conversation to one of morality rather than expediency.

Liberalism is for the most part reactive rather than pro-active, though the opposition will often paint it as an assault on our democracy. In truth, it is more of a response to corruption, falsehoods and the distorting of our founding documents than an activist movement of its own.

Generally, a liberal ethos boils slowly below the surface until the abuses of power and the consequences of a quick fix become difficult to ignore. Then it will provoke a national conversation to right the ship of state.

CONSTITUTIONAL NORMS

While the Constitution did not necessarily foresee this ongoing process of corruption and course correction, it did elevate 'liberalism' as the higher power in our national dialogue. For this document was written at the height of the Enlightenment, trusting in those liberal precepts that fought against monarchy and undue influence either an individual or a class...actual and implied.

Those precepts included fealty to the rule of law, limits on inherited privilege, constraints on arbitrary power, freedom of conscience and speech and an aristocracy based on talent and not on birth. And all of this was premised on unleashing individual potential while at the same time striving for the common good. (Capitalism was the system, according to Adam Smith, that would help to unleash that potential in the economic realm.)

As stated in Madison's Federalist Papers #57, which was the roadmap to understanding the meaning of the Constitution, we should strive ' to obtain as rulers, men who possess most wisdom to discern and most virtue to pursue the common good of society'.

But the philosophers of the Enlightenment were no fools when it came to evaluating human nature. Even good men were subject to corruption. To avoid problems, philosophers like John Locke proposed 'separation of powers'...writing 'it may be too great a temptation to human frailty apt to grasp at power ... for the same persons who have the power of making laws, to have also in their hands the power to execute them.'

That concept, to tame certain human instincts was embraced wholeheartedly by Madison when he sketched out the document that would be written in that steamy summer of 1787...creating three co-equal branches of government.

And then there was Federalist #10, Madison's other brainchild, taking another page from the Enlightenment's theory of checks and balances and projecting this onto a society of multiple and varied interests that would create a level playing field of competing ideas and influence.

Despite all of this planning, the Founders did not foresee a time when these interests might be out of balance...often due to Adam Smith's economic model of free enterprise and capitalism, which we embraced from our earliest days, thanks to Alexander Hamilton's vision of a credit-worthy nation.

AN INHERENT CONFLICT

We have come to know there will always be an inherent conflict between this concept of 'wealth creation', known as unbridled capitalism, and the virtues and aspirations of a vibrant democracy. For liberals, unlike conservatives, it is only when they are grossly out of balance, as in the Gilded Age, that progressive ideas are most likely to surface

Such was the case in 1901 when Theodore Roosevelt assumed the presidency on the death of William McKinley. (Note that he was an accidental president and not one that the plutocrats of that era would have otherwise embraced.)

TR saw government as the intermediary between capital and labor to resolve the excesses of either party. He did not deny the benefits of capitalism, he merely sought to tame them by elevating the role of the President as the ultimate judge... through arbitration or any other means, including reactivating a dormant Sherman Anti-Trust Act.

The next president to restore the balance between capitalism's wealth creation machinery and the aspirations stated in Federalist #10 was FDR. He had an easier time in reforming the system, thanks to the Great Depression. That cataclysmic event destroyed the credibility of unfettered capitalism including its side effects, such as rampant, unregulated speculation in the stock market, t overproduction and monopolistic price fixing.

Everything about FDR's so-called 'New Deal' screamed 'liberalism', giving dignity back to the average man by creating workfare programs such as the Civilian Conservation Corps and Social Security to grant a satisfying retirement.

It is worth mentioning that FDR, a very cunning politician, launched Social Security as a bona fide government program, under the constitutionally approved taxing power, in order to confront various demagogues of the day... always a danger in times of economic uncertainty. That included men like Huey Long, who were already a political threat to FDR's chances for re-election.

The liberal agenda was less of an assault on capitalism than an attempt to restore the hopefulness that was inherent in our founding documents. Despite the rabid reaction of the plutocrats of the day, it never entered their minds that FDR had in effect saved 'capitalism' from self-destruction, by tempering its excesses.

Nor was it surprising that a conservative Supreme Court was anxious to overturn his methods as well. Perhaps the greatest gift FDR gave us ... and one that moved us towards that more perfect Union...was in reconciling the negative liberty enumerated in the

Bill of Rights as compatible with the government's role in creating a more compassionate society.

THE VALUE OF LIBERALISM

For that is the role that liberalism should play. It corrects the blatant shortcomings that years of promoting unbridled self-interest can create. Out of the chaos of the moment, something unexpected happens that moves the country forward...as with the COVID 19 pandemic of 2020.

In the social realm, it makes democracy relevant by spreading the rights and privileges of citizenship to the many, rather than the few. In the area of economics, it finds ways to keep capitalism relevant by having the government cushion and control the worst in terms of human nature, restoring the balance in a functioning democracy, as foreseen in the Constitution (and in Federalist #10).

But at its worst, it can be excessive, especially when frustrated for decades in making inroads. At times it can overcompensate in making that course correction by forgetting who we are as a people. In that case, the solutions suggested may be subject to accusations of 'socialism' that simply muddy the waters with meaningless phrases. For it is a given that Social Security and Medicare have become highly popular programs that work effectively side by side with capitalism.

We are and always will be a marketplace of ideas and actions. While government can and should step in to restore that balance, the course correction must have the support of the people and reassure them of its continuity in the traditions of America.

REVISING THE LIBERAL MESSAGE

Liberalism should be careful not to confront duplicity with righteous indignation, as though it alone can fix all the ills of modern day society. The danger lies in believing that Lincoln's phrase, spoken at Cooper Union ...'right makes might'...can be the last word. It may galvanize a particular group or party to 'fight the righteous fight'. But, still the message to convince others of your cause must be crafted in a subtle and non-confrontational manner.

While Lincoln understood this, he never crossed the line in accusing others of being unpatriotic or even treasonous, as many others did. In fact, that is in large measure why Lincoln won the Republican nomination in 1860. (Seward called the differences North and South 'an irrepressible conflict' and lost all southern support.)

Today's Democrats must be careful not to repeat Hillary Clinton's 'deplorables' faux pas, which immediately closes down the conversation and turns it into 'know-it-all elitism'...condescending of the beliefs of others, including their religious beliefs.

It is no mystery why today's Democrats have difficulty connecting with white working class voters, while their message clearly resonates with the young voter. Despite the fact that Republicans have continually frayed our meager safety net, challenging Medicare and Obamacare as budget busting giveaways, those who have been hurt the most do not necessarily see things that way.

Appearances can be deceiving. The most vulnerable among us do not see a Republican Party controlled by big money that has little in common with their needs. All they see is a connection with cultural issues and support for guns and their religion. And that is enough.

Ultimately, they are the ones who will need to be persuaded, gently and over time, that things need to change. There is a difference between building this argument sensibly versus promising all sorts of blatant giveaways. This is simply another iteration of 'we know best' elitism to the most marginalized. Those left out do not want to hear about the sudden utopia they have been deprived of ...including free college, free health care, and freebies to illegal immigrants.

Utopia can wait for now for those who have watched their incomes and way of life stagnate for far too long as the wealthy game the system. This over-stepping also makes it easier for the opposition to demagogue these issues, let alone ask who will pay for all of this.

In short, progressivism must take a grass roots common sense approach that seeks common ground on 'kitchen table concerns'. That is essential if liberalism is to re-connect with what used to be a solid core constituency. Grandiose promises from a bully pulpit only allow the opposition to paint these as an elitist betrayal of American values.

THE FUTURE
OF IMPEACHMENT

AN HISTORIC PERSPECTIVE

The subject of impeachment has been on the radar for some time... so perhaps it is time to evaluate the history behind this constitutional mandate and its effectiveness in today's world.

Impeachment was an ancient relic used by Parliament to wrest power from the king by charging his ministers with abuse of power. A conviction would then result in removal from office and, on occasion, a jail sentence.

The various times when impeachment was acted upon by Parliament included charges of 'certain high treasons and offenses'...with the phrase 'high crimes and misdemeanors' appearing somewhat more than a century before the drafting of this American Constitution.

Those attending the Constitution Convention in 1787 were obviously intent on dealing with abuses of power. And impeachment seemed the perfect antidote as it had already been written into many of the various state constitutions, starting with that of Massachusetts...drafted by none other than John Adams.

It was intended to limit the authority of elected officials who acted more like kings...and mainly focused on the chief executive under Article ll, Section 3, who was almost unanimously assumed to be Washington at that point. The most obvious offense at that

time...for those crafting a document to ensure the future of a fragile democracy...was betrayal of the trust of the people by colluding
with a foreign power.

A FIRST TEST CASE

It was a work in progress...as exemplified by its inappropriate use in
1805, with the impeachment trial of a Supreme Court Justice named
Samuel Chase. The fact that the charges were brought against this
member of the judiciary rather than a sitting president, tells you that
the process was hardly perfected at the time. Instead, it had been
activated in a moment of righteous indignation by Jefferson and
his fellow Republicans ... when there were surely better alternatives
to deal with the supposed insult.

The times were ripe for such overstepping of constitutional
norms. For we were still dealing with the aftermath brought on by
the Alien and Sedition Acts, foolishly passed by the Federalists during the Adams administration of the late 1790's and limiting freedom of speech in the lead up to the so-called quasi-war with France.
Many Republicans were thrown in jail, including James Callender,
one of Jefferson's many surrogates sent out to slander the Federalists
at every opportunity. In some sense, this trial was therefore seen as
payback by the Republicans, and Jefferson in particular, for Justice
Chase's intemperate attacks on the opposition party.

The trial of Justice Chase did at least add some additional
ground rules to a process ill-defined at best under the Constitution.
It confirmed that it had to be an offense worthy of being called
'high crimes and high misdemeanors and related to the office in
question. It was also established that the crime in question did not
have to be one that qualified as any indictable crime'. This further
recognized that presidential powers were different from those that
mere mortals could only dream of.

Although he came close to being impeached on the shaky
grounds of 'partisan zeal', Justice Chase was ultimately acquitted...

establishing the immunity of judges in their judicial work from the process, as well as the immunity of the judiciary as a whole.

What we can take away from this early trial on the grounds of impeachment is the obvious political nature of the process, an element that remains with us to this day...one that has always made the process risky as dissolving into partisanship rather than purpose

PRESIDENTIAL IMPEACHMENT

The first president to be impeached was John Tyler in 1843. And the reasons were purely political, having little to do with 'high crimes and misdemeanors'. For Vice President Tyler had ascended to the presidency upon the death of President William Henry Harrison, only one month into his term in office. (Harrison had the misfortune of giving the longest inaugural address to date on a cold, blustery day in March and catching a fatal case of pneumonia.)

Had someone done a better job of getting his running mate's political credentials, he would have discovered that John Tyler was a dyed-in-the- wool Republican and not a member of the President's Whigs. His pushing the opposition's agenda as president may have been offensive to those fellow Whigs, but it hardly qualified as 'treason or high crimes and misdemeanors'...a point the House agreed to in voting not to continue the process.

The next accusation of crimes worthy of impeachment was brought against Andrew Johnson, who became President upon the tragic death of Lincoln. In truth, it is doubtful that anyone could have filled Lincoln's shoes to the satisfaction of those Radical Republicans who now controlled the party apparatus.

But Johnson fell so far short that a trial for 'high crimes and misdemeanors' was probably a foregone conclusion. In effect, he negated every wartime goal that had cost both North and South hundreds of thousands of lives...putting the 'slave-ocracy' back in a position of authority and trashing the 13th, 14th and 15th Amendments.

Still, the grounds for impeachment were in large part political, as 'outrage' rather than 'treason' better suited the supposed crime in question. Johnson dodged conviction in the Senate by one vote... and only because those Republicans chose to bring the proceedings under the obscure and ill-conceived 'Tenure of Office' Act. This act unconstitutionally expanded the Senate's oversight of the Executive Branch to include the right to control the dismissal of Department heads.

We had to wait more than a century for the next mention of impeachment. That of course dealt with the malfeasance of President Richard Nixon's involvements in the Watergate cover up. Were it not for the 'smoking gun'... the serendipitous discovery of White House tapes that had already been tampered with, yet still yielded damning evidence...there would have been no resignation and no potential impeachment.

It is the bipartisan nature of the Senate's findings that marks this as distinctly different from prior impeachment proceedings. Senators put the nation's interests above partisanship and stood together in visiting the White House to advise Nixon of the potential verdict.

The next impeachment trial may well represent an all time low when it comes to grounds for impeachment. For the charges against President Clinton for the Monica Lewinsky affair represented strictly personal transgressions to be dealt with by a husband and wife.

Numerous presidents have had marital affairs that would have qualified for impeachment based solely on the hyper-partisan nature of today's politics. But, the public quickly figured things out for themselves. Clinton's approval ratings soared midst the folly of special prosecutor Ken Starr's farce of a trial... based on Clinton's lying under oath about 'not having sex with that woman, Miss Lewinsky', while triangulating on the meaning of that word.

The upshot of that trial was to further diminish the importance of impeachment in the eyes of the public, turning it into high political theater rather than 'high crimes and misdemeanors'.

THE TRUMP SITUATION

And thus we arrive at the presidency of Donald Trump, perhaps the man least qualified emotionally and intellectually among all our presidents to occupy that office. In the hyper-partisan atmosphere that allowed him to game a vulnerable public into electing him ... with the acknowledged assistance of a foreign power...his gross misdeeds ended up not warranting impeachment in the Senate, despite a mountain of evidence accumulated by the Mueller Commission.

The case is even more damning...in terms of falling within the constitutional benchmark of 'treasonous behavior'. Yet, despite an impeachment proceeding in the House, with many highly qualified witnesses detailing the President's colluding with a foreign power to enhance his re-election prospects, the Senate voted to acquit.

Once again, partisan politics intervened, further diminishing the prospects of ever having the impeachment process rein in the behavior of a renegade president. This process has actually elevated and broadened the grasp and reach of executive authority, thanks to unforeseen circumstances and the assistance of an Attorney General who, himself, has knowingly and purposefully broken long-standing norms.

ENTER WILLIAM BARR

In late 2018, Bill Barr was nominated for the position of Attorney General, to replace the weak and conflicted Jeff Sessions, who had incurred the President's wrath in recusing himself during the Mueller investigations. In truth, he had been auditioning for the position for some time, having been a late convert to 'Trumpism'. (He originally supported Jeb Bush as the Republican nominee in 2016.)

To prove his loyalty, the characteristic most esteemed by the President, he had written supportive Op-Ed's in the Washington Post and criticized Mueller for hiring prosecutors who had donated to Democratic politicians. Nevertheless, having served in the Justice

Department under Reagan and both Bush presidencies, Barr was looked upon as an institutionalist. On that basis, his confirmation by the Senate was looked on as little more than a 'rubber stamp'.

Had those senators done their homework, they would have seen that Barr held many views that were far out of the mainstream. Decades ago, he had taken issue with legislation passed after the Nixon era to empower independent counsels and inspectors general to investigate presidential misdeeds.

When the Supreme Court validated this process as 'not unduly interfering' with the powers of the executive branch, only Justice Scalia dissented, citing this as nothing more than partisan politics, a viewpoint with which Barr agreed.

It should therefore not be surprising that President Trump found his soul mate in Bill Barr, a man who believed that years of liberal corruption had infected our country and weakened our institutions, primarily the presidency.

A devout Catholic, Barr believed that liberals were guilty of godlessness and removing religion from the public square, despite the constitutional mandate of separation of church and state.

This in fact put him totally in sync with a Republican Party that had totally abandoned bipartisanship in favor of a constant war against godless liberals. In a fortuitous Faustian bargain, both men found what each was looking for...an Attorney General who would be more devoted to supporting a president's interests than following the law, and a president who would put conservative religious values front and center in his appointments and his actions.

Now, Barr would show no inclination to temper Trump's worst instincts.

TRASHING MUELLER

It was with this in mind that he misquoted and distorted the long-awaited findings of the Mueller Commission, leaving the door open for the President claim that there had been 'no collusion'. This, despite the fact that the report documented many acts that screamed 'obstruction of justice' and a very cozy relationship with the Russians in great detail.

Barr's concerns were clearly focused on so-called political opponents, fueled by illegal leaks and seeking to undermine the presidency. The Mueller Report was simply one more iteration of this scourge. At the President's urging, he even launched an investigation of the FBI's Russia probe and the CIA's assessment that Russia had intervened on Trump's behalf in the 2016 election. When this yielded no evidence of such behavior, he then made sure to question the results and continue digging.

A SECOND ATTEMPT AT IMPEACHMENT

Barr went so far as to interpret Article ll as giving a President such exalted control over the executive branch as to include his right to oversee investigations into his own misconduct...in effect shredding the meaning of the impeachment clause.

When a whistleblower came forward to report the details of the President's conversation with the President of Ukraine, more of a shakedown for dirt on his political opponent, Barr made sure to try to bury it.

While damning testimony was given by highly reliable State Department officials, Barr was giving a speech before the ultra right wing Federalist Society, turning the tables and calling this 'a scorched-earth war of resistance against this Administration... shredding norms and undermining the rule of law'.

Barr set the stage for ignoring subpoenas from the House for documents and testimony from Administration officials, shredding the Constitution in order to elevate his long held theories and denying the legitimacy of another branch of government in challenging executive supremacy.

This goes far beyond any precedent, including Andrew Jackson's elevating the Chief Executive above both the legislative branch and the judiciary as the only individual at the time, truly elected by the people. (Even Jackson couldn't avoid being censured by the Senate for killing the federally approved Bank of the U.S.!)

Trump has delivered what Barr covets most. More than any president in recent history, he has promoted the Christian cause, pandering mercilessly to the evangelical community. Conservative Christian values are now paramount in the appointment of judges, most importantly to those to the Court of Appeals and the Supreme Court. Ironically, given this scenario, Barr's drive to have presidents free of the constraints of Congress could well be successful if and when these claim reach a Supreme Court of like-minded ideologues.

FINDING A NEW WAY TO DEAL WITH 'IMPEACHMENT'

It would be ironic if the impeachment process, mandated under the Constitution to deal with presidential acts, has had the opposite effect. Perhaps the appellation of 'high crimes and misdemeanors', has unleashed a backlash on the Right that now elevates presidential prerogatives far beyond constitutional norms, completely shredding the concept of 'checks and balances'.

Perhaps it's time to re-examine new and revised guidelines to re-establish that balance and restore what the founders intended to accomplish in that steamy summer of 1787. Not being confined to a rigid historic process may have its benefits... if we again hark to 'constitutional norms' that have yet to be specifically defined.

Let us remember that Article ll (in defining the powers of the Chief Executive) was written in fairly spare prose. It only included Commander-in-Chief and foreign policy powers, which seemed appropriate given that Washington was expected to be the first President.

The rest was to be fleshed out through the various phases of our history, as presidential powers have grown, based on accepted precedent, rather than strictly defined text. We must ask, what are the 'powers' bestowed directly or by precedent on a president, as well as the constraints, created in the same manner?

Which brings up the unspoken issue of values and morality, something not mentioned in the Constitution, but which we are clearly entitled to expect of our presidents. In fact, this began with Washington, our most revered citizen who valued his reputation as a man of character more than any other attribute.

Impeachment proceedings were initiated to investigate Clinton for questionable morality in his personal affairs, and his lying under oath, having nothing to do with his performance in office. Would it therefore be much of a stretch to conduct impeachment, or some other proceedings, for immoral behavior in the conduct of the office?

Those presidents who attain so-called 'presidential greatness' are generally seen as temperamentally suited in dealing with the demands of the office.

What would this constitutional 'temperament' consist of, among other things:

1. Leaving partisan politics behind and speaking to and for all the people.

2. Being open and available to the media and honoring its role as the 'Fourth Estate' in keeping the people informed.

3. Honoring the right of every American to pursue his or her religious beliefs without fear of retribution.

4. Eliminating fear-mongering and divisive rhetoric and always seeking to speak truth, based on the facts.

Nor should adhering to these values come as a surprise. After all, the Constitution, as documented by Madison in his invaluable notes, adheres to the values of the Enlightenment. Primary among these are the concepts of rational reason, religious freedom, our common humanity and equality for all in the 'pursuit of happiness', all of which informed Madison's script.

Whether it is Lincoln's words of 'a more perfect Union' or appealing to 'our better angels', or Obama's singing 'Amazing Grace'... the way a president speaks to the American people is emblematic of his honoring his oath to uphold the Constitution. Failure to do so, in documented multiple settings, is a betrayal of that oath and worthy of being 'dismissed' from office under impeachment or some other proceedings.

Perhaps that case should be made before the Supreme Court, rather than a highly partisan chamber of Congress, with the facts carefully laid out in oral argument that would be published so that the people were kept informed, as would be their right in this case.

HISTORIC COMPARISONS

Abraham Lincoln, well before he rose to prominence, addressed an organization in Illinois called the Young Man's Lyceum. There he spoke of an incident in nearby Alton...where a pro-slavery mob had killed an editor for challenging slavery as a moral outrage. (They then threw his printing press into the Mississippi.)

Young Lincoln cleverly used his moral outrage to focus not on the divisive issue of slavery, but on what was at the heart of any healthy form of government. That is, the 'rule of law' as a sacred tenet in our democracy. His concern was that once we abandoned that precept, our democracy would ultimately fall apart.

John Marshall also had an opportunity to address a major 'conspiracy' case that threatened our democracy in Jefferson v. Burr. It was well known that Aaron Burr (post the duel with Hamilton) was a schemer and possibly intent on building an empire for himself in the interior of the Louisiana Territory.

But Marshall also knew that Burr was 'washed up' and no longer a threat. His greater concern was with President Jefferson, who had not responded to various subpoenas while holding himself above the law.

Marshall was a genius at crafting the right airtight legal argument that always took into consideration the primary needs of the country to move us forward as 'a more perfect union'. And so he looked at the case and strictly defined the elements that would constitute 'conspiracy', allowing Burr to go free. That was simply because he saw Jefferson as a greater threat to our democracy in his imperious ways as president than the scurrilous Burr.

It is a shame that Robert Mueller did not consult history, whether it was these two examples or others in order to use his authority to do the 'right thing', which was to thwart the clearly destructive and treasonous behavior of a renegade president.

Finding against Trump would have been easy, based on all the facts and circumstantial evidence. It would also have provoked a showdown, long overdue, between the rule of law and out-of-bounds presidential behavior, while sparing the country a partisan debate under the moniker of impeachment.

Mueller clearly refuted arguments that the President has the constitutional authority to terminate federal prosecution and cannot theoretically obstruct justice. That on its own, would legally elevate the president beyond the bounds of the law, something never imaged in Article ll.

Mueller wisely distinguished this questionable power 'when in the nation's interest' as opposed to 'wrongdoing to avoid embarrassment or for personal gain', which was Trump's obvious motive in this case. Ironically, some have called Mueller an institutionalist, as though going rigidly by the book represents a higher calling. But in effect, Mueller's lack of a firm and decisive finding, despite the mountain of evidence, allowed others to pervert the process and purity of this so-called 'institutionalist'.

One has to wonder what it takes, beyond damning circumstantial evidence, to find a nexus of a conspiracy and collusion. Surely John Marshall would have found a way!

Nevertheless, it is ironic that a President without any regard for the law and institutional barriers was granted a reprieve by a man who had far too much regard for the narrowest strictures of the law... particularly when another approach (both legal and conclusive) was easily available and very much in the country's interest.

CONSTITUTIONALLY MANDATED SECTIONALISM

In terms of potential presidential greatness, there needs to be another 'Lincoln' arriving on the scene in the near future to address today's highly toxic hybrid form of sectionalism that is breaking down traditional norms and threatening our democracy.

As with the era preceding the Civil War, this may ultimately lead to an outbreak of violence that brings matters to a head. Based on the demography of today, the most vulnerable and disenfranchised portion of the population often lives in the least populated (non-urban) sections of the country which also puts them out of touch and susceptible to misinformation.

Yet, under the Constitution's mandate for a bicameral legislature, this segment of the population is able to control the selection of a preponderance of senators and thereby be over represented in this august body. This power includes the Senate's role in approving or rejecting Supreme Court justices with lifetime appointments, thereby exerting undue influence over the third branch of government.

A BRIEF REVIEW OF HISTORY

Sectionalism has been with us since the days of the founding fathers. However, at the time, we had an open frontier to move on and give the disenfranchised a new lease on life by moving West. Actually,

James Madison looked upon sectionalism as a plus when crafting the checks and balances of the Constitution.

In Federalist #10, he explained that a country with a variety of sectional and other interest groups would balance each other out, without any particular one dominating the conversation. Thus, despite the nation's size, this would allow a democracy to thrive in much the way it did in a small Greek City State.

Throughout our history, one section has often been pitted against the other...starting with North versus South and the Hamilton/Jefferson schism that drove Washington crazy in Cabinet meetings.

Many times, the fighting was over economic hegemony. That usually involved a limited money supply courtesy of the banking community or tariff laws that favored Northern manufacturing over an agrarian economy in the West and South.

It was the famous Tariff of Abominations in the Jackson era that first provoked talk of secession. Fortunately, President Jackson revered the Union more than he did the white supremacy of his native Tennessee. And so he made men like South Carolina's John Calhoun back down and abandon his threats of secession.

While money can still influence sectional issues, it is only when various cultural issues are added to the mix that we reach a potential boiling point.

Such was the case with the Civil War, when a North, now viewing slavery as a moral issue, challenged the South to abandon its attempts to expand this economic system beyond the area where it had been sanctioned under the Constitution.

The South in turn balked at having its way of life (both economic and cultural) challenged and looked down upon. That was basically the cataclysmic event that broke down the possibility of a constructive dialogue, leading inexorably to war.

Yet it is instructive to note that the North's winning the Civil War did not put an end to this issue, despite legislating an end to slavery through the 13th Amendment. The South fought back with a cultural war under the banner of 'The Lost Cause' and outlasted the will of the North in re-imposing another form of slavery under a policy of 'Jim Crow'. The lesson here is that sectionalism based on cultural differences cannot be bludgeoned out of existence.

Rather, it requires a dedicated and collaborative effort over time to change ideas and traditions... mostly focused on the next generation.

THE CONSOLIDATION OF WEALTH

Today, it is the consolidation of corporate power that threatens the Madisonian theory of social. This has created a non-constitutional power center of sorts that can bypass the people through a cadre of lobbyists to enact its own self- serving agenda.

That includes opposing issues vital to the nation's well being that may be antithetical to the interests of big business. Such is the case with solutions to climate change that require the oversight by the federal government and threaten the myth, perpetuated by the business community, that 'government is the problem, not the solution'.

REAGAN ERA'S UNDOING OF AN ACTIVIST GOVERNMENT

Today's sectionalism is further aggravated by changing economics. Wealth creation once meant benefitting all of society. Where the barons of the Gilded Age produced goods that enhanced the GNP, today's winners in globalization are the financial markets composed of bankers, hedge funds, private equity managers etc.

These moneymen simply manage and remove funds from the overall economy, rarely adding a penny to our national wealth. Nor does this bode well for tomorrow. Today's shiny object of wealth management simply detours and diverts talented individuals from careers and professions that might add to our national wealth.

The undue influence of this new moneyed class in affecting government policy has halved tax rates and eliminated Glass Steagall regulations on investment banking, while keeping minimum wages stagnant.

The New Right's current rant against 'demonic government' interfering with their interests, hawked endlessly by right wing vehicles, depends on a massive dose of amnesia and revisionist view of American history. It also depends on putting together a vital Republican coalition of convenience. This includes many of those living in those over-represented rural communities, fearful of a multi-cultural society and opposed to abortion.

With the explosion of social media, the job of stoking the fire of distrust of government, begun in earnest under Reagan, is already easier. This generation also has fewer memories of major events such as The Great Depression and World War II that required our standing together, rather than counting on our own self-interest to meet any future challenges.

THE JUDICIAL PLOT OF ORIGINALISM
Another element in our national conversation that has dulled our sense of communalism is the judicial theory of 'originalism'. This term was invented by Robert Bork and has been called 'arrogance cloaked in humility' by Justice Brennan. It has continued to elevate individual rights above those of the collective whole. In effect, it has created spurious First Amendment freedoms that were never intended under the Constitution.

Funded again by the wealthy, through so-called intellectual think tanks, it represents its own form of judicial activism.

In the <u>Heller Case</u>, it transformed gun ownership into a sacred right of the individual by setting up a straw man of impending doom and implying that government was coming to get your guns. In the <u>Citizens United</u> decision, it elevated corporations to the equivalents of persons entitled to free speech (another throwback to the Gilded Age of 1890).

In short, 'originalism' distorts our history, rather than defining it. All of this under the guise of a so-called constitutional doctrine that John Marshall would not recognize. At a time when issues like income inequality, climate change, globalization require a national response and federal action, five justices may well claim that their hands are tied by the paramount rights of individuals.

With a Congress ineffective and locked in cultural gridlock, in part due to sectionalism that overstates the voices of the most under-populated states, we may well continue to thwart the will of the people ... or at the very least, doing what's good for the country in terms of loss of jobs and dignity in the global economy.

Yet these are the ones who have voted for a party that has recently enacted a huge tax cut that totally favors corporations and the wealthy. These voices will now insist that this requires cuts in social security and an already meager safety net of other benefits in order to balance the budget.

TODAY'S NEW BRAND OF SECTIONALISM

Today's sectionalism seems different and more dangerous from that of the past. It represents a situation that is part culture war, part economics and part racially motivated. This makes the so-called 'red/blue' divide even more susceptible to demagoguery by the various interest groups, aided by the vastly increased social media's ability to target a specific audience and harden opinions.

It also preys on some of the intrinsic weaknesses in our Constitution, threatening to make the document less relevant at a time when we need more than ever to have it hold the nation together. The question is, who will address the issues that underlie these so-called sectional problems? Will it be an activist president or an activist court, under cases that lay out the issues to be adjudicated?

If so, these might include:

1. Growing income inequality between the haves and have not's.... who are largely separated geographically between urban and rural areas.

2. A geographic and racial divide between a rural white America and a growing multicultural urbanized America.

3. A growing politically active evangelical America in the hinterlands versus a less ardently religious urban audience.

In short, we seem to have two America's talking past each other and having little in common, other than occupying the same country. Perhaps this will require a re-working of the Constitution's mandates under Article I Section 2 that sets the ground rules for electing representatives in the House. Perhaps these have to be reworked in order to make the government work more efficiently for all the people based on today's demographics.

These might include:

1. Drafting a constitutional amendment to move confirmation of Supreme Court justices to the House...a body more representative of the entire country.

2. Building a more activist and robust House with a larger representation, noting that the current 435 members was established in 1911...with half of today's population.

   - This might include apportioning votes, rather than a winner-take-all process, in order to divide it among the various candidates and better express the will of the people.

3. Empowering a federal commission to establish new congressional districts composed of the broadest set of demographics

that encourage political compromise to satisfy a variety of constituents.

It is now almost forty years since this pro-business, anti-government ethos has been embedded in the national psyche.
The question will be:

- Has the public suffered enough income inequality, wage suppression, lack of bargaining power and loss of benefits?

- Will we take back the agenda and make the Constitution more 'perfect' with our votes or will we allow today's sectionalism...cultural and economic...to mask our common interest?

A NEW CONSTITUTIONAL PARTNERSHIP

Achieving presidential greatness has never been in the hands of the president alone. It requires that he be surrounded by an experienced White House team to implement his agenda, led by an effective Chief of Staff, who has experience in dealing with Congress to pass the necessary legislation to ensure his legacy. It obviously helps if the President's party also has a majority in both houses of Congress. If not, strategy and competence on the part of the Chief of Staff is even more imperative!

Today, an effective president may well require a different alliance and lines of communication, and a policy expert within the White House to forge new ground. That would include one between the executive branch and the judiciary to initiate important cases with the right facts to reach the Court for a decision based on constitutional grounds.

While the two branches of government have often been at odds for a variety of reasons...with the Court clipping the wings of the chief executive when necessary...ironically there were times when the two branches worked together, sometimes for the wrong reasons.

In the case of 'Dred Scott' of 1856, the Court attempted to settle forever the issue of spreading slavery throughout the country, a political decision if ever there was one. It was calculated to please the Buchanan Administration and shut down a national discussion that was about to destroy the fabric of a nation. Lincoln attacked the decision as immoral and favoring a lave conspiracy of expansionism. He never called it unconstitutional.

The Supreme Court may be the third branch of government under Article lll of the Constitution, determining the constitutionality of legislation or executive action. It has most definitely been involved in politics ever since John Marshall elevated it as a co-equal branch of government.

Starting with his decision in <u>Marbury v. Madison</u> in 1804, the court under Marshall enshrined the right to constitutional review, only hinted at in the Constitution. But Marbury was not merely a case that afforded Marshall this opportunity. By pledging his fealty to interpreting a Constitution, he gave himself greater latitude to be free of the restrictions of common law or precedent in guiding a nation toward that more perfect union.

He also used his talents in making savvy political decisions to satisfy both Federalists and Republicans, at war over who would control the judiciary. In the end, it assured each that the Court would calm the waters and give both parties equal judicial consideration. In fact, Marshall's major decisions over the next three decades were unanimous, despite the fact that there were more Republicans than Federalists on the bench.

They were also highly political decisions, calculated to give the federal government greater authority over the states, leaving them with what was called 'residual' authority. In the process, the Marshall Court unleashed American commerce across state lines, building the sanctity of contracts to promote business and commerce as well as forging a nation as much as Hamilton or Lincoln.

THE AMBIGUITY OF JUDICIAL ACTIVISM

Some would call the Marshall Court 'activist', a term intended as a pejorative. However, its decisions have been upheld over more than two hundred years, all that time setting precedents for other decisions to build on this legacy. (And is a supposedly non-activist court any less political in not taking action to craft 'a more perfect union' for the public good?)

Again, let us look at the <u>Dred Scott</u> decision of 1856, where the Court followed the implicit mandate of the Constitution's 3/5's clause, declaring Negroes to be property! That certainly showed a lack of judicial activism. But it also denied the intent of other founding documents...namely the Declaration of Independence, with Lincoln finally winning that argument in the court of public opinion.

For Lincoln understood that there is a higher law than sustaining a decision that refutes morality, even if that requires citing another founding document to embrace that higher authority.

We have only to look at <u>Bush v. Gore</u>, the decision of a supposedly non-activist majority to note the diminution of judicial authority in its disregard of judicial precedent that motivated a seat-of-the-pants decision. Was it a fear of chaos in the political process that warranted this intrusion into 'pure politics'?

Ironically, this represented the height of 'activism', especially when there was well-established precedent to let the House decide the outcome of an election without a sufficient majority in the Electoral College.

A FRAGILE ALLIANCE

Presidents have long recognized the Court's power to contradict their actions, based on constitutional issues. But some of our greatest presidents have also chosen to ignore those decisions when they felt that the people or the sweep of history was on their side.

Such was the case with Jackson in the <u>Cherokee Nation Case</u>, when he said, 'Marshall has made his decision. Now let him try to enforce it!' He knew only too well that the manic land grab of settlers moving west was unstoppable. Lincoln as well ignored the Court when it disputed his suspending the writ of habeas corpus during the Civil War, claiming a wartime necessity as commander-in-chief.

There are times when the Court may be out of sync with the times to the detriment of the nation or again guilty of violating a moral edict enshrined in the Declaration of Independence. Such was the case with the Court's 'separate but equal' decision in 1896 in Plessy v. Ferguson.

It took another fifty years to set the stage to reverse that verdict. Rather than rely on that higher morality to overturn the decision in Plessy, Brown v. Board of Education represented a new type of carefully prepared test case. It provided reams of data proving that 'separate' education for blacks and whites was inherently 'unequal'. Perhaps this approach is needed today to get government moving toward establishing that 'more perfect union'.

Nor was this decision to reverse an ill-conceived judicial standard out of the mainstream. Truman had already set the stage for re-evaluating race relations when he integrated the armed forces. Brown was simply building on prior precedent established by the executive branch and taking it to its natural conclusion, a true collaboration of sorts between the two branches. The same could be set of the recent march toward equality in 'matters of sex', including gay rights.

THAT NEW ALLIANCE

With Congress unwilling or unable to resolve many of today's issues through sensible bipartisan legislation, perhaps it is time to look to a novel relationship. In truth, while all three branches were put in place to act as a check in overstepping constitutional norms...there is nothing in the Constitution that prohibits collaboration in search of a worthy and constitutional goal.

To paraphrase, the great John Marshall, any action required by the Chief Executive to bring to fruition a constitutional mandate under Article ll, is assumed to be valid under the 'necessary and proper' or 'implied powers' clauses. Let us assume that both branches have an interest in moving the country forward in a positive manner as equals. Certainly, each branch, Judiciary and Executive, have enough 'carrots and sticks' to make this work.

The Court will not seek to make decisions that break with constitutional norms according to solid precedent no matter what the current president requires. In fact, its decision may give something of value to the Chief Executive while rewarding other interested parties in this national debate. Such was the policy in many of Marshall's greatest decision in elevating the position of the judiciary.

Likewise, the Chief Executive has ways to gaining cooperation of the Court. Such was the case when FDR threatened to 'pack the Court' with additional justices at a time when they seemed determined in the midst of the Depression to overturn important 'New Deal' legislation.

Nor would adding to or subtracting from the Court be unprecedented, as the number of justices varied from 'day one', particularly in the early years of the Court. FDR's threats in and of themselves were quite effective. Although public opinion forced him to abandon this ploy, the justices understood the message and began to deem much of this legislation as constitutional. (As some clever observer wrote at the time, 'a switch in time, saved nine!')

While the current make-up of the Court tends to be highly conservative, an alliance that gives added stature to the Court in a partnership in resolving thorny issues, could be quite enticing as well as productive. That is a solution the Founding Fathers would likely applaud in demonstrating the flexibility of a document never intended to be the final word.

MAPPING OUT SOME MAJOR ISSUES TO BE ADDRESSED

Let us test this theory with the issue of gun control, which has defied congressional action, despite mass killings at movie theaters, concert venues and in our elementary public schools, where innocent children were the victims.

If a hypothetical test case were put in motion under 'the equal protection ' clause of the Fourteenth Amendment, perhaps the Court could begin to incrementally cut back on various types of weaponry on a number of grounds, including the adverse affect on the rights of many innocent victims.

The Administration would need a strong, knowledgeable Solicitor General with a team of researchers to make a convincing case, one that was full of historic data to prove their case as to the intent of the founders. This was what Lincoln masterfully accomplished at Cooper Union in 1861, when he proved that a majority of those crafting the Constitution disapproved of the spread of slavery.

Even an inveterate 'originalist' looking at the second amendment would be faced with reams of documentation from that era surrounding the writing of the Constitution. It would be difficult to deny that the right to possess muskets was proposed on any other basis than the right to assemble a state militia on short notice, when no standing army was available. Supreme Court might well decide that any firepower exceeding this equivalent level would require congressional action. The Court would then review this legislation at a later date, giving the legislative branch a 'buy-in' on the decision. Again, as with Marshall, everyone would receive something of value

That same sense of balance would be equally important in the Court's revisiting its decision in <u>Roe v. Wade</u>. Perhaps the Court acted too boldly in declaring a right to abortion (under the right to privacy). It might have been better to grant this right incrementally, while suggesting safeguards and limits (to be written into law) to prevent this from becoming a lightning rod to awaken the passions of the religious community.

The timing for this new approach may actually be fortuitous. It appears that the Court might be ready to look toward its legacy in the eyes of history. It may well be the Judiciary's moment to elevate its constitutional ranking when it comes to the workings of the three branches of government.

It would certainly please the Founders to know that the document they crafted in 1787 was dynamic and fluid enough to address the challenges of the future in keeping a vibrant democracy afloat. Perhaps that is why Chief Justice Roberts, a confirmed conservative as well as a wily political operative, opted in recent decisions to find grounds to support the Affordable Care Act and other legislation that might be called 'liberal' in its intent. As John Marshall knew only too well, the Court's strength is ultimately based on that moral standing in making wise decisions that benefit the country as a whole, rather than one particular interest group.

Perhaps a wise chief executive will seek that alliance to jumpstart a bold legislative agenda and have us moving in the right direction toward collective justice for all rather than individual rights for the few. Only time will tell.

UNIQUELY AMERICAN ISSUES

E very nation is seen as having its own unique qualities, its own foibles, its own special characteristics. Some of these are part myth ... part stereotype ... part exaggeration. Nevertheless, they pervade the thinking of that particular society.

These perceptions are built over centuries. For Americans, that process began in 1776, at the nation's founding, with that Declaration of Independence.

Our best presidents have known how to play to those unique American qualities and use them to bring us together. They have also known when to take us beyond our 'comfort zone' and dismiss some as irrelevant. There have also been times when presidents have used qualities or beliefs baked into the American psyche to serve their own ends and move us backward, at least for the moment.

Those words in the Constitution, 'to form a more perfect Union', require that our leaders continue that uniquely American conversation. We as well are challenged to assess our progress from time to time in reaching that goal. And if that forces us to face a harsh reality from time to time, that too is part of the process.

Benjamin Franklin

BENJAMIN FRANKLIN: THE FIRST AMERICAN

N o one personifies American uniqueness more than Benjamin Franklin. Born thirty years before Washington, he was in some ways the elder statesman among the founding father, advising the others, usually with a sly twinkle in his eye, based on keen understanding of human nature.

Whether through good fortune or cunning, he seems to have turned up at all the right moments to add his name to more of our revered documents than any other founding father.

THE EARLY YEARS

His life begins on Milk Street in Boston, where he is born above the family store in 1706. His father is a chandler, a soap and candle maker with seventeen children between his first and second marriages. His mother, that second wife, is a scrappy Puritan from a prominent Nantucket family.

Franklin, the youngest son, is a bright little mischief-maker, never lacking for an audience to entertain and play tricks on. Family circumstances limit his horizons when it comes to education, studying at Boston Latin for a few years without graduating. Nevertheless, he will be sure to tweak those students at Harvard from time to time and remind them what a more modest education can produce.

Franklin grows into a large, barrel chested young man and goes to work for his older brother, the founder of The New England Courant, the first independent newspaper in the colonies. Never one to stay idle for long, he decides to spice up it up with a little gossip, writing earnest yet humorous letters to the editor under the name of Mrs. Silence Dogood.

Everyone is greatly entertained...except for Franklin's step-brother, forcing him to flee to Philadelphia rather than face penalties under his apprenticeship.

THE PHILADELPHIA YEARS

And thus a young, scrappy entrepreneur in the newspaper business is born, ready to take the biggest city in the colonies by storm.

By the age of twenty, he is already networking with others in his profession, creating what he calls The Leather Apron Club. It is dedicated to self-improvement through 'Socratic methods' and what Franklin calls the use of strategic silence for indirect persuasion.

Throughout his life, he will practice the art of self improvement, writing a list of the virtues that can help a man succeed... something many of the founding fathers are intent on as well, particularly John Adams, another man with a New England upbringing.

He finds order and humility the hardest to achieve, which plainly plays out in life when he enters into a common law marriage while fathering a child in an out-of-wedlock relationship. He is sure to then memorialize the moment by writing an amusing pamphlet on the rules and maxims for promoting matrimonial happiness.

He and his wife Deborah will have one son, who dies early of smallpox and a daughter Sally, who will remain eager to please her father despite his continuing absences from her life.

Franklin, always a believer in communalism, continues to change the face of Philadelphia by creating a number of organizations, including a lending library, a voluntary fire brigade and ultimately, a college and a hospital.

He writes prophetically, 'What good men may do separately is small compared to what they may do selectively'. When battles with Indians break out on the perimeters of the country, Franklin harkens to this message and attempts to forge an alliance with other colonies. He even puts a cartoon in his paper of a snake cut into pieces along with the words, 'Join together or Die'.

His experiences will serve him well in ultimately helping to craft the birth of a nation, reconciling the disparate themes of individualism and communalism to live a satisfying life.

Always sensitive to a changing society, he takes up his pen to write another amusing tract to skewer a growing middle class. It is called 'Poor Richard's Almanack' and will outsell the Bible with its tales of Richard Saunders and his nagging wife Bridget.

One might call it the nation's first 'sitcom' as it proudly promotes the virtues and foibles of the American way of life with what will be known as 'cracker barrel' humor.

A MAN OF SCIENCE

By now, Franklin has built a newspaper empire by sending his apprentices up and down the coast to establish their own newspapers and share the profits with him. One might therefore call him the first media czar, long before the Hearst's and Murdock's earned that title.

This leaves him free to retire and spend his life pursuing what he calls 'scientific amusements'. For these are the times when the philosophy of the Enlightenment has prophesied an orderly world that can be explored through experimentation and a political system that man can establish through an orderly process of checks and balances.

For Franklin, both concepts are inexorably tied together, one promoting individual experimentation and the other requiring a communal approach... which will ultimately come to fruition with the Constitution Convention thirty years later.

While he lacks the academic credentials to be a great theorist, Franklin's keen and probing mind unlock the cosmic secrets behind electricity as a single fluid, leading to his practical invention of the lightening rod. These experiments turn him into America's first international celebrity, now known as Doctor Franklin, provoking a famous French statesman to say of him later in life, 'He snatched lightening from the sky and the scepter from tyrants'.

AN AWAKENING PATRIOT

As the most prominent citizen of Philadelphia, he is now sent abroad to renegotiate the terms under which the Commonwealth of Pennsylvania is governed by the Penn family. This will be Franklin's introduction to the issues that soon engulf other colonies in their dealings with the King of England and a Parliament that writes arbitrary legislation to impose a host of increasingly onerous taxes.

Once again, Franklin's unorthodox family relationships are at play when he is accompanied by his illegitimate son, William, and conveniently sets up a second household with another woman and her daughter. William will now follow in his father's footsteps and father an out-of-wedlock child of his own, William Temple Franklin, to be known as Temple.

Doctor Franklin is still abroad as the situation grows tense back home with the imposition of additional taxes. While others are speaking of breaking with the King, Franklin remains loyal, while humorously chastising Parliament with pamphlets such as one titled, 'Rules by which a Great Empire may be reduced to small one'.

He finally returns to America with his grandson, Temple, while William remains in England as a committed loyalist. This is a propitious moment, as the battle of Bunker Hill enflames patriotic zeal.

A COMMITTED FOUNDING FATHER

By now, Franklin is finally ready to join the combatants, proposing a strong central government and put in charge of establishing a paper currency, which will ultimately prove to be worthless.

He attends the First Continental Congress, along with John Adams and Thomas Jefferson, and takes part in drafting the 'Declaration of Independence'... crafting the phrase, 'We take these truths to be self evident'.

With the Revolution ongoing, and Washington as Commander-in-Chief, the Continental Congress is fast at work, trying to craft a document to establish a workable government. It is known as the Articles of Confederation, giving all the participants, determined to retain their autonomy, the right to veto any proposed legislation.

The Revolution creates a government desperate for funds to fight the British. Franklin is sent to France to seek financial assistance from Britain's arch-enemy. All of his personal attributes are at play as he charms the French, acting out the part of that authentic American and even donning a coonskin cap to make the point. He uses those skills he has honed to perfection in the art of persuasion to charm the French Foreign Minister and extract the necessary funds. Only his fellow Ambassador, John Adams, remains uncharmed, as his hardworking, humorless approach fails to yield results.

With our victory at Yorktown ending the war, the clever Franklin sidesteps the French and opens backdoor negotiations with the British ... leading to his being one of those representatives signing the final peace agreement.

Again timing is on his side as he returns home to attend a convention called for the summer of 1787, supposedly to amend the Articles of Confederation. But first, he stops in Britain to settle affairs with his son, William, who remains as a loyal Tory. Franklin shows another side of his personality as he strips his son of his assets, including Temple, who returns home as his grandfather's official secretary.

His presence as well as Washington's at the Convention in Philadelphia will prove vital to success in drafting a new Constitution to replace the ineffective Articles of Confederation.

He, along with Washington, sit on a dais, elevated above the fifty five delegates who will be engaging in a contentious debate on many points. Franklin wisely suggests opening each session with a prayer to cool tempers and bring everyone together in a spirit of compromise. Much of the work to craft the final document will take place in the shaded garden at his home on Market Street.

As the convention winds down, many are disappointed with the results. But, Dr. Franklin is ever the optimist as he views the future prospects of the nation. He looks at the carving on the back of the chair he has been sitting in for the past four months and declares that he sees a rising sun.

With the Constitution now signed by all the delegates who are eager to leave for home, he has the final word, acknowledging that the process has been difficult and that it will be up to future generations to perfect this imperfect document. His words may be somewhat ungrammatical, yet prophetic, as he says, 'I consent to this Constitution because I expect no better and because I am not sure that it is not the best.'

And now this man, the only one among the founding fathers to sign the Declaration of Independence, The Peace Agreement with Britain and the Constitution, completes his autobiography. He intends for it to serve as another self-help manual, this time as a guide for America's middle class, whom he regards as the future guardians of this fragile democracy.

CONCLUSIONS

Benjamin Franklin dies but a year later, having presided over the writing of the nation's most important founding document. We salute him today for his service and for his continuing relevance in our ongoing national conversation that occasionally strays from those founding concepts.

He heralded the importance of a vibrant middle class as a unique attribute of American Democracy. He fostered the development of a unique American culture, including a homespun sense of humor that allows us to laugh at our foibles. He embraced science as an asset, rather than a threat, in charting our course and guiding us toward the future. He saw no conflict between advocating on behalf of individualism while embracing communalism, the belief that we were stronger when we worked together to promote the needs of our Democracy. And he was unfailingly optimistic as to the future of this experiment in man's ability to control his worst impulses and govern himself.

AN AMERICAN Q&A

We have always prided ourselves on each generation participating in a robust conversation as to its vision for America.
That is part of the mandate of our Constitution, a constant effort
to perfect that 'more perfect Union'.

Today's conversation seems more heated, as though we are more
apt to disagree on fundamental issues than prior generations. If
so, perhaps the questions (and answers) noted below can highlight
some of the issues to be resolved.

**Question: What is the defining characteristic of American
'Uniqueness'?**

Answer: That has always depended on the times, always changing,
but in general, it is about 'exceptionalism' of sorts.

In the founding era, it meant establishing a unique form of government, based on the ability for people to rule themselves without
the intervention of kings or despots.

As the nation grew in population and wealth, it meant the
self-confidence to believe in the 'Manifest Destiny' of the country
to become a transcontinental power and spread the message of
democracy.

In the Gilded Age (1870-1900) it represented the right of the
wealthy to teach the benefits of unbridled capitalism to the nation
and to the world.

In the 1940's, under FDR, it meant the pride in banding together as a nation to defeat a Depression and the threat of fascism.

In the next decades, it meant leading the free world in opposing the threat communism with a superior political ideology and economic system. Domestically, it meant crafting a bipartisan agenda to build the middle class and increase the scope of long dormant civil rights legislation.

Beginning in 1980 through today, it has meant reduced government, in part through lower taxes, and honoring unbridled capitalism and individual rights to unleash 'the best and the worst' in America.

Question: How do we best define the unique aspects of American character?

Answer: While there are many subheadings when it comes to describing ourselves as 'Americans'...perhaps 'resilient and optimistic', best defines our place in the scheme of things...the ability to rise to our own level of competence without impediments placed in our way.

For that is what a free enterprise system supposedly promises in a marketplace of ideas and opportunities, overseen by a central government, where capital and labor have an equal voice.

The question is whether that premise still exists.

Question: Is today's multicultural society a unique experience in our history?

Answer: In truth, we have always had different ethnicities coming to our shores. Our earliest immigrants were from England and Ireland. But by the later half of the Nineteenth Century, many were arriving from southern and Eastern Europe, creating a great deal of displeasure and discrimination.

However, more than cultural differences, skin color and the shape of one's eyes have incited much greater antipathy.

The Chinese Exclusion Act of 1890 was the earliest iteration of this. The continuing wave of immigration from Mexico and Central America is the latest, aggravated by some crossing borders illegally.

When combined with the nation's black population...not a factor of immigration but rather the moral issue of slavery...the totals presage a majority population of color in a previously white America, a prospect that many find unsettling.

Dealing with this requires balancing the positive aspects of immigration to the American economy and to society with the negative aspects, to create an informed 'bucket' of solutions.

Question: Have we properly honored the Constitution's words regarding the separation of church and State?

Answer: Since the founding era, many have come to these shores in search of religious liberty. It is therefore ironic that today many feel entitled to impose their religious values on others.

The founders were by and large deists, believing in an orderly world watched over by a higher power, without accepting specific religious dogma.

Washington believed that we come together in the public square as Americans, to honor the words of the Constitution. We are then free to exercise the beliefs of a specific religion in our homes and in our houses of worship.

The reasons this is has been questioned of late are complicated, in part by party politics that have stoked the fires of dissent in search of votes. The Supreme Court may be the 'court of last resort' to deal with this issue on constitutional grounds.

Question: Have we always been a country of one-issue voters?

Answer: Parties used to stand for a different philosophical view as to the role of government...one party preferring an activist government versus another wanting less government and more self reliance (i.e., another variation of Hamilton vs. Jefferson).

Now, emotional, hot-button issues have come to define parties, rather than philosophical or regional differences. Instead, issues like racial purity versus multi-culturalism are more like the pro versus anti- slavery issues of the 1850's.

The intrusion of religion has turned pro-abortion sentiment into a godless and hedonistic point of view without room for compromise.

Freedom to bear any type of weapon versus strict controls is a replay of another unique American issue, fear of government intrusion to take away one's rights. This is also part of a larger issue where so-called individual liberty has been elevated over the rights of the collective whole.

Question: Are we losing the ability of government to represent the will of the people ... through current demographics... or gerrymandering and voter suppression? And is this a new phenomenon?

Answer: We have often had unrepresentative government ... starting with a Constitution that, through the three-fifths clause, elevated the South's population and gave it far too much power in the House of Representatives.

That problem was supposedly 'solved' by giving blacks a full vote under the Fifteenth Amendment. Obvious voter suppression under Jim Crow, implementing such tactics as a poll tax tells us that local issues are always at play without federal oversight.

As voting rights are not specifically enshrined in the Constitution, other than hinted at under the Fourteenth Amendment, it may be time to enact a Twenty-Eighth Amendment to create one consistent mandate rather than a fifty state patchwork of state and local rules.

While those representatives in the House were to be based on a state's population, the current level at 435 vastly understates the voice of the most populous states.

Question: Is the current assault on a free press, with terms like 'fake news' and 'deep state' to denigrate its reliability, something new?

Answer: We have long had 'press wars'... all the way back to Jefferson's starting the Republican Party to challenge the reigning Federalists. And Andrew Jackson virtually owned the press in his creation of the Democratic Party.

It comes as no surprise to have Fox News supporting a particular point of view vis a vis CNN and leaving the people to decide who best represents their interests.

However, the best of our presidents have a respectful working relationship with the Fourth Estate, realizing that it was their job to keep the people informed. Attacks on the press would usually come from outside the Oval Office ... from those with a specific agenda. Now attacks on the press come from the Chief Executive, a dangerous phenomenon that may one day be defined as grounds for impeachment.

Question: Is Donald Trump an aberration in our political life or the logical extension of party politics?

Answer: In demeanor, Trump represents the grossest but still logical extension of a divided electorate...similar to the caning and acts of violence that went on in Congress in the lead up to the Civil War.

However, in actions taken, he is totally in line with the objectives of today's Republican Party... unbridled capitalism, free of regulation and disregarding the need to fund safety net programs, while grossly favoring the wealthy.

Question: How and when did the working man and woman lose the ability to have someone represent their interests vis a vis business?

Answer: As in the Gilded Age (1870-1900), a new iteration of 'Social Darwinism' has come to prevail under the assumption that business knows best when it comes to the interests of the nation and its workers. In fact, the courts have validated this concept in decisions like 'Citizens United', while rendering no decisions as to expanding workers' rights.

What has been most unusual is the passivity of both the public and the workers in accepting the demise of unions, mandated to represent the interests of labor. This despite a long history of fighting for these rights throughout the 1930's and 40's when America successfully constructed a huge middle class of equal opportunity and a thriving economy.

The reasons for this are vast and varied. But paramount among them is the clever messaging of business interests that now dominate the media with their messaging and their money to spread patent falsehoods and myths.

Question: Why are large segments of the sinking middle class so vulnerable to a false narrative that doesn't meet their concerns?

Answer: In part, this is due to the denigrating of our government institutions, begun under Reagan, with his famous remark that 'government is the problem, not the solution'.

This opened the way to the so-called 'majesty of the market place', free of those irksome 'hindrances' (i.e., government oversight and regulation) and having the lion's share of economic growth end up in the pockets of the wealthy.

Today's egregious and growing income inequality has left a sinking middle class seeing themselves as somehow unworthy, rather than entitled to benefits as a right not a privilege.

Question: Is today's sinking middle class different from that of prior decades, and in what ways?

Answer: Yes! For income inequality and the loss of a living wage previously affected the most vulnerable...immigrants and blacks. But today, it affects the heart of the white working class and therefore destabilizes an entire economy.

The symptoms are manifold, including a falling life expectancy, especially in rusted out factory towns and rural areas left behind by globalization.

This in turn has created a crisis in society with disadvantaged whites turning inward, focusing on their personal struggle and addressing the emotional pain with opioids or other drugs that the pharmaceutical companies are happy to provide, thereby preventing their even having to look for a job.

Question: Have we always placed individualism over a belief in our federal institutions?

Answer: Again, that misplaced myth of self reliance has long had many of our most vulnerable assuming the role of 'lonely warriors', leading them to carry guns and focus their anger on the false narrative of a faceless government that neglects them, while allowing shiftless immigrants and minorities to feast at the public trough.

Question: Are we destined to embrace nationalism versus a globalized communal interrelated world and what are the risks of each?

Answer: Individualism is a liberal creed, celebrating the uniqueness of each human being. Yet it can often come into conflict with the values of communalism, given that selfishness is a part of human nature, especially when left untamed.

Globalization has brought prosperity to many countries. It risks being burdensome when it breaks communal ties that give people's lives meaning.

Ultimately, the job of a state, other than social cohesion, is to provide economic remedies for those who are left behind with a sense of alienation. This is also the antidote for the rampant individualism promoted by unbridled capitalism.

When that economic machinery benefits the few, the fundamentals of a national consensus come into conflict with individualism, leading to setting class against class. The question is whether we can get back to establishing a national consensus that values the role that government will play in that process.

John Quincy Adams

NON-IMPEACHABLE
MISDEEDS

With all the talk of impeachable behavior or other acts that might well qualify as 'high crimes and misdemeanors' under the Constitution, it may be helpful to lighten the conversation and review so-called presidential misbehavior of another sort, that does not rise to that level of concern.

In some cases, that might include a personal failing that may cloud a legacy. In other cases, the accusation may say more about the accuser than the perpetrator. Or perhaps the misdeed may be more of a sign of the times, one that would not receive a passing glance today.

So let us take a moment to both amuse and edify ourselves as we review the various scandals, missteps or unintended consequences that history has recorded or possibly missed, regarding various presidents.

GEORGE WASHINGTON was known as a man of good, solid judgment and of impeachable integrity.

Had he not been deified by the public as 'the father of the country', he might well have been impeached for signing the Jay Treaty with the British in 1794. For according to the great mass of public opinion, this treaty was virtually treasonous, giving everything to Britain that was demanded, with little but a few crumbs to a proud, young nation.

Today, there would undoubtedly be endless hearings to delve into the machinations that had taken place behind the scene by various culprits.

Yet, history applauded the Treaty for settling various festering issues and allowing us to concentrate on growing a fragile democracy.

JOHN ADAMS had the unfortunate fate to follow a virtual deity into the White House. Where Washington was tall and of regal bearing, Adams was short and plump. He also possessed a volatile temperament that was hard to control.

The only so-called scandal that might have surfaced could have to do with so-called 'dereliction of duty'. For as President, he spent more than a third of his term away from Washington, licking his wounds back in his hometown of Quincy Massachusetts when attacked by rivals or Congress.

THOMAS JEFFERSON was wont to attack his various rivals through dutiful surrogates...while making sure that his hands appeared clean when it came to intrigue. Once in a while he got caught, as when Washington discovered a letter in which Jefferson described him as 'the shorn Samson' and broke off any future correspondence.

One of those surrogates, a man named James Callender, turned against Jefferson, writing of his relationship with that 'African Venus' named Sally Hemings, who shared the President's bed. Weeks later, Callender was found dead, floating in the Tidal Basin. If the Vince Foster suicide warranted scrutiny during the Clinton Administration, one can only imagine the hearings and FBI investigations that might have ended the Jefferson presidency.

JAMES MONROE was more the victim rather than the perpetrator in terms of the misdeeds perpetrated by a President. Ironically, he was perhaps the most put upon of presidents in terms of his spending his own money during his many trips abroad in the service of his nation without being properly reimbursed.

This actually severely diminished his resources and required his spending his older years living with his daughter. In fact, a spiteful Andrew Jackson only exacerbated the situation. As president, he was still nursing a grudge against Monroe for not backing him in a particular dispute. He therefore further delayed the reimbursement that Congress had already approved, knowing that Monroe was clearly entitled to it.

JOHN QUINCY ADAMS, the son of our second president, was perhaps our most adept Secretary of State, serving under James Monroe and crafting the Monroe Doctrine as the President's Farewell Address.

However, his election as President caused a scandal that could well have had its legal authority questioned in an impeachment or other proceeding. He was the first president to reach the White House without winning the popular vote.

Andrew Jackson had actually won a plurality of the vote (among several candidates) when the House was called upon to decide the winner. Jackson labeled the results as 'The Corrupt Bargain' when Henry Clay awarded the presidency to Adams, a charge never proved, but which nonetheless haunted the presidency of Quincy Adams.

Quincy Adams was the only President to leave the White House and take up a second career as a member of House of Representatives. He was also one of the few to face censure in the House ... as close to impeachment as any other proceeding. However, the act for which he was censured was more of an act of bravery than deceit. He managed to enrage the South by challenging the 'Gag Rule', calculated to close down any discussion of slavery. It took him nearly ten years of continuous effort, but in the end, he succeeded in getting the gag rule reversed and thwarting the South.

Another footnote of history includes Lincoln's being present in the House as a one-term congressman in the 1840's and watching the passion that Adams brought to this subject of moral reckoning. It might not be surprising that this lit the flame of passion within Lincoln as well.

ANDREW JACKSON controlled the votes in Congress during his reign as president. Otherwise, he would clearly have faced impeachment proceedings for not renewing the tenure of the Bank of the U.S. Instead, he was censured, still a severe reprimand, by Henry Clay and his fellow Whigs.

What might have received greater scrutiny today was his outsized sense of chivalry. This caused him to fire his entire Cabinet and reap chaos for the country for a protracted period of time. All because he disapproved of the way a particular Cabinet member's wife had been treated by the wives of other officials.

JOHN TYLER was one of those ill-chosen vice presidents, selected for all the wrong reasons to balance a ticket. He then ascended to the presidency upon the death of William Henry Harrison.

The threat of impeachment was based less on 'misdeeds' than the fact that he was never truly a Whig and would not support the party's agenda. The lesson here is that 'sour grapes' does not justify the accusation of 'high crimes and misdemeanors'.

JAMES POLK was a one-term president who expanded the landmass of the United States further than any prior president, Jefferson's Louisiana Purchase included.

Jefferson merely accepted the offer made by Napoleon to sell it to us at twenty-three cents an acre, while Polk concocted a story about Mexico's invasion of U.S. territory and started a phony war to execute a land grab. (Even Lincoln took issue and challenged Polk to show us 'the spot' where this took place...in what was called the 'Spot Resolutions'.)

Today that might be considered another 'Iraq' with lots of congressional investigations and possible impeachment proceedings. But in 1844, Polk's acts were seen as a display of 'Manifest Destiny' and our right to claim any land that completed a transcontinental nation.

JAMES BUCHANAN always ranks at the bottom of the list as to 'presidential greatness'. This has to do with two elements. First, the multiple scandals and incompetence that took place during his Administration. And second, his being a 'doughface'... a northerner who sided with the South in the lead up to the Civil War...leaving Lincoln to face an emboldened Confederacy.

No one ever discusses the fact that he may well have been our first gay president, living openly with a congressman in rooming house. It is therefore surprising that in that day and age of less tolerance, a man like Buchanan could rise to the presidency, despite all the rumors.

If he had turned out to be an excellent president, think of all the doors he might have opened for other like-minded men or women to seek higher office. Perhaps we wouldn't have had to wait another 170 years for a man like Pete Buttigieg to arrive in the scene.

ABRAHAM LINCOLN would definitely have faced impeachment proceedings if he had not been a man of such high moral character. He had enemies in many quarters...the South, in Congress and even in the North where many 'Copperheads' sided with the South. It was not surprising when members of Congress accused his wife Mary of everything from being a Confederate spy to spending excessively on frivolous items.

If the Clintons faced scandals like 'Travelgate' and 'White Water', imagine what the Lincoln's would have faced if his reputation as 'honest Abe' had not been so 'rock solid'. His overwhelming sense of morality saved him more than once ... as when he walked into Congress and offered to repay his wife's debts from his own pocket. With that, the matter was settled then and there without a peep.

ANDREW JOHNSON was a prime candidate for impeachment. He he managed to skirt that by one vote, only because Congress commenced the process based on the wrong grounds.

Johnson had basically thumbed his nose at the North's victory and sought to reward the southern slaveholders by restoring the status quo. This should certainly have qualified as 'high crimes and misdemeanors', especially considering the loss of life to win the war that was being betrayed, including Lincoln's legacy.

Instead, the House decided to rest its case on a flimsy piece of legislation known as The Tenure of Office Act, which extended congressional authority far beyond the limits of the Constitution.

ULYSSES GRANT has been viewed by history, until recently, as being a weak and pliable President, at the center of a corrupt Administration. Not that this was ever sufficient grounds for impeachment, especially given his popularity among the people.

For he was also perhaps the most bona fide of Civil War heroes, often fighting on the front line and inspiring his men not to retreat when things got tough. Without his skills as a strategist and a warrior in battle, Lincoln would probably not have been re-elected, and the war would have ended in a stalemate or worse.

It is now recognized that as president, he pushed on against great odds to realize Lincoln's legacy and reward former slaves with citizenship and dignity. But the Civil War had unleashed a wave of prosperity, commerce and corruption throughout the private sector and government. It was 'doing business' that interested the masses, not doing right by these former slaves. And so, through no fault of Grant's, the South ultimately defeated Reconstruction and restored the status quo with Jim Crow.

Where Grant did fall short was in not weeding out that corruption when faced with the facts and standing too firmly by his army friends, when men like Orville Babcock continually betrayed him. Nevertheless, he was cleared time and again of any malfeasance other than being a true and loyal friend, a fault perhaps, but also an indication of his character and his great sense of loyalty.

The so-called Gilded Age of great wealth and income inequality spawned a series of presidents between 1870 and 1900 who mirrored the times.

CHESTER A. ARTHUR deserves mention, although none would ever rank among the greats or near greats. It is ironic that his earlier career included his presiding over the Customs Houses of the Port of New York, a hotbed of corruption, greed and payoffs to politicians.

Yet once in office (upon the assassination of a President James Garfield), Arthur ran an honest administration and helped pass the Civil Service Act to appoint capable individuals in various government positions and end the curse of rampant patronage.

THEODORE ROOSEVELT was not one to be bullied even by the press. If he was unhappy with a story written by the king of 'yellow journalism', William Randolph Hearst, it was not beyond him to sue for libel, though he was likely to lose more often than not.

What galled him most were accusations that he had somehow profited in the building of the Panama Canal. Especially as he viewed this as his 'gift to America', turning us into a two-ocean naval superpower.

As history has recorded, the party that should have been offended was Columbia. It was only by staging a revolution within that province of Panama that we managed to wrest it from Columbia and turn it into a separate nation. As one of his Cabinet members said of the entire affair, when asked about the President's clever dealings, 'It wasn't seduction. It was rape!'

There was not a peep from Congress for going far beyond the precepts of the Constitution or the norms of diplomacy, although he clearly violated the territorial integrity of another nation.

WOODROW WILSON was by far our most academic president, having written copiously on various aspects regarding the role of the various branches of government. As president of Princeton University, he also brought that institution great scholastic renown.

Based on these qualifications, his rise in Democratic politics, attaining the governorship of New Jersey and then the presidency in short order, was really quite astounding.

It was his techniques in mobilizing the country to enter World War 1 that are viewed as somewhat questionable, particularly his stirring up pseudo-patriotic xenophobia and 'fear of the other' that played to our lesser instincts. In the process, all so-called 'hyphenated' Americans, especially those of German origin, were made to feel uneasy when their loyalty to America was constantly questioned.

Nevertheless, a troublesome precedent had taken flight, one that would play out in World War ll with the Japanese community in the West Coast. But most of all, it was ironic indeed that this should have taken place under an enlightened academic.

Perhaps Wilson's greatest misdeed in terms of diminished moral authority occurred when he screened a preview of the racist film, 'The Birth of a Nation' in the White House. His actions gave voice to the Ku Klux Klan elevating its standing and leading to a march on Washington, with thousands of members dressed in the garb of white nationalism.

WARREN G. HARDING is one of the most recognizable among that list of 'worst presidents'. But in truth, the country should not have been surprised by his mediocrity. They had knowingly elected 'an average Joe' and that is what they got.

Nor did the times help. The end of World War 1 and the fight in Congress over whether to join the League of Nations had worn down the country in terms of any glimmer of idealism. Harding's pledge to restore 'normalcy' seemed like the right medicine. With lots of money in circulation, graft and good times was naturally the order of the day. And Harding's cronies, known as the Ohio Gang, were just the right type to take advantage.

But unlike Grant, who suffered a similar fate of being betrayed by friends, Harding had few redeeming qualities other than affability. He was

therefore doomed to reside in the dustbin of history, without the taint of impeachment.

CALVIN COOLIDGE, a man from Vermont, was best known for saying everything in as few words as possible, and only when silence did not work. Fortunately, his presidency occurred midst the boom times of the Roaring Twenties or he might have been accused of withholding vital information from the American public…possibly more than a presidential misdeed in other times. However, it is interesting that Ronald Reagan, the great communicator, looked to Coolidge as one of our best presidents.

HERBERT HOOVER is someone who peaked prior to reaching the presidency, having served as the Secretary of Commence in two prior administrations, a time of great innovation. His fate, in running out of answers to cure the Depression at a time when the country needed new ideas, was somewhat tragic, but not impeachable.

FRANKLIN ROOSEVELT, one our greatest presidents in the eyes of history, certainly deserves plaudits for getting us through the Great Depression and then through World War ll...two cataclysmic events. But to a degree, as a member of the gentrified class on both his mother and father's side, he undoubtedly inherited some prejudices that were hard to dispel.

Not that he was clearly prejudiced. In fact, there were so many Jewish advisors in his Administration that the more bigoted often referred to it as 'The Jew Deal'. Still, many historians have rightly questioned FDR's not bombing the rail lines leading into camps like Auschwitz, especially as bombing raids were already under way in the vicinity. The excuse often given is rather feeble...that FDR did not want to favor one group of wartime victims over another and was more interested in simply winning the war as quickly as possible.

The other blot on his record includes gross discrimination against native-born Japanese. The Executive Order, removing them from their homes and consigning them to camps on the West Coast, is another blot on our history and FDR's legacy. But truth be told, the war hysteria and the fear of an imminent invasion was difficult to tamp down, a legacy carried over from World War l under the Wilson Administration.

HARRY S. TRUMAN was totally unprepared for the presidency when FDR died of a cerebral hemorrhage at Warm Springs Georgia in April 1945. He knew practically nothing about the ongoing conferences between FDR, Churchill and Stalin to create a new world order. Yet he surprised everyone as a quick study and more than held is own at Potsdam against a wily Stalin.

Although Truman had overcome the stigma of starting out as a machine politician from Kansas City, Missouri, he emulated Grant in keeping his cronies from Missouri close and remaining loyal to them, despite mounting evidence of their misdeeds.

Still, unlike Harding, Truman accomplished much where it mattered...enough to place him among the near-greats as president.

DWIGHT EISENHOWER was the first bona fide war hero since Grant to occupy the White House. The hero of D-Day and the liberation of Europe assured the public that he would avoid all those scandals of the Truman presidency and run an honest administration.

He learned the hard way that there was often a cozy relationship between members of an elite, when his Chief-of-Staff, Sherman Adams, was caught accepting favors and gifts from an industrialist friend from New England.

Perhaps his greatest misdeed occurred when he was campaigning for the presidency. He failed to confront the witch-hunt being conducted by Senator Joseph McCarthy on communist sympathizers...particularly when he was targeting General George Marshall, one of the most esteemed men in the country and the one who had nurtured Eisenhower's career.

JOHN F. KENNEDY and his stunning wife Jackie dazzled the public with their youth and good looks. His brilliant inaugural address heralded a new era, including certain lines that are still quoted today ... such as, 'ask not what your country can do for you.'

But appearances are deceiving. Actually, JFK was somewhat of a dilettante, absent from the Senate on more important votes than any other senator. In fact, even Khrushchev viewed him as weak when they first met in Vienna, which convinced him to try placing Soviet missiles in Cuba.

It also turned out that JFK was somewhat of a playboy in other ways as well, with multiple scandalous affairs while in the White House. If Bill Clinton is any example, in today's world and with the 'MeToo' movement, that misdeed alone might have ended his political career and perhaps his presidency.

LYNDON JOHNSON was a larger than life political figure from the oversized state of Texas with a significant legacy in the arena of civil rights. What ultimately could qualify as 'misdeeds' was his letting the military (and his Secretary of Defense, Robert McNamara) overwhelm civilian authority in the lead up and execution of the Vietnam War. For four long years, the American public was kept in the dark as to the realities of this growing disaster in blood and treasure that diminished our prestige abroad.

RICHARD NIXON is a poster boy for presidential 'misdeeds', long before Watergate landed the fatal blow with his voiding impeachment only by resigning.

During the 1968 campaign, he used various surrogates to undercut peace talks in Paris with the Vietnamese, knowing that a favorable result would limit his chances of winning the presidency.

His paranoia ultimately led to the creation of an 'Enemies List' and schemes to 'get even' in multiple illegal ways. This included having so-called burglars breaking into the Democratic headquarters in the Watergate in DC...and the start of the scandal that forced him to resign to avoid formal impeachment.

It was his using his presidential authority to involve the CIA and the FBI in this criminal ruse that counted as 'high crimes and misdemeanors' and 'abuse of power'. It is, however, ironic that his respect for the office and his legacy ultimately triumphed in his not destroying the most damning evidence, those White House tapes.

GERALD FORD was left to clean up the Watergate mess and restore faith in government, which he accomplished admirably in his scandal free brief time in office. His one so-called 'misdeed', pardoning Nixon from facing criminal proceedings, is actually viewed by many today as honorable in putting this episode behind us and not having the country endure an endless circus.

JIMMY CARTER, a former governor from Georgia was elected as the Democratic political outsider to sweep away the taint of corruption and cronyism of the Nixon era. Between the questionable behavior of insiders from Atlanta and family issues, including his brother Billy making deals on behalf of the government, the spell was quickly broken.

Perhaps his greatest misdeed was in diminishing the natural optimism of Americans by speaking of 'malaise of the spirit' ... something Americans would never appreciate. In the end Carter proved that too much of an inexperienced outsider was not the solution to our problems.

RONALD REAGAN, known as the 'Great Communicator', heralded a new era of supposedly less government and greater reliance on the majesty of the marketplace to solve our problems, a theory known as 'trickle down economics'.

History may one day look back on this era as the beginning of the end of the American Dream of equal opportunity for all...a huge 'misdeed' in terms of the American creed of equality for all.

His very cynical credo, saying that 'government is the problem' not the solution', lessened the people's confidence in our institutions, including the Environmental Protection Agency put in place to protect clean water and clean air and secure the future of a healthy planet.

It was the Iran-Contra affair that nearly qualified as an impeachable offense...his greatest 'misdeed' that created a near constitutional crisis when an out-of-control right wing cabal, working out of the National Security Council, decided to trade arms with Iran in order to supply cash to fund a revolution in Nicaragua.

GEORGE HW BUSH was also involved in the fallout of Iran Contra. As a favor to Reagan, he pardoned of many to stop the continuing investigation that was leading right to the door of the former President, now suffering from Alzheimer's.

The other misdeed may have involved his choice of Clarence Thomas, a cynical move at best when he replaced the retiring Thurgood Marshall, the defender of black rights with another black man who had no intention of taking up that cause.

BILL CLINTON took office just as the media landscape was changing. With the advent of the cable networks, and a thirst for stories to titillate the public, both Clinton and his wife provided plenty of fodder.

The Clinton's responded with a 'War Room' to combat these accusations, which only led to a more suspicious press and right wing conspiracy theories. Indeed, friends of the Clinton's went to jail for obstruction of justice.

The upshot of all of this was to open a new era where the personal affairs and behavior of a president became a subject worthy of being considered an impeachable offense.

GEORGE W. BUSH, the president on 9/11, dealt with that traumatic event in ways that broke many Constitutional norms. First, he vastly changed the ground rules as to each American's right to privacy. In the process, he greatly expanded the reach of the government into the lives of ordinary Americans. That much of this was done furtively, without explaining to the public, will further put a blot on this presidency.

Add to this, the Iraqi War as another ill-advised response to 9/11, based on fabricated information. It is rather astounding that President Bush did not face impeachment proceedings for violating a number of constitutional norms.

President Bush also allowed his Vice President, Dick Cheney, to acquire power for decision-making far beyond prior norms, creating a destabilized presidency. While this may not be a violation of constitutional norms ... given the fact that the duties of a Vice President are vaguely enumerated at best under Article ll ... it is still noteworthy as a dangerous precedent.

BARACK OBAMA was one of the few presidents to avoid any major scandals that could taint him personally. This, despite the fact that Republicans were determined to make sure that our first black president would only serve one term at best. That meant conducting endless hearings at the slightest provocation, which could never deliver the intended goal.

DONALD TRUMP is a president who has already perpetrated more potentially impeachable offenses than any other predecessor...from violating the emoluments clause to publicly attacking the press and threatening the First Amendment. But perhaps the most obvious is his abandoning his oath to defend and protect the Constitution by refusing to address Russia's highly documented interference with our electoral process.

Yet, it is perhaps the Republican Party's refusal to confirm the impeachment process, based on party loyalty over fealty to the Constitution, that represents the greatest scandal of the day.

THE DNA OF
SELF RELIANCE

DEFINING THE RIGHT TO 'HAPPINESS'

While Americans have been promised 'life, liberty and the pursuit of happiness' in their founding documents, there has always been a question as to what that 'pursuit of happiness' should include. Lincoln defined that as giving every individual, at a minimum, the right to be entitled to the fruits of his own labor.

Of course, he was addressing the scourge of slavery in that quotation. The question still lingers: What should 'happiness' include as a right of citizenship?

Is it strictly an individual goal, leaving every person on their own to determine what happiness means? If someone falls short, is he or she then subject to the penalties of life including the loss of the most meager benefits?

FDR was the first President to expand the guaranteed rights of 'happiness' beyond Lincoln's words, starting with the aptly named 'social security'. His successor, Harry Truman then tried to add medical benefits, which was finally achieved by Lyndon Johnson with Medicaid and Medicare, both programs to guarantee medical benefits to the elderly and the disadvantaged.

A CONFLICTED PUBLIC

Nevertheless, many Americans are conflicted about accepting these safety net benefits as nothing more than coddling and threatening their independence from an intrusive government. Add to that, the fear that government won't stop with this, but find ways to strip away their independence and their guns!

To change that mindset, we must ask the following:

- Why benefits provided by our government that supply everyone with a basic dignity are suspect as part of a creeping 'socialism'?

- Why do people favor programs like Social Security and Medicare without realizing that these are in effect the beneficial aspects of so-called socialism?

Obviously, those who oppose these benefits, usually the very wealthy who perpetuate this myth by calling them 'giveaways', have done a good job of perpetuating the myth of self-reliance. In the process, those who need these programs most will vote against their own self-interest.

Part of the answer lies in the ethos of Americans, that we have always done things on our own to build our lives. This includes a culture that has turned the American cowboy, more often than not a loner who lived a hardscrabble life, into an American hero. In actuality, we should be celebrating the average person who fled west in search of a better life, crossing the plains in a Conestoga with his family and possessions. Apparently, that is not heroic enough to celebrate as an American myth.

PRESIDENTS AND THE MYTH

So let's look into this unique American belief in 'self-reliance' and realize that even our past presidents have perpetuated this myth...

often having to do more with appearance that substance. After all, imagery has always been important in viewing our presidents favorably as real Americans.

Let's start with Washington and Jefferson who were known as the two best horsemen in the country, sitting in the saddle with a great sense of authority. Washington was always known for making an exalted appearance, even from his earliest days in the French and Indian Wars, as a military man on the rise.

Andrew Jackson was another military hero. But it was also well known that he carried some pieces of lead in his body, the result of gunfights and confrontations with anyone who was foolish enough to challenging him. Obviously, the cowboy myth has intrigued us in one way or another from our founding days. And our presidents are clearly part of this 'American ethos'.

Another president who fits this mold is of course Teddy Roosevelt. Through grit and determination, he transformed himself from a sickly asthmatic child into a strapping young man. He made sure to complete the process by going out to the Badlands of North Dakota to live the life of a real cowboy. He returned several years later with a barrel chest and bull neck of which he was duly proud. For the rest of his life, he continued to prove his worth in battle, conquering the wilds of the Amazon and Africa in a life of supposed self-reliance.

In the modern era, other presidents have emulated the cowboy myth in more mundane ways, including owning a ranch and clearing brush, as Ronald Reagan and George W. Bush were proud to do before a line up of photographers.

RURAL SELF-RELIANCE

Like the cowboy who came from under-populated areas and relished relying on his resources, many living in today's rural areas cling to the same myths that unfortunately limit their options. To add to this, these communities are often the most left behind in the process of globalization or unnecessary tariff wars.

Yet thanks to a bi-cameral legislature, dictated by the Constitution, this segment of the population retains outsized political in sparsely populated states and can tilt the balance in the Electoral College. Though needy, they are often too proud to vote for a more robust safety net without the proper urging of a president like an FDR or a Lincoln, who can explain why certain myths are simply not right for the times.

Instead, egged on by political interests that play to this myth of self-reliance, they will vote against their interests, denying themselves all the benefits that can give them a better life...including robust health care, extended unemployment benefits, retraining programs and apprenticeships in lieu of college to give them a chance for gainful employment.

And all because they still believe these rights and entitlements are nothing more than a handout that makes them seem less worthy as individuals. In the process, their voting power in the Senate deprives the rest of the country from receiving these benefits as well.

The real question is whether the fragile populations of these regions will continue to rage against inevitable change or continue to see government assistance as nothing more than big city condescension. And will they continue to vote against their interests to at least cushion the impact of a changing world, while holding the rest of us hostage?

TODAY'S DILEMMA

Today we are faced with more of an interdependent world, the antithesis of self-reliance. We are also faced with egregious income inequality and an evolving work place where automation, artificial intelligence and robotics will inevitably limit job and income opportunities.

Yet, those factors may well increase our GNP and our national wealth, leading to several critical questions:

1. How do we deal with the myth of self-reliance and the so-called majesty of the market place in justifying minimal safety net benefits?

2. How do we re-waken the ethos of the New Deal to celebrate self- worth? These should include government initiatives to create new industries in alternative energy, workfare on vast infrastructure programs or other alternatives.

3. Do we fund these programs through deficits or a more equitable tax policy that redistributes arbitrary wealth creation of capitalism for the benefit of all?

And most of all, is there a president in our future who can explain all of this to a public that is often wary of government intrusion in their lives?

STYMIED BY MYTHS

ADDRESSING THE CORONAVIRUS CRISIS

We as a nation like to call ourselves tough, resilient and innovative. We often use these terms as a badge of honor to highlight the difference between us and the rest of the world. This so-called American exceptionalism is not the entire story. In truth, we are also tethered to quite a few 'myths' that have often sapped our strength and our ability to handle major challenges at times of crisis.

It is only when a president inspires us to rise above these uniquely American myths that often divide us and face a crisis in a united fashion that he can truly bring out the best in us and in himself.

This task has been accomplished by some of our finest presidents...men like Washington, Lincoln and FDR, all of whom dealt with a major wartime crisis and constantly rank at the top of the list in evaluating 'presidential greatness'. There are also presidents who have burnished their careers by actually encouraging us to believe these myths that often divide us.

DEALING WITH CORONAVIRUS

Many of these widely held 'American myths' have already colored our response to the coronavirus pandemic, a unique event in our history that has been called the equivalent to war. For like war, it has already touched the lives of all Americans, but this time almost like a tidal wave versus the lead up to actual war, which often transpires over a much longer period of time.

Nevertheless, the impediments in addressing this crisis versus real war are often quite similar. They are in many ways symptomatic of those deeply held and oftentimes highly destructive beliefs that have long been part of the American ethos.

FEAR OF "THE OTHER"

History supplies many examples of these, starting with what can be called 'fear of the other'. This has at critical moments allowed suspicion and distrust to be sewn among the populace, something that is particularly harmful in keeping the country united in times of crisis.

As a nation of immigrants, this has been easy to employ by our worst leaders. But 'fear of the other' became even more virulent when skin color (brown, black and yellow) was added to the equation, starting with the Chinese (and Asian) Exclusionary Act.

The unintended effects of heightening this fear are multifold, not only sapping our strength as a nation but also damaging our image abroad as that beacon of hope to the world. Even today, it is not unusual to find one particular party pandering to the racist sentiments that still prevail throughout the South. This was in fact known as 'the southern strategy', pursued by Republicans in the 1970's to build their base after LBJ's Civil Rights legislation lost the 'Solid South' for Democrats. (It is not surprising that Donald Trump won these states overwhelmingly in 2016.)

ISOLATIONISM

This is another strongly held belief that has often left us unprepared and divided in addressing various. It is actually a form of ultra-nationalism, the belief that we are somehow superior and that our interests alone must dictate our actions.

This 'theory' began in our earliest days, as part of the belief that we were different from a corrupt Europe and needed to keep it at bay, as documented most notably by the Monroe Doctrine, written back in 1824. That belief has lingered way beyond its 'shelf life', when two oceans can no longer protect us from events abroad.

Isolationism left us drastically unprepared to enter both World Wars 1 and 11. Gearing up for World War 11 in particular became a mammoth task, due the delays in recognizing all the warning signs coming at us from abroad. Even so, it was only 'Pearl Harbor' that finally broke the isolationist fever for the moment.

Yet 'isolationism' is with us today in the widespread belief that 'bad things' only happen abroad to 'inferior peoples'. You could also call this a form of racism, but surely it qualifies as gross 'ignorance'. As with 'fear of the other', it infects a large segment of the American population and can be pandered to with abandon by the wrong person at the helm of our ship of state.

SCIENCE-DENIAL

Another widely held belief that saps our will to act at times of crisis is the continuing suspicion of scientific data. This again relates in part to the unique American experience that makes some believe that we should reject what some would call 'the corrupt ways of 'modernity'.

This myth, unusual for a modern highly industrialized nation, has long been part of our history. This often stems from strongly held religious beliefs among a large segment of the population that often see biblical references as a 'higher authority'.

Today, more than ever, there has been an increased intrusion of religion in the public square by the evangelical community, contrary to the founding principle of separation of church and state. This agenda has been embraced cynically and wholeheartedly by Republicans to boost their numbers at election time, despite the cost to our founding principles and our ability to address critical issues that will plague our future.

Perhaps the best illustration of this anti-science bent is the ease with which large numbers of Americans reject the concept of climate change, regardless of the overwhelming scientific data that supports this premise. While this is highly unusual for a wealthy, industrialized nation, it shows how deep seated this anti-science myth is among a large part of the country and how it has been kept alive by blatant demagoguery.

In addition to those who reject clear-cut scientific evidence, there is another segment of the population that knows better. However, they prefer to view this as a threat to the economy, which apparently takes precedence in this era of 'greed is good' versus the ethos of 'we are all in this together' of a bygone era.

THE EVILS OF ACTIVIST GOVERNANCE

This is the most disturbing myth, for it basically negates the hopefulness of the Constitution, written in the Age of Enlightenment under the premise that man could curb his baser instincts and live and thrive under the rule of law.

This latest myth diminishes the value of our founding documents and untethers us from the past, as if we should forget our history and chart our course based only on the expediency of the present. Actually, it fits quite nicely with the growing belief among many that government is a useless morass of inefficiency that needs to be drained.

Another aspect of this myth, combining fear of the other and fear of an activist government, is the frenzied push back against gun control, despite the multiple shootings annually that highlight the need for reform. This myth is embraced nearly wholly by Republican voters and pandered to by Republicans in Congress, simply to acquire votes at election time.

In this case, the twisting of precise constitutional language by the Supreme Court has opened the floodgates for acquiring 'weapons of war'. This highlights an era of Court decisions that threaten constitutional norms by elevating the so-called rights of the few over those of the many.

There has long been a deep-seated skepticism about the value of an activist government, beginning with the heated debates between Hamilton versus Jefferson back in the 1790's. That should have been settled almost a century ago, with FDR's approach in confronting the Great Depression.

Embracing our unique form of government, bequeathed under the Constitution, seems to have taken a back seat today to the myth of 'the majesty of the market', including a blind allegiance to its workings by Republicans in particular. This has put the private sector, the wealthy and corporate America, in an elevated position versus the role of government to maintain that level playing field as envisioned by Madison under his brilliant Federalist #10.

Once again, a conservative Supreme Court is not blameless in promoting this myth in cases like <u>Citizens United</u>, granting corporations a voice in the public square with a First Amendment right to free speech. Never mind that John Marshall, our most esteemed Chief Justice, labeled corporations as 'artificial entities' to promote commerce under the sanctity of contract law, a term today's justices seem to have overlooked.

This has also allowed many in their ivory tower to possess a larger voice in our national affairs and look down on others as somehow 'unworthy'. This appears to validate shredding an already fragile safety net, including programs like Obamacare, and elevating the health of the stock market over the health of average Americans.

THE MYTH OF INDIVIDUALISM

It was Herbert Hoover who, during the Great Depression, counseled Americans to rely on their 'rugged individualism' to restore the economy. Again, this outdated myth harks back to our earliest days, when pioneers set out to cross the Alleghenies and chart a new life. They were on their own in this veritable wilderness. Nor did they expect anything from a fledgling government that was thousands of miles away.

But today, we live in a very different world where virtually no one can make it on their own. Yet, that same myth of 'rugged individualism' and 'self reliance' is still with us, implying that we don't need government programs to get us through tough times, despite the majority of Americans today living paycheck to paycheck.

Is it any wonder that many of the neediest still believe this myth, blaming themselves rather than the economic system for their lot in life and seeking consolation in opioids to drown their lack of self worth?

EVALUATING TRUMP AND THE REPUBLICAN PARTY
In evaluating the Trump Administration's response (or lack thereof) to the coronavirus pandemic, it is safe to say that the American myths noted above did not start, and will not end with Donald Trump.

He has pandered to many of them mercilessly over the past three years in order to take control of the Republican Party. Unfortunately, that was rather easy, considering the Party has abandoned those core values of traditional conservatism, preferring only to put more money into the hands of corporations and the wealthy.

In the process, Trump has damaged the country's ability to address the current situation in a satisfactory manner, one that has already resulted in far more deaths than might have been. It has already been noted that it is the poorest among us who are suffering the most from this pandemic, people who do not have the means or the living space to self isolate. In that regard, the virus has only highlighted the fact that we are a two-tiered society that has ignored the basic needs of the many.

It should come as no surprise that the President has been quick to assign blame for his ineptitude to others, based on his disdain for effective government.

REAPING WHAT WE'VE SOWN

Let's review those myths that have allowed the current president to take us down this path, with the approval of nearly half the country.

First, it would only be natural that we would ignore all the warnings that a pandemic was about to envelop the nation. For according to the myth of isolationism, we Americans are supposed to be immune from the scourge of those inferior societies from abroad. Calling it the 'China virus' is simply a way of validating this claim and activating the xenophobia and race baiting that still plays to a large segment of the Republican base.

Dismissing the approaching storm was also made easier, in that those warnings were coming from scientists, allowing the Right to mock their fears and lose a full two months in addressing this impending crisis.

Pandering to the 'Religious Right' made it easy for Trump to dismiss this as mere scare tactics, delivered by corrupt and suspicious forces. This reaction has been widely applauded by evangelists who continue to urge their flock to believe in salvation by that higher power, namely religion and godliness.

The long term affects of dismissing constitutional norms and elevating the majesty of the marketplace has also made it easier to view this pandemic as simply an impediment to a booming economy, another iteration of the elevation of unbridled capitalism as the new 'founding value'.

Nor can the effect of these myths in dividing the nation into two separate camps be denied. For many, the words and warnings of scientists and reporters represent nothing more than another political assault on Mr. Trump, now that impeachment has failed.

TODAY'S REPUBLICANISM

While Trump may represent a gross caricature of what we could ever envision as a president, in actuality, he is quite ably enacting the Republican agenda, one that relies on these 'American myths' to divide the country and maintain its grip on power as a minority party. One would have to ask, why one of the two major parties in a two-party system that has endured over the past two hundred twenty years, would seek to pull us back to the past and promote myths that have never represented reality.

The only comparable times in American history when this transpired was the lead up to the Civil War...when the issue of slavery created a breakdown in a national dialogue. At that time, the South, like today's Republicans, were ranting that 'federal government was the problem, trampling over states' rights. Secession and war became the inevitable answer, after years of pointless compromise and deflection.

Today is much the same, as the elevated role of the religious right in shaping the conversation has turned Democrats into sinners and liberalism into a godless creed. Hence, a meaningful conversation is totally out of the question. What will it take for the Republican Party be reconstructed as the centrist party it once was before moving further to the Right, and clinging to myths, without any of the core values that once defined the party?

If Trump represents anything, it is a wake up call as to where the Republican Party has been trending for decades. His failure to activate the full authority of federal government to address the coronavirus is simply an acknowledgment that the Republican embrace of destructive and obsolete myths has had the intended effect.

Frankly, if Trump were to use the resources of the government, that would be contrary to his mission of stripping many government departments of competent personnel while appointing officials who are basically antithetical to the mission of that particular department.

LOOKING AHEAD

Ironically, ceding the mission of dealing with the coronavirus to various talented governors may in the end prove that good governance is possible. Perhaps it will give voice to the proper role of government in commanding the necessary resources and soothing an anxious nation with the truth, delivered with empathy.

This would not be the first time that scenario played out. For it was New York Governor, Franklin D. Roosevelt who, like other governors in 1929, looked to President Hoover to lead the way in solving the plight of the Great Depression. But Hoover was unfortunately wedded to the failed economic policies that had elevated capitalism to a righteous dogma and was willing to let the market resolve the problem, despite the fact that the people were dealing with a daily crisis of their own.

And so, FDR was free to experiment within New York State with various policies and legislation to ease the burden on ordinary Americans. When elected president in 1932, he was fully prepared to embrace new ideas, including Keynesian economics, which encouraged government intervention.

This once again elevated the role of the federal government to tame the excesses of capitalism and restore people's faith in an activist government as the solution, rather than the problem. Yet, those policies were still vehemently opposed by many Republicans throughout FDR's first two terms, until World War ll united the country against a common enemy.

Having proven their value in bringing greater prosperity to all the people, including building a robust middle class, FDR's 'New Deal' and Truman's 'Fair Deal' were accepted as the given wisdom by the next Republican President, Dwight David Eisenhower. He then built on that legacy with true conservative values that preached fiscal restraint and middle-of-the-road policies that kept the country united in its belief in a workable two party system.

For that is the way politics should work if both parties have rational ideological differences in their core beliefs, rather than clinging to outdated myths that represent more of a cult, than a political party.

Perhaps the obvious incompetence of the Trump Presidency, most notable in his handling of this pandemic, will lead the way back for the Republican Party to once again be a party of ideas and hopefulness rather than anger and division.

BALANCING FICTION
AND REALITY

IDEAS: MYTH VERSUS REALITY

In the world of ideas, 'power' can at times be uncomfortable in changing perceptions or 'the given wisdom'. Such was the case with the theory of evolution destroying the religious theory of creationism.

Yet many will still prefer to cling to myths that provide social cohesion. That is the essence of a religion.

Let us admit that embracing both truth and non-truth is two sides of our dual nature. We often switch between one and the other multiple times within a day. Yes, we can be both smart and intentionally gullible. In fact, fictions (or myths) often enjoy distinct advantages over truths. If shared by a group, it creates identity and a sense of belonging that generic universal truths cannot supply.

Fictions have been used throughout our history for better or for worse. When the South lost the Civil War, it developed a myth known as 'The Lost Cause'. This allowed it to claim that the war was about being invaded by the North to take away their rights. Naturally, any mention of slavery was omitted, while incorporating aspects of racial inferiority that explained the rationale and benevolence behind 'Jim Crow'.

Those statues of Confederate generals in town squares were part and parcel of perpetuating that myth for future generations and further degrading the black community. Though the logic of the myth of the 'Lost Cause' was easily refuted elsewhere, it took hold in the South, where the cultural landscape was hospitable.

As demagogues know only too well, most myths that are perpetuated on a larger scale must be somewhat metaphysical, grandiose or even outrageous, requiring that leap of faith so as not to be easily disapproved by physical evidence.

That concept can be applied to politics as well as religion. Hence Hitler learned quickly the power of the ' big lie'...and the bigger the better. For adherence to the 'big lie' indicates loyalty over reason, and loyalty is all that is required to keep the herd intact. The constant use of outrageous falsehoods can also be useful in separating true believers from the rest of the herd...and indicate where disloyalty lies and must be dealt with.

THE LIMITS OF TRUTH

Our psyche does not require that politicians supply us with a constant dose of reality, which can seem elitist to many in destroying myths that hold us together.

Certainly our dealing with COVID-19 demonstrates that truism with those resisting wearing masks and not social distancing. Their preferring this alternate reality is a natural human reaction. The only thing that is shocking is a president's encouraging this behavior ... perhaps as a would-be demagogue to test the loyalty of his followers.

Even in normal times, reality has always required tact and clever messaging by a president. Telling Americans about our worst moments, such as our savage treatment of Native Americans, would not be a politician's best calling card, unless explained in a very artful manner, as Lincoln did in appealing to our 'better angels'.

While John Adams feared the mob and wrote of this in several tracts, Jefferson preached the myth that a little rebellion here and there 'refreshes the tree of liberty'. It is obvious who won the hearts and minds of Americans, as Jefferson went on to be an adept politician in founding the Republican Party, while Adams never understood the game of politics.

Jimmy Carter talked about 'malaise' in our economy, which might have been true, while Reagan spoke of 'morning in America'.

NATIONALISM: A DANGEROUS FICTION

We often walk a fine line between fiction and reality. Some fictions, like 'Washington cutting down that cherry tree' are harmless additions to a national culture that we all share. Yet, when a fiction is intended to divide us into sub-groups and creates suspicion, it can do great harm.

Take the word 'nationalism', which is being used today to combat the strides that have been made to create a more interconnected world. While it sounds patriotic, it can be anything but. In the early part of the 20th century, a surge in nationalism made us fearful of hyphenated Americans and gave rise to a re-empowered KKK.

Today the word 'nationalism' is part and parcel of the slogan 'Make America Great Again'. Both are about the rise of white nationalism and being fearful of anyone who is of a different skin color.

NATIONHOOD VESUS NATIONALISM

The word 'nation' and 'nationalist' have little in common. Lincoln's words at Gettysburg spoke of a 'nation conceived in liberty and dedicated to the proposition that all men are created equal'. Words like these echo the works of philosophers like Locke and Montesquieu, which formed the underpinnings of our Constitution. They reflect the belief in our common humanity, not the attributes that divide us.

Nations are based on a common history as well as sharing certain myths, all of which bind us together with laws that guarantee our rights and our common humanity. And yes, that is about 'liberalism', which all the philosophers of the Enlightenment applauded.

GLOBALISM: NATIONHOOD ON A GRANDER SCALE

Globalism is a form of that same 'liberalism' played out on the world stage ... believing that all nations also have more in common than divides them. It promotes discussions that lead to multi-lateral agreements, in politics and economics, that benefit the many rather than the few. It also creates a more stable world order, the value of which is incalculable.

And yes, the global community of which we are a part, is responsible for the earth's clean air and clean water and addressing climate change. Nationalism, the idea that we are only responsible for our country winning every day, cannot accomplish this on its own. That is another myth that some may wish to perpetuate. However, there comes a day when we have to pay the bill for the folly of our ways when reality trumps myths.

In fact, globalism has made the world richer, a fact rather than a myth. Yet, it has also created dislocation as jobs migrate to places where they may be more cost-effective, a hallmark of capitalism.

But there are other truths to be faced. The growth of incomes in third world nations, through globalism, will naturally come at the expense of jobs in industrialized nations. In that limited sense, we become poorer, although the jobs lost are generally not the jobs of the future that we wish to preserve. To stop this process, which benefits far more individuals than it hurts, and revert to the myth of nationalism would be a prescription for disaster.

What we should be addressing are the options to cushion this negative impact. For these are plentiful and in the end may well be highly beneficial. These include among others a more robust safety net that addresses growing income inequality, retraining programs in hi-tech growth industries and massive infrastructure programs that benefit the entire economy.

But again, explaining these benefits is more difficult than sound bites that talk of losing or being conned and outfoxed, especially When most who listen are ignorant of the pitfalls of nationalism in our past.

DEMAGOGUES FEASTING ON MYTHS

At the height of the Depression, a desperate nation was relieved to hear the voice of FDR tell us that things would be okay. And yet, he was aware of demagogues nipping at his heels while peddling a false narrative of get-rich-quick schemes. For that reason, the concept of Social Security was developed to thwart their divisive impact on far too many gullible souls.

Demagogues are always likely to thrive in perilous times and encourage myths that seem to explain the chaos of the moment, when the herd is less inclined to question. A man like Joseph McCarthy could never have alarmed the country in the early 1950's with tales of communists taking over the State Department unless we had already been prepared to accept these words.

Though we had just led the world community in a battle against fascism, the old familiar pattern of seeing intrigue and betrayal abroad soon surfaced. We were exposed to tales of FDR selling out the country at Yalta and handing Eastern Europe to Stalin on a silver platter. We were told that George Marshall, the General who conducted the war effort with unfailing skill and integrity, had sold us out in allowing the communists to take over China.

Our faith in our leaders had already been diminished by organizations like the well-financed 'China Lobby', making unfounded accusations to save the corrupt regime of Chiang Kai shek. We then received distressing news regarding individuals with access to nuclear secrets betraying the nation and sharing this with the Russians. We read of seemingly normal everyday Americans like Julius and Ethel Rosenberg, ultimately sentenced to death in the electric chair for this betrayal.

Of course that made all the untruths seem all the more logical when Wisconsin Senator Joseph McCarthy stepped in with his accusations. Adding daily with more exaggerated claims only amplified his standing and his believability with the American public.

Even Eisenhower, in the midst of his campaign for the presidency, did not dare to offer words of praise and support for Marshall, the man who had propelled him to that leadership role in the war.

If we wonder how a man of principle like Eisenhower could be cowed by a demagogue at a given moment, it was because a false narrative had little by little gained credibility and captured the imagination of a public that had lost the ability to reason.

While certain harmless myths can bind people together, feeling a sense of community and common purpose, others like those McCarthy was spreading can destroy that very sense of community and pit one group against another.

If that process continues for long, dry rot sets in and a society will destroy itself from within. In the case of Joseph McCarthy, we were lucky. He was brought down by televised hearings that exposed his bullying witnesses and even demeaning officers in the military. Otherwise, he might have been headed for the presidency.

Fortunately, at that time we still lived in an open society that valued truth and possessed a cadre of questioning reporters who were still admired by the public. Most prominent among them was Edward R. Murrow, who had been the one to report the news out of London during the heroic Battle of Britain.

It only took a few brave voices to oppose those demagogues who thrived on rumors and myths that sought to confuse and divide. Murrow's warnings about the character and intentions of McCarthy began to take hold, as did a lone voice from the only woman in the Senate, Maine's Margaret Chase Smith.

TODAY'S DEMAGOGUES

Today's Republican Party has thrived on myths for years to unify the party faithful ... many of which become more outlandish, including rumors of a satanic cult initiated by the opposition party. That has opened the door for a man like Donald Trump, today's version of Joseph McCarthy, to spew his venom to 'Make America

Great Again' by attacking our institutions and our allies while cozying up to autocrats.

Those who applaud his 'telling the truth' are the unquestioned true believers who, as he claims, would support him even if he were to 'shoot someone on Fifth Avenue'. For truth and reason fled the stage long ago for a Party that has elevated falsehoods and myths to replace the truths of our founding documents.

Nor will this be gone when Trump is no longer President. This alternate reality will still be with us, continuing to threaten the viability of our two party system...and a nation's future viability that requires thought and reason to triumph over divisive myths.

COMPONENTS OF PRESIDENTIAL GREATNESS

What makes a President 'great' in the eyes of history? Does it require a crisis to be mastered or a battle to be won? Is it his or her character that elevates the conversation and has us listening to our better angels in that march toward a more perfect Union? Or can it be more subtle...simply maintaining that critical balance between all three branches of government, as envisioned by Madison in his brilliant concept of 'separation of powers'?

And what will it take for today's Chief Executive to deserve that accolade in the eyes of history? These are all questions, worthy of further exploration.

Theodore Roosevelt

PRESIDENTS WHO MIRROR THE TIMES

There are presidents whose words or actions define (and are defined by) the times in which they live. This can be a calculated move on their part or a random, fortuitous event, which accrues to his benefit.

A president's legacy may be celebrated in the eyes of future generations or scorned for pandering to the present, while ignoring problems that loom on the horizon. Exploring these different possible outcomes may help unlock those qualities that we value most in those presidents who embody the times in which they live.

THE MONROE DOCTRINE

Certainly James Monroe's enunciating the words of the Monroe Doctrine in 1824 was right for the times and has continued to resonate as that 'coming of age moment' for a nation that was no longer a fragile democracy. For the first time, we would be taking our place in world affairs and contradicting Washington's cautious approach of 'neutrality'.

Monroe, serving from 1816 to 1824, had followed Jefferson and Madison, as the last of the three Republicans presidents to serve two terms. The country would soon look elsewhere for leadership, with the emergence of Andrew Jackson, the first commoner President... poorly educated yet hugely adept as a natural political force.

Monroe's tenure had been fairly mundane, as the Republicans left their ideals of small government behind and embraced more of the Hamilton agenda. If not for the Monroe Doctrine, he would leave office as a competent, but uninspired chief executive.

Drafting this document was a serendipitous event. The credit belongs to his Secretary of State, the very able John Quincy Adams. Ironically, Adams would go on to succeed Monroe; but his presidency would be a mere shadow of his success as Secretary of State in commanding the international stage as an exceptional and savvy diplomat.

Adams was the one who keenly understood the desire of the British to meddle in the affairs of our hemisphere, particularly with those burgeoning democracies of South America.

With Monroe nearing the end of his second term and about to address Congress in his State of the Union Address, Adams seized the moment to have the President caution Europe against intruding in our affairs.

He was adept in making this a righteous plea, warning Europe not to taint our hemisphere with its corrupt ways. At the same time, he spurned any interest in meddling in the affairs of South America, saying that we were simply the 'well-wishers' of those seeking to create their own democracies. (Our expanding the

Monroe Doctrine to become the policeman of the hemisphere would only come later, with Teddy Roosevelt.)

The Monroe Doctrine has continued to shine, giving James Monroe a definite boost in the eyes of history, despite the fact that he did little more than stand before Congress and read the handiwork of John Quincy Adams.

JAMES POLK

Another President who benefited from the times was James Polk. Unlike The Monroe Doctrine, which mirrored the times and elevated us in the eyes of history, Polk's actions in fomenting a war with Mexico in 1844 basically represented a land grab that breached constitutional norms.

However, the story is far more complicated. For Mexico had been part of Spain's colonial empire for centuries, stretching all the way from Texas to the West Coast. We had even wrested Florida and portions of the Gulf Coast from her grip during the Monroe Administration, again with the clever Quincy Adams handling the negotiations.

Now that Mexico had finally broken free and been granted her independence in 1824, that land out west looked more attractive to a nation entranced with the concept of Manifest Destiny and spreading westward. By then, thousand of Americans settlers were already occupying Mexican land and living in an uneasy alliance side by side with native Mexicans.

The fact that the prior administration had already annexed the Texas Territory, gave Polk the ability to stage a series of events that would justify a war to seize even more of Mexico's land. He sent some very capable generals down to the border on the Rio Grande to provoke an impasse without seeking Congressional approval, as required by the Constitution. No one would ever identify the exact spot where Mexican forces supposedly invaded our territory. It was only young Abe Lincoln, in Congress for a brief term who stood ready to question such duplicity.

A quick war, handled rather adeptly by Generals Taylor and Scott, had us annexing huge swaths of land all the way to California and up the West Coast. We even demanded and received reparations from Mexico in the final peace treaty!

In the end, history has applauded Polk's actions and given him a pass for expanding presidential authority. For, Polk performed the inevitable task of creating a trans-continental power, from the Atlantic to the Pacific. If he hadn't done this, someone else would have.

As far as the public was concerned, this was already part of our destiny under the celebrated doctrine of 'Manifest Destiny'. But this mantra came with specific responsibilities as well...to spread the benefits and bounty of our American democracy with others, by way of all the ports we had just acquired along the Pacific Coast.

THEODORE ROOSEVELT

With that expansion came the responsibility to bring our way of life to those savages in Asia through a benevolent sort of imperialism. That would be the task of Teddy Roosevelt in the early part of the Twentieth Century, another president who more than suited his times ... a story best illustrated in the way he went about building the Panama Canal.

By then, possessing a colonial empire was in fashion among the nations of Europe. And Teddy Roosevelt was not one to be left behind. He had already proven his military mettle in the Spanish American War, as well as his vision in building an impressive fleet to acquire the Philippines and other Spanish possessions.

He also understood that projecting American power in both oceans required a canal through Central America to enable us to move ships from one ocean to the other in the shortest amount of time. There was one particular spot in Central America that was ideal, located in the Panama region of Columbia.

When Columbia reneged on a deal that included the payment of a significant sum, Roosevelt decided to act. He paid off some local revolutionaries, while stationing battleships off the coast in case the Columbia government was foolish enough to oppose us.

The Canal was completed in 1904, a dazzling feat of engineering in moving millions of tons of dense clay to create a unique waterway that transformed worldwide commerce. As Teddy Roosevelt flashed that dazzling smile and proclaimed 'Bully!' with great satisfaction, a Cabinet member was more blunt in describing what had taken place, saying, 'It wasn't seduction. It was rape! '

And yet, once again a President has received great praise to this day for doing what was inevitable. And better to have the U.S. do it than allow another nation to 'invade' our territory and set the terms.

NEGATIVELY MIRRORING THE TIMES

There are other presidents whose actions matched the times, yet their legacy was diminished for doing so. This is perhaps best illustrated in the years preceding the Civil War, when a series of Presidents sought various solutions to prevent the Union from breaking apart.

First was Millard Fillmore, who ascended to the Presidency in 1850 upon the death of General Zachary Taylor, one of the heroes of the war with Mexico. He acted quickly to support what was known as the Omnibus Bill, containing five major pieces of legislation calculated to appease the South. This included a stronger Fugitive Slave Act to hunt down those runaway slaves fleeing to freedom.

When the Bill failed to pass, a Senator from Illinois named Stephen Douglas cleverly broke the bill into five separate pieces of legislation. A grateful President Fillmore thanked Douglas, now known in the Senate as the Little Giant, for saving the Union.

The next President, Franklin Pierce, was a northern Democrat from New Hampshire. Again, the country breathed a sigh of relief, for Pierce was known as a 'doughface', someone who openly disdained those troublesome abolitionists who were threatening to break the Union apart. Finally, the South seemed satisfied with a President who sympathized with its plight and would work to calm its concerns.

The next President, James Buchanan, was another Northern Democrat. Once again, the public looked on with optimism. After all, Buchanan seemed to have all the right credentials. He had served admirably in several administrations as an Ambassador to Great Britain and as a Secretary of State, noted for settling some thorny issues abroad.

He was known for his agility in triangulating to reach the right decision and enhancing his reputation in the process. This was to be his crowning moment in settling perhaps the most divisive issue to ever face the nation. Buchanan had watched the past two presidents fail to pass legislation to accomplish this. He knew that something more definitive would be needed, perhaps something other than another act of Congress.

On the day of his inauguration, after taking the oath of office, Buchanan was seen having a private conversation with Chief Justice Roger Taney. Only days later, the Court delivered its long awaited decision in the 'Dred Scott' case, putting an end to the question of whether slavery would be legally sanctioned outside of the South.

The decision cleverly avoided any discussion of the rights of states or territories to have a say in that matter. Instead, it declared that slaves were 'chattel' and as such, could be taken anywhere in the country, including those states and territories that banned slavery.

This of course went far beyond the three-fifths clause, that blot on the Constitution that classified certain individuals as less than a whole individual. Now, they would be nothing more than a mere possession, never considered capable of enjoying the full rights of citizenship.

Buchanan believed that he had found the right solution to finally lay to rest questions as to the rights of slaveholders. He was greatly offended to be accused of being a part of a 'slave conspiracy', a term used by a former Congressman from Illinois named Abraham Lincoln.

ENTER LINCOLN

Lincoln had spent the last decade as a successful attorney, certain that his days as a politician were over. But his moral outrage grew as he watched a succession of presidents only make matters worse. Even his fellow Illinoisan, Stephen Douglas, was being applauded for turning slavery into a simple issue that people could decide with their votes. Now the President had involved the Supreme Court in these devious schemes, poisoning yet another branch of government.

Lincoln, a man with only six months of formal schooling, understood the gravity of the situation. He would challenge Stephen Douglas for that Senate seat, using Euclidean logic to perfect his arguments. He would build his case slowly so that the common man would understand the fundamental task at hand.

Still, he didn't expect much, having been disappointed far too often in life. Yet, people began to listen as he spoke of the Declaration of Independence granting the promise of 'life, liberty and the pursuit of happiness' for every individual, regardless of color.

He ultimately lost that Senate race. But his speeches in those seven debates with Stephen Douglas piqued the interest of influential men in the East. For here was a man with a different message, not one suggesting another clever solution. Instead, Lincoln was speaking of a moral issue that we seemed to have lost sight of...being true to the underlying hopefulness of our founding documents.

CONCLUSIONS

As the preceding historical review indicates, achieving presidential greatness may include 'mirroring or enhancing' the times. Certainly, the Monroe Doctrine marked a prideful moment in our history, one that deserves to be applauded even today. It has afforded future presidents the opportunity to alter or expand its reach to suit the times. This too is the hallmark of a great document...one that remains relevant in defining America's role in the world.

Even if a particular theme does not endure, we generally applaud bold words and actions by a president that gives the nation a sense of well being, although these actions may include some questionable elements. This description certainly fits the War with Mexico, a rather duplicitous act that nonetheless netted the desired result, transforming the nation into a potential world power.

It also includes our 'stealing' the land to build the Panama Canal, transforming that potential into the reality of a world power, both in military might and as a commercial force to be reckoned with.

There are also times when trying to enhance the status quo is simply a prescription for failure. Such was the case with those three presidents in the lead up to the Civil War. None of them had the vision required to chart a new course when a decade of compromise had only worsened the situation. Those times required a leader to forge a different path, one that was yet to be defined. Even so, Lincoln's actions triggered a cataclysmic event that would rip the nation apart. He would be taking the nation on a journey without the guarantee of success, making the task even more daunting.

For sometimes, a president's job is not to bask in the glory of the times, but to change them through his role as the moral conscience of the nation. For that is the ultimate mark of presidential greatness.

Dwight Eisenhower

A NEW BIRTH
OF FREEDOM

SETTING CONSTITUTIONAL NORMS

We have always been a nation born in the hopefulness of a future full of new possibilities, one of eternal optimism regarding our freedoms...of speech, worship and reaching our true potential.

There has also been an assumption that this dream of a brighter future would be passed on to the next generation, thanks to a highly productive, and competitive economic system anchored in capitalism. It is balancing these two sides of the American experience, our aspirations and the machinery of wealth creation, that often leads to a contentious debate.

Such was the case with Alexander Hamilton and Thomas Jefferson in the founding era. One envisioned an agrarian paradise with a minimum of commerce while the other foresaw a credit worthy nation with a strong central government and a vibrant economy.

In truth, the Civil War was fought to settle once and for all the issue of a wealth-creating economy, based on enslaved labor. This of course represented the most egregious form of inequality. But throughout history, when the benefits of capitalism are captured disproportionately by one segment of society, social upheaval of one sort or another becomes a distinct possibility. Restoring that balance, before we lose the essence of that democracy, then becomes the task of the right leadership at the top.

Our Madisonian democracy is premised on creating a balanced landscape of various interest groups coming together to map out the common good. Diversity was our strength in providing a multiplicity of viewpoints to sort our complex issues. That was the objective underlying the creation of three separate branches of government to promote this uniquely American dialogue.

The Executive Branch was to set a course with an agenda to be enunciated in various forums.

The legislative branch was to debate the pros and cons of that agenda and craft legislation...along with the Chief Executive's right to veto and the legislature's right to override that veto.

And, overseeing that process, the Judicial Branch was to question the constitutionality...as members of the Supreme Court viewed the meaning and intent of that document.

THE IDEAL PROCESS

That process would supposedly air multiple points of view in search of the common good, free of dogma and preconceived ideas that did not bear the scrutiny of our collective wisdom. This phrase is at the heart of that process. It was to be a collaborative process that did not keep a scorecard as to winners or losers. The only winner would be the American people, who had a voice in the process through their representatives.

This national dialogue was based on the premise that this huge country had enough voices with various points of view to create shifting majorities rather than monolithic power centers unwilling to compromise. This vision requires leaders at the top, those elected and appointed figures who share this American ideal and are masters at guiding us toward what unites us. Those iconic phrases that Lincoln enunciated in our darkest hour, including 'those ties that bind' and 'those mystic chords of memory.'

FACING IMPEDIMENTS

There is no question that there may be times when this journey is impeded, when particular issues divide the participants to a degree that thwarts this conversation. How Americans resolve these issues with the right leadership at the top is perhaps the defining moment for a generation in moving toward that ever-present goal of a more perfect Union.

But today, to a growing degree, that question has been removed from our hands by globalization...a process that has brought increased prosperity to the world, at the cost of ceding a portion of that unique American dialogue to outsiders, faceless members of a global over-class.

There has always been a sense of entitlement among those who are most adept at 'wealth creation'. But today's meritocracy is different. It is less obvious and less subject to restraint. Many within this group have gained their wealth, not by building new industries, like an Andrew Carnegie, but by inventing new forms of financial speculation.

Having little allegiance to the norms or aspirations of society, much of their assets are stashed in tax havens rather than being reinvested to build a national war chest for worthy projects like modernizing infrastructure or converting to a green economy. In recent times, as the economy grows by an average two percent annually, the lion's share of the wealth created has gone to the owners of capital, leaving crumbs for the workers who toil daily for stagnant wages.

THE SCOURGE OF GROWING INCOME INEQUALITY

The growing income inequality created by this form of 'hyper capitalism' cannot possibly be justified as benefiting society. On the contrary, it has further detached this class of elitists from reality, with a 'let them eat cake' attitude toward those who labor in the real economy while facing constant economic insecurity.

By elevating the voice of this faceless segment of the economy, today's economic theories that boast of the 'majesty of markets' have lost sight of the fundamentals of a healthy society. These include full educational opportunities regardless of class...investing in our younger generation through a generous health care system that leaves no one hungry.

Instead, we are left feeling frustrated and powerless, distracted by issues that have little or no bearing on the plight of the average American family...issues that are calculated to divide us and paralyze the ability to have a constructive dialogue. This 'blame game' includes nativist chants and racial slurs to explain the plight of the most marginalized...seeing the government in a conspiracy that favors 'welfare queens' or immigrants who are supposedly stealing those low paying jobs that can barely support a family.

RESTORING BALANCE

How to tame the hubris of the 'over-entitled' for the greater good has always been the job of great presidents like Teddy Roosevelt, who broke the 'fever of greed' during the Gilded Age by acting as the honest broker between the needs of industry and labor.

But it is the 1950's, the decade following World War ll with Eisenhower as president, which we should turn to as representing a time when constitutional norms were in balance. It was then that a wise steward presided over great prosperity throughout all levels of society, along with a steeply progressive tax rate that was paid willingly.

THE QUALITIES OF LEADERSHIP

Eisenhower exemplified a host of constitutional norms, including bipartisanship, character and good solid judgment. This helped in finally ridding the country of a demagogue like Joseph McCarthy, exposing his true character to the country in televised hearings.

Nor would Eisenhower have enacted those huge corporate tax cuts of 2017 that were supposed to pay for themselves by unleashing investment. Vague, unproven theories were not of interest to Ike. He would never have bought into that 'trickle down' economics, begun under Reagan, which stripped the middle class of its fair share of economic growth. On the contrary, building a healthy middle class was his main objective.

He spoke common sense as a military man who feared an overly ambitious military. When Congress insisted on more weaponry to fight the Cold War, he cautioned that each new fighter jet would mean building one hundred fewer schools. When industry and Congress colluded to establish a military-industrial complex, he questioned the values that would turn us into an armed camp, with little left for the betterment of society.

Yet he did not turn away from our responsibilities as the leader of the free world. He had been the first Supreme Commander of

NATO, recognizing the need for a mutual defense pact to thwart Soviet ambitions. He prepared the alliance for a long, difficult confrontation that would simply wear down the opposition without firing a shot.

A globalist with the bona fide credentials of the ultimate World War ll hero, he would have created an alliance to deal with the effects of climate change, treating it as the new battle to be waged to save the world from a disaster comparable to nuclear war...one that could destroy our planet and our way of life.

Still, Eisenhower was one who knew how to differentiate and calibrate. He would never waste American resources on foolish regional wars, especially when they reeked of colonial ambitions. He realized that our moral authority was too valuable to be squandered on the wrong value system.

But perhaps his wisest and most cunning ploy was to use our nuclear capability to bluff our adversaries and keep them guessing as to when and where he might use nuclear weapons. He then used this policy with purposefulness to reduce military expenditures and invest elsewhere, including huge infrastructure programs such as the St. Lawrence Seaway and Interstate Highway System that continue to benefit the country.

HONORING OUR INSTITUTIONS

Eisenhower was a man who always sought compromise, abjuring the extremes and favoring the so-called 'Middle Way'. He believed in consensus and avoiding the more radical approach. Above all, he was an institutionalist, making sure that all three branches were respected and expected to do their jobs properly.

He might disagree with the timing and extent of a Supreme Court decisions, as in <u>Board v. Board of Education</u>, voiding the concept of 'separate but equal' in terms of segregated schools. But he felt constitutionally bound to enforce it, even if this meant sending federal troops to Little Rock to do so.

Where many orthodox Republicans saw his victory in 1952 as spelling an end to FDR's New Deal, Eisenhower considered it valid precedent and enlarged social security to cover the self-employed. In fact, we was constantly critical of the Far Right wing of his party for being out-of-step with the needs of the people and, in his words, headed for the dust bin of history. Would he not have found it ironic that these views now reign supreme in an out-of-kilter economy.

When the Russians launched Sputnik, the first man made satellite to circle the earth, Eisenhower did not look for scapegoats to blame. Instead, he created a Scientific Advisory Commission and soon regained the lead in space exploration.

CURING THE ILLS OF INCOME INEQUALITY

If he were president today, Eisenhower would use the cumulative wealth in this country to address the needs of the many. He would set up a commission to come up with a host of innovative solutions and then decide which would most likely gain the bipartisan support of Congress.

These might include a universal monthly child allowance, a federal wage subsidy to ensure every worker a life of dignity for a family or reforming housing assistance to eliminate sub-standard accommodations in ghetto-ized communities. These are programs some might label as socialist. But Eisenhower was never interested in labels. In fact, His party affiliation was not know until the very last minute, when he turned down Truman's offer to succeed him and ran as a Republican.

Considering that he presided over an era when a 90% tax on the wealthy benefited the average person without diminishing economic growth, he would certainly be open to redistributing wealth through tax reform of various sorts to create an acceptable threshold of benefits for every American.

As a student of history, he would reaffirm our commitment to honoring Jefferson's words in the Declaration of Independence: 'life, liberty and the pursuit of happiness.' He might even see this as 'a new birth of freedom', those words spoken by Lincoln at Gettysburg to justify the loss of life during the Civil War.

A President who had invested so boldly in infrastructure would certainly see the worth in investing in people...health care, education and social advancement, knowing it would yield great dividends in the workplace and in the constant 'pursuit of happiness'.

Although Eisenhower was a true believer in capitalism and the role of business in benefiting the nation, he would be aghast at the types of fortunes possessed by a relative few, particularly those gained through financial manipulation. Capping these fortunes at a specific dollar amount might well be considered, yielding billions for worthy projects that had failed to be addressed because of Congressional gridlock...another manifestation of the power of the wealthy to use a cadre of lobbyists to close down the conversation.

Perhaps another Eisenhower is out there to restore the balance that our institutions were mandated to adhere to. Perhaps a man with his moral authority and belief in the promise of America can reform the current Republican Party to once again be a party of ideas, rather than monolithic dogma. and regain a belief in bipartisanship.

Abraham Lincoln

PRESIDENTIAL MESSAGING

I n general, our presidents have never been known for their oratorical skills. Certainly not Washington, who was more often praised for his 'taciturnity' and sense of dignity. Nor Jefferson, who avoided speaking in public whenever possible, even delivering his Annual Address to Congress in writing, at which he clearly excelled.

Andrew Jackson, whose skills were always being underestimated, was definitely capable of rising to the occasion with fine oratory, as in his first inaugural and standing up to South Carolina's secessionists.

It was clearly Lincoln, our sixteenth president, who excelled at the art of writing and delivering sublime oratory, despite the fact that he had barely six months of formal education and was otherwise basically self-taught. Instead, he read voraciously, memorizing the most memorable passages from the Bible, and the works of Shakespeare, polishing that off by incorporating Euclidian logic to express those eternal truths.

To better understand what made Lincoln's writing so artful and articulate, let us look into the times in which the great man lived.

TRANSFORMING THE OLD DISCOURSE

Nineteenth century America was a speech-making nation, a culture of long sermons and orations. Paper and print were still the best means of disseminating a message. But Lincoln was 'aural'...always more interested in how a speech sounded, rather than how it was written. He cared about commas because they were often his way of signaling a pause that lent gravity to the next phrase.

It was language after all that had enabled him to gain credibility among those who saw him as just another frontier politician, especially when the old platitudes no longer worked in political discourse to defend the indefensible.

It was Lincoln who was unique in bringing the words and phrases of moral authority to his speeches, starting with his 'House Divided speech'.

He understood where good writing was headed as it purged language of the nineteenth century flourishes, as exemplified by Edward Everett at Gettysburg. All the more reason that his chaste and spare Gettysburg Address shimmered with grace and passion after Everett's two-hour oration.

A natural classicist, Lincoln balanced phrases gracefully with touches of alliteration here and there. He never made them sound forced or calculated... giving them a drumbeat and cadence of energy from within.

Lincoln was more than simply a man of his times. Just as Mark Twain crafted his fiction to mirror the common man, Lincoln also had an ear for new simpler phrases.

Interestingly, Twain and Lincoln shared even more. Both were raconteurs who used humor to mask a melancholy nature. And both were born in border-states, making their way East to gain acceptance, as Lincoln did to great acclaim at Cooper Union.

Lincoln also knew how and when to sound conversational, without sounding casual, speaking as if being overheard while talking to himself...something called the art of 'familiar dignity'. As when he says in his first inaugural, 'suppose you go to war...you cannot always fight.' In responding to Stephen Douglas in those famous debates, he made sure to sound conversational and full of obvious common sense, in order to reach the everyday man. The style was blunt, and easily understood, yet the content was never banal.

Lincoln was also hugely adept at using humor, not only to push away his own melancholy, but as a means of communication between speaker and listener. This allowed the audience to share a more intimate moment and establish greater personal rapport. It also served to lighten a moment of great insight and lessen the sting in delivering a serious message.

Among our best at writing his own speeches, Lincoln was perhaps most like Churchill, a man who was praised widely for 'mobilizing the English language, and sending it into battle'. As with Churchill, the moment could not have been better timed, with both nations facing a crisis of monumental proportions. Sadly, in today's era of sound bites, it is highly questionable as to who would have listened to either of them.

As with Churchill, galvanizing his sceptered isle to stand up to Nazi atrocities, Lincoln set the stage in his second Annual Message to Congress for the need for new solutions, when he said, 'The dogmas of the quiet past are inadequate to the stormy present. So we must think anew and act anew.'

THE POWER OF HIS WORDS

Lincoln, like Churchill, believed that words describing a future yet to be realized could have the power to bring it into existence ... converting imagination into reality. At the same time, he was always aware of that higher power, admitting as the war lingered on that 'events have controlled me'.

Of course, as president, he also wielded enormous power to use his talents to shape public opinion and move it toward a new reality. Nevertheless, he freely expressed his gratitude when that reality came to pass, as Union troops welcomed blacks into the army without violence or cruelty.

Lincoln was secure enough in his craft to take the words and suggestions of others. He did this with many of Seward's ideas, transforming them into those soaring phrases in his first inaugural, including 'the mystic cords of memory' to indicate the ties that bound us together and could not be severed, even in war.

He not only knew how to use his words, he also knew when to withhold them. There were many times during the war when he was impelled to write a rather passionate letter regarding military ineptitude. Then he would wisely decide to put it in the drawer for history to take note of his passing thoughts.

Such was his letter to General George Meade, when he failed to pursue Lee after his retreat at Gettysburg, allowing him to cross the Rappahannock back to Virginia. Lincoln practically moaned, 'It looks as though the war will be prolonged indefinitely. Your golden opportunity is gone, and I am immeasurably distressed by it.'

Considering how many generals had disappointed him in their failure to match the skills of Southern generals, we must once again salute Mr. Lincoln for his self-restraint.

ADDRESSING CHANGING TIMES

Perhaps we can relate to Lincoln because he also lived in a time of government paralysis, a breakdown in public trust in the Republic itself. As today, it was a time of great technological change, rendering traditional forms of communication obsolete and raising questions as to the public's willingness to listen.

It would have been easy for Lincoln to be cynical or appalled as the norms of the day were splintering, both on the battlefield and between the races. Yet, this tortured soul who constantly sought to bury his melancholy beneath humor was always seeking to explain that cosmic plan over which he had no control. Ultimately, he found a transcendent meaning from the carnage in his Second Inaugural, spreading the blame between North and South as he looks toward a more just time of healing.

CLEVER AT MESSAGING

Lincoln was a canny politician, adept at using new technology to spread a 'message' and elevate his standing with the public. Prior to making his New York debut at Cooper Union, he visited the studio of Mathew Brady, who took pictures that still stand the test of time. They project the image of a man of substance and intellect.

He also knew when to take additional pictures at various critical moments ... as wartime aims changed and the public yearned to view Lincoln as he evolved into 'Father Abraham' in the public consciousness.

One cannot help but contrast this with today and a president who constantly lowers the bar, appealing to our basest instincts on race and distrust of our institutions. This includes President Trump's disturbing inaugural address, talking about 'American carnage' in some dystopian alternate universe that few can relate to. Again, let us contrast that with Lincoln over 150 years ago when he actually faced a daunting national crisis that was about to rip the country apart.

Let us celebrate Lincoln's use of language to calm those divisive forces, not exacerbate them...explaining why we as a nation could not go our separate ways as members of a sacred pact that over a century before had forged a perpetual Union.

It took Lincoln his entire first term to convince the North that these ideals were worth fighting for in what appeared to be an endless war. Lincoln was a cunning man. His words were constantly positioned to keep us united in spite of constant disappointments on the battlefields and a war weariness that invaded the nation's soul.

LOOKING THROUGH THE LENS OF TODAY

One can only wonder how Lincoln would have dealt with today's technology, calculated to give rise to disinformation. With the Internet and social media accelerating the process, the younger generation has abandoned thoughtful newspapers and the printed word in favor of these alternative sources. Sound bites have replaced carefully crafted articles and editorials that seek to inform and educate, building a reasonable case and defending a particular point of view.

Inaccurate information or 'fake news' as the expression goes, can now be spread with impunity and without attribution, molding our opinions and shaping our decisions. It is bad enough when domestic interests play that cynical game to serve their own interests. Now we have discovered that hostile overseas interests can invade this new media with impunity, pitting one group against another and sowing discord to distort election results.

How might that have impacted Lincoln, a man who was convinced that the people would always seek the truth and judge him accordingly? Once again, the only antidote lies with us. Lincoln's words in the lead up to the Civil War still ring true today. We are engaged in a national debate as to what kind of nation we want to be ... one that honors our founding documents and the promise of the Declaration of Independence or one that sees a nation as 'us' versus 'them'.

Walls cannot be built that will be high enough, nor technological barriers strong enough, to prevent the flow of information to distort a national conversation. It can only succeed if we allow it to. Perhaps we need another Lincoln, a person who can elevate the conversation to appeal to 'our better angels' and take us through difficult times in search of the best of America. Yes, words still matter and the nation still yearns to hear the right ones.

Andrew Jackson

PRESIDENTIAL SWAGGER

FROM JACKSON TO TEDDY ROOSEVELT TO TRUMP

We are currently living through a highly unorthodox presidency, based on the personality, temperament and unpredictability of the current White House occupant. That is not unusual. There have been several instances in our history of navigating through unchartered waters with a particular chief executive.

Let's call them men with 'presidential swagger', a characteristic that can work quite well or be a huge detriment, depending on the times and other characteristics of the individual in question.

Andrew Jackson was one of these, a man who, as president, was still walking around with lead in his body from multiple gunfights in the Wild West. He was also a man who, as a general, had so exceeded the orders of then President James Monroe that he had almost precipitated a war with both Spain and England.

From that day forward, he would be a man whom other feared would destroy the government with his impulsive, dominating ways.

Nevertheless, Jackson was highly notable as a Chief Executive, capable of greatly expanding presidential authority and facing down threats of nullification by South Carolina long before others failed miserably at the same task. More important, he was a man of great character and certitude, incorruptible, courtly with women, able to turn enemies into lifelong friends and dedicated to the well being of a nation that had provided him with endless opportunity.

What is unusual about a president like Donald Trump are acts that speak to character issues. These include childish tweets and insults...lying compulsively while questioning the right of a free press to hold him accountable...admitting vile behavior toward women and garnering a reputation for unethical business practices. Here we are in unchartered waters.

This is nothing Andrew Jackson would have tolerated. Yet, we do question his presidential judgment in initiating events leading up to the tragic 'Trail of Tears', dispossessing Indians from their land and sending them out West on a long march that many would not survive.

Another President who was a disrupter of the norms of the day, as well as an unpredictable force of nature, was Theodore Roosevelt. When serving in the State Assembly in Albany, he quickly mastered the legislative procedures and elbowed his way around the political bosses, going after what he called 'the wealthy criminal class', a product of the Gilded Age that had a lock on entitlement.

As Police Commissioner in New York City, supposedly a dead end job, he turned it into another success ... walking the beat to get to know the system and putting regulations in place to end corruption and graft.

Like Jackson, his unpredictability was generally aimed at setting things right for the public good...not on self aggrandizement for its own sake, as when he told the titans of industry that they should police themselves for 'crimes of cunning'.

According to Roosevelt, the Constitution had to be thought through anew in dealing with today's corporations, which put him right in line with Hamilton and John Marshall...both of whom saw this document as capable of being interpreted to suit the times.

Roosevelt also elevated the role of the executive above the other branches in representing the will of the people under what he called 'The New Nationalism'. As a disturber of norms, he established the Department of Commerce and Labor that housed a Bureau of Corporations to investigate further malfeasance. He also established commissions composed of experts in a particular field to bring him their findings on issues like urban housing and public health.

However, he had no patience for what he called 'sentimental humanitarians'. On the other hand, when presented with compelling information, such as Upton Sinclair's expose on the meat packing industry, he took immediate action.

Jackson was highly unpredictable as a military man in not following orders. Roosevelt was the same when it came to expanding the American footprint abroad...a swaggering, unapologetic imperialist. He felt that building the Panama Canal was his greatest accomplishment, giving us access to another transcontinental route that would transform American commerce. One can look at that as providing international infrastructure for an America that was now committed to joining the international community.

Never mind that, as with Jackson, the ends often justified the means, including stealing the land and fomenting an uprising in a breakaway section of Colombia.

His actions clearly implied that no one should stand in the way of America's destiny, including Congress.

Roosevelt's saving grace was his dual nature...a thoughtful, caring man who had constructed a coat of armor to project to the world. Inside that carapace beat the heart of a highly intellectual man who cared deeply about the environment and the plight of the downtrodden. A dedicated conservationist, he began a crusade to save our wetlands and expand our national parks. When Congress refused to make the Grand Canyon a national park, Roosevelt simply ignored them, using executive authority to set aside 800,000 acres as a 'national monument'.

In foreign affairs, under what was called the 'Roosevelt Corollary', he expanded the reach of the Monroe Doctrine to allow the U.S. to intervene in the affairs of other nations in our hemisphere. Again, acting more like Jackson, he meddled in Cuba...sending marines to restore order under something called the Platt Amendment, while declaring the island a protectorate.

But he lived in the right times. All of this was looked upon approvingly by a world that understood and supported expansionism. Given these credentials, Roosevelt was even asked to broker a peace agreement between Japan and Russia, winning a Nobel Peace Prize in 1906 to add to his international swagger.

His exploits overseas were part of a 'coming of age' moment for the country. As with Jackson, when a president is in tune with the times, he gets a free pass for better or worse. Yet throughout all the turmoil he managed to initiate, like Jackson, Roosevelt saw himself as the voice of the people. He represented them in fighting against moneyed interests that thought themselves above the law and the interests of the people. This Jeffersonian message of fighting for the underdog resonates to this day with voters who feel themselves dismissed and neglected by a changing society.

SUMMARY

To be authentic, swagger has to come from some place deep inside an individual...born of conquering not just adversity, but those internal demons to be dealt with. Certainly Jackson and Roosevelt both met that standard, acquiring a life possessed of military glory. Jackson accomplished this at the Battle of Horseshoe Bend, where he earned his nickname as 'Old Hickory', a man who would bend but not break. Teddy Roosevelt met that test at the Battle of San Juan Hill, where he and his Rough Riders defied the odds to win a crucial battle against far greater numbers on the Spanish side.

History gives Roosevelt and Jackson's swagger not just a pass, but grudging praise as well, as it was always within the bounds of a broader interpretation of a constitutional prerogative under Article ll...well almost!

For that matter, both men had a deep understanding of the Constitution and its concept of 'separation of powers'. Roosevelt was a scholar in the workings of government. And Jackson more than once astounded those doubters when he, a man of little education, wrote long counter-arguments to those accusing him of overstepping executive authority. We judge that today as increasing the power of the presidency to achieve constitutional goals, the same tactic used by John Marshall to elevate the Court's authority within constitutional norms.

TRUMP'S UNIQULEY UNAMERICAN SWAGGER

Let's contrast this with Trump's gratuitous verbal assaults on the workings of the courts and their decisions, having nothing to do with constitutional issues that affect the Chief Executive. His actions go to the heart of questioning our institutions' proper workings and province under Articles I and lll. To say that this violates the credo of 'separation of powers' under the Constitution would be an understatement.

The more Trump does this without pushback from the courts or Congress the more he dulls the public's understanding as to the damage that goes to the very heart of American democracy.

Trump's 'swagger' appears to revolve around short term divisive pandering rather than focusing on what is in the nation's best interest. He lacks a moral compass that we crave in a president, endlessly engaging in petty attacks on those who do not offer sufficient praise.

'Swagger' must be backed up with more than constant hyperbole. Unlike Jackson and Roosevelt, Trump is not a bona fide military hero, a prerequisite in carrying off the art of 'swagger'. Nor do his business dealings indicate anything approaching a sense of fair play. On the contrary, he seems to be a poster boy for just what Roosevelt railed against ... titans of industry with a sense of entitlement and being above the law.

In short, Trump is simply not capable of true presidential 'swagger', an art form of sorts to accomplish important national goals. Instead, his swagger represents egregious behavior calculated to hold onto a narrow political base for the purpose of self-aggrandizement.

John Adams

ADDRESSING MOB RULE

Our First Amendment enshrines the right to free speech, a term far too broad not to require the Court's intervention to determine where that right is not applicable. Such is the case where the Court has chipped away over the years, saying, for example, that yelling 'fire' in a crowded theater without good intentions is unacceptable behavior and does not warrant first amendment protection.

Assembling in public to represent a specific cause also requires certain limitations as to 'free speech', as when an unruly mob threatens others with violence.

Whether we view the right of assembly as an example of free speech or as 'mob violence' depends on one's perspective. To those protesting, even with a provocative threatening air, it may still feel like exercising the right to free speech. To the disinterested observer, or the object of the anger, it may look like mob violence.

Expressing public opprobrium has always been a right of America's citizens. We were founded on a certain amount of anger, if you count events like the Boston Tea Party as a rather strong display of dissent. After all, it was our anger at British taxation without representation that provoked the American Revolution.

Thomas Paine's pamphlet on 'The Rights of Man' gave voice to that anger and became a rallying cry for many as it laid out the complaints of Americans in a highly understandable and galvanizing way. At our nation's founding, many of our leaders understood the risks and consequences of inciting mob violence and walked a narrow path between inspiring and inciting.

We valued those firebrands among our founding fathers. Men like Patrick Henry almost single-handedly came close to having the Constitution voted down at Virginia's ratification convention, a result that might well have buried the document in the tomb of history, perhaps forever.

Even firebrands can go too far. When Paine, who highly approved of the mayhem of the French Revolution, went abroad to preach his 'rights of man', he found himself threatened with the guillotine without a friend to help him, except for Jefferson, who was always sympathetic to such rhetoric when it served his purposes.

Since our founding days, presidents have had to deal with the wrath of the mob in one way or another. Washington's loathing for overheated dissent was well known, whether in his Cabinet or the body politic. It was mainly out of concern that incidents such as Shay's Rebellion in Massachusetts were all too frequent and a threat to the Nation that he attended the Constitutional Convention in Philadelphia. That alone finally convinced him of the need to modify the ineffective Articles of Confederation and replace them with a strong central government.

As President, he was always aware that Europe was watching this experiment in democracy and rooting for its failure. That is in part why he personally took action during his second term in 1794 to put down the Whiskey Rebellion in Carlisle, Pennsylvania. Anyone other than Washington would have then been accused of being a monarchist and betraying the eternal message of America. However, he alone possessed such elevated stature as to be immune to such accusations.

Not so with other founding fathers. No one was more aware of the dangers of mob violence than John Adams. Prior to the Revolution, when British troops were still patrolling the streets of Boston, it was Adams who risked his career as an attorney and a future patriot to defend them after firing on a mob of angry Americans. For Adams recognized that they had been unreasonably provoked and did not deserve to be hung for their actions.

Prior to his presidency, Adams had written broadly on the subject of man's lesser nature. In 'The Davila Discourse', he warned of the inherent evil in man and his susceptibility to the wrong impulses. Of course, that gave Jefferson additional ammunition to brand all Federalists as 'monocrats' who demeaned the common man.

Adams never learned that lesson when it came to leaving a paper trail expressing his doubts as to the ability of the people to govern themselves. Hamilton was also guilty of this shortcoming, which in part explains why he never attained public office. He was better at advising a president than being one.

Hamilton's debut six-hour speech at the Constitutional Convention...where he praised the British monarchy and endorsed lifetime appointments for the chief executive ... ended his chances to play any significant role in Philadelphia. He did however go on to write the bulk of the Federalist Papers to explain the logic behind the words of the Constitution. This ultimately garnered the necessary votes at critical state ratification conventions.

One president who had no fear of the mob was Andrew Jackson, whom Republicans (and Whigs shortly thereafter) were happy to slander with the approbation of 'King Mob'. He willingly embraced the name, inviting the underclass back to the White House to celebrate his inauguration in 1828. The rabble more than lived up to its reputation, jumping out of windows, tearing down the silk drapes and destroying the furniture...thanks to Jackson's barrels of liquor to heighten their enjoyment.

Jackson was a new kind of president. While Jefferson played to the ordinary man with his rhetoric and lived the high life of a slave owner from the planter class, Jackson genuinely felt himself to belong with ordinary folk. He knew their ways and appreciated their contribution long after he had acquired a plantation manor and slaves of his own.

He also knew that the mob was on his side and was adept at manipulating it through his control of a robust Democratic press. But he too drew a line in the sand that was not to be crossed. When and if the mob got out of control by threatening to destroy our sacred Union, as South Carolina did in 1832, he was quick to threaten total annihilation, without anyone doubting his words.

Lincoln, another man of the people, began his career as a young politician, speaking out against mob lawlessness in his famous Address at the Young Men's Lyceum. He drew the line when a mob attacked and killed the editor of an anti-slavery newspaper, saying 'There is no grievance that is a fit object of redress by mob law'.

On the other hand, when the Draft Riots broke out in New York and other major cities in July of 1863, with many blacks being slaughtered, Lincoln wisely counseled caution, saying, 'one war at a time' and leaving the local police to handle the matter. It may be difficult to understand Lincoln's measured reaction to this outrage, when it was obvious that his emotional bias was clearly with the Negro community that his Proclamation had liberated earlier that year.

Context, however, was always important to the politically savvy Lincoln. He knew that the Democrats were likely to pounce and make this an issue in the upcoming election. He was bound to be accused of overreacting with federal troops and abusing his powers as Commander-in-Chief, especially when he had already bent the rules in suspending the writ of habeas corpus.

The fair-minded Lincoln was also expert at gauging human nature. He knew that the Irish immigrants who had rioted and hung Negroes from trees were feeling victimized by a draft that allowed the wealthy to buy their way out of serving.

Now let us fast forward to the Great Depression of 1929, with Herbert Hoover in the White House. Hoover was a man of great administrative skills, but clearly tone deaf as to the people's woes in being stripped of their financial well-being by events beyond their control. Virtually every week, he would tell a frustrated and fearful American people that prosperity was just around the corner, while the banks were using government funds to prop up their balance sheet.

When the Bonus Army of World War 1 veterans marched en masse to Washington to protest and demand back pay, they set up makeshift shanties down by the Tidal Basin, known as 'Hoovervilles'. Unfortunately, the President could not understand or sympathize with their plight and mistakenly outsourced the remedy to General Douglas MacArthur, who viewed this as simply mob violence. His forces then moved in, destroying tents and shredding the dignity of patriotic Americans.

As a result, Hoover lost the public for the balance of his term, assuring the election of FDR in 1932.

The events recounted above can perhaps shed light on another president's words and actions regarding mob violence in Charlottesville, home to Jefferson's University of Virginia. In that case, a band of skinheads and neo-Nazi's carrying torches descended on an interracial crowd protesting peacefully. It was said that these white supremacists had received a license to peacefully protest in the park. Clearly their behavior had exceeded traditional norms and incited opposition, with the death of one woman by a car driven by a neo-Nazi.

Where this could have been a teachable moment for not tolerating obvious bigotry, President Trump chose to wink at neo-Nazis, saying there were fine people on both sides and making this episode one of moral equivalence.

Evaluating this though the lens of history, one would have to ask:

1. Was this a case of supporting a valid minority point of view too long ignored, one that needed to be heard and honored?

2. Did the President's words elevate the conversation toward that goal of 'a more perfect union'?

3. Did the President's words educate and explain where he would draw the line on moral equivalence?

4. Were the President's words devoid of political influence and intent?

Unfortunately, none of these questions can be answered in the affirmative.

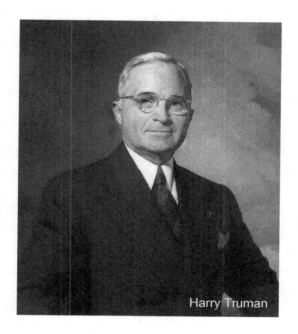

Harry Truman

A PRESIDENT'S
UNTOLD STORY

INTRODUCTION

When it comes to evaluating presidential candidates, we generally know very little other than the standard biography that anyone can read on line and the less conventional stories covered by the press.

Where campaigns are happy to feed the public with a steady stream of information calculated to inspire a spate of campaign donations, we are seldom exposed to a candidates formative years... those experiences that often create core values and mold aspirations. Yet, these are often what that individual will draw upon at that moment of crisis to color his judgment and his actions.

WASHINGTON'S FORMATIVE YEARS

George Washington has been revered throughout our history for his calm in the midst of those revolutionary battles as well as his wise decisions as our first President. However, these qualities did not miraculously appear. They were acquired over time through hard work and unrelenting self-discipline, often to overcome obstacles life had placed in his way.

Washington was the least favored of the children of Augustine Washington, the product of his second marriage to Mary Ball, a cantankerous woman who reserved her affections for her daughters and seldom praised her only son.

According to the laws of primogeniture, the bulk of Augustine's estate would go to Laurence, his eldest son from his first marriage. Nor would George enjoy the benefits of a proper schooling. What he did possess was height, athleticism and the regal bearing to make an impressive entrance. He soon realized that these assets could best be displayed in a military setting, where his limited schooling would count for little.

Despite those deficits, Washington burned with ambition, perhaps motivated by the desire to prove his mother and father wrong in their assessment of his future potential. Toward that end, he dedicated himself to a life of self-improvement, memorizing all the precepts in a book titled 'The Rules of Civility'. He had his well-connected brother introduce him to the Fairfax family, the largest landholders in the nation, who would be there to do him favors in the future.

CLIMBING THE LADDER

Washington's anger smoldered, watching British generals look down upon Americans such as himself. He learned to keep his temper in check as he studied military strategy, committing much of it to memory. At the same time, he would remain skeptical in applying those rules of war to an unusual landscape he knew intimately.

His moment to gain fame of sorts came soon enough during the French and Indian wars, when British General Braddock disregarded his advice and insisted on marching his troops in formation. When Indians descended on an easy target, scalping the British, including Braddock, it was Washington who projected the appropriate calm under pressure to lead an orderly retreat.

He was also clever enough to publish the story of these feats in 'The Journals of Major George Washington'. For he knew he would always be auditioning for the next step up the ladder of success. He added to his prestige by marrying one of the wealthiest widows in Virginia, transforming himself into a member of the upper class he long admired.

When others began to speak of separating from the Mother Country, Washington, knowing his deficits, made it his business to learn the issues from his more knowledgeable neighbor, George Mason. They would ultimately separate over Mason's refusal to ratify the Constitution, something Washington considered a badge of honor.

By the time the colonies convened the first Continental Congress in Philadelphia, Washington made sure to attend in full military regalia, knowing that he alone possessed the credentials to be the commander-in-chief of revolutionary forces. This included the 'Fabian strategy' he had learned from the Indians ... the ability to fade into the landscape when dealing with overwhelming British force.

When the war ended and Washington retired to Mount Vernon, he wisely remained above the fray, using his prestige to call for the writing of a new Constitution. His presiding over the crafting of that document enabled him, as our first President, to make fealty to its every clause his first priority.

PRESIDENT WASHINGTON

As President, he displayed the same excellent judgment in creating a cabinet of esteemed men to help govern, similar to the aides-de-camp that had served him well during the war. Once again, this allowed him to evaluate the information supplied by those better educated and more knowledgeable on a particular subject.

What others described as 'the gift of taciturnity' in truth reflected his wisdom in letting others try to impress the regal Washington, a man who always knew how to make an impressive entrance. Throughout his two terms, he displayed the lessons learned in his youth, being unfailingly courtly with women and in control of his considerable temper, except perhaps when mediating the heated discourse between Hamilton and Jefferson.

It should come as no surprise that he favored Hamilton above all others, as much for his wisdom as for who he was as a person ... someone who had also been overlooked based on his questionable birth status and who yearned for military service to give himself a sense of self worth. For those same experiences were embedded deep in Washington's soul from his earliest years, never to be forgotten and always part of what drove him to excel.

TRUMAN'S UNEXPECTED PRESIDENCY

While the people of his time expected much of Washington, there are other presidents of whom little was expected. Yet, in spite of this, some defied the odds. Once again, if the history of their formative years were better known, people may not have been quite so surprised with the successful presidency of Harry Truman, the ultimate 'accidental' President. For he was called upon to step into the shoes of FDR just as Germany was about to surrender and a new world order would need to be established.

Eleanor Roosevelt summed up that moment best when Truman came to the White House to pay his respects to the family upon FDR's death. Dressed in black, she responded to his condolences with words that rang true for Truman and the entire country, saying, 'What can we do for you, Harry? For you are the one who is now in trouble!'

Yet, within his first hundred days in office, this grossly underestimated man from Missouri made many of the most important decisions that saved the world from chaos. Again, much of this has to do with those qualities and beliefs nurtured during his youth and reinforced long before he entered the national spotlight.

THE EARLY YEARS

The story begins in 1884, when Truman is born in Grandview, Missouri, a farming community just outside of Independence. In this way, Truman's life will always be part of the story of America, a product of the heartland and people with the simple values of hard work and integrity.

Even as President, he would continue to revere his mother, known to the world as Mamma Truman, a strong-willed woman who taught him to read at the age of five. She was the one who first noticed his poor vision, finally diagnosed as hypermetropia or what one might call 'flat eyeballs'.

Like Teddy Roosevelt, whose world as a child was limited by severe asthma, Truman's time indoors lights his imagination as he reads voraciously, including biographies of famous generals like Andrew Jackson, Grant and Lee. He memorizes passages from the Bible that echo the phrases he hears at home, phrases like 'say what you mean and mean what you say'...'never get too big for your britches' and 'never forget a friend'.

When hard times hit the family, a teenage Truman quits his job at a bank in Kansas City and returns to the farm. Over the next five years, he will rise at five in the morning every day to plow the fields, an experience that, in his words, 'gave me time alone to think and settle all the ills of mankind'.

He enters politics almost by accident only because the Pendergast Organization in Kansas City needs a man known for his integrity to win the farm vote out near Grandview. He serves as eastern judge in Jackson County and honors his pledge to watch over the taxpayer's money, refusing the machine's request to give out contracts to friends. When his term expires and Pendergast offers him a Senate seat, he proves himself to be a scrappy campaigner, beating some better-known candidates.

SENATOR TRUMAN

He enters the Senate with the press assuming he will be a pawn of a political machine. But Truman ignores the implications, hanging a picture of Boss Pendergast in the entrance to his Senate office. For Truman, loyalty to a friend is still a bedrock commitment.

He goes on to surprise those doubters. He is the first Senator to arrive early in the morning a habit he developed during those years on the farm. He does his homework, taking fifty books from the Library of Congress to be better prepared for his work on the Commerce Committee.

But it is his Committee on Wartime Waste and Fraud, known to the public as the Truman Committee, that wins plaudits from the press and the country for conducting hearings with great efficiency that save billions of taxpayer dollars.

That is all the public knows about Harry Truman when FDR, seriously ill with advanced heart disease, selects him as his Vice President for his fourth term. After the election, the President basically ignores his Vice President, despite all the momentous decisions being made to forge a new world order as the Allies defeat the Nazi

War machine. It is therefore no wonder that Eleanor Roosevelt greets the new President with words of concern.

CHARACTER COUNTS

Harry Truman is a man of character in many ways, big and small. He delays his marriage to his childhood sweetheart so that he could serve in World War 1, even though he could easily have dodged service at the age of thirty-three. He even memorizes the eye chart, knowing that, with his poor eyesight, he would otherwise have flunked the test.

In France, he serves as captain of Artillery Battery D and transforms it into one of the best in the 129th Regiment. He leads his men safely through the Meuse Argonne offensive, one of the bloodiest battles of the war.

Like Teddy Roosevelt, who took his Rough Riders to victory on San Juan Hill in the Spanish American War, Truman remains close with his buddies in Battery D, especially Eddie Jacobson, who will be instrumental in one of his most important decisions as president.

Despite Eleanor Roosevelt's concerns, on his first day in office, Truman impresses the men who surrounded FDR. They find him highly knowledgeable on the men and the decisions that have preceded him into the Oval Office. He is already knowledgeable on the critical details of the Yalta Conference, where FDR supposedly gave away too much to Stalin.

To hold Stalin to account, he travels to another Big Three conference at Potsdam, just outside of Berlin and makes another highly favorable impression... this time on a skeptical Churchill. Where FDR used his personal charm to win the day, Truman is plain-spoken in letting Stalin know where he stands.

The very same day, a blinding flash of light at Alamogordo, New Mexico heralds the first successful test of an atomic bomb. Now Truman will have to make another momentous decision, whether to use this weapon to end the war in the Pacific. Already his own experience is vital, having lived through the carnage in the Meuse Argonne in World War 1 that killed over fourteen thousand Americans. In the end, he decides to drop the bomb on Hiroshima in order to 'shorten the agony of war, and save the lives of thousands of young Americans.'

With the Japanese surrender, many in Congress think that things will go back to business as usual. But they don't know Harry Truman, someone who has always fought for the little man, even back in his hometown of Grandview. He launches a 21 Point program to increase the minimum wage, enact tax reform and provide new housing for millions of disadvantaged.

He is equally diligent in foreign affairs, as he assembles a first rate team, starting with the appointment of the greatly respected George Marshall as his Secretary of State, someone he calls 'the great man of the age'.

Marshall and his Under-Secretary, Dean Acheson, transform the State Department and craft what is known as the Truman Doctrine to oppose the Soviet ambitions to expand the grasp of communism in Western Europe. This is followed with another bold initiative enunciated by Marshall to rebuild a war torn Europe. But again, Truman displays the modesty of a true leader, insisting that it be called the Marshall Plan.

He displays a unique capacity to grow when faced with injustice of any sort. This son of southern society turns his back on his roots when he hears of Negro troops returning from Europe and being beaten in Mississippi. He appoints a Civil Rights Commission to renew the promise of the Fourteenth Amendment, knowing it will negatively affect his chances of being re-elected in the South.

Perhaps his standing up for the forgotten has something to do with his past...a boy whose handicap forced him to spend time in-doors reading of the great moments in America's past, moments he is inspired to emulate. He sympathizes with the dreams of a Jewish homeland in Palestine, thanks in large part to his long friendship with his wartime buddy, Eddie Jacobson. He ultimately refuses to back down in recognizing Israel as the fruition of that dream, despite the opposition of Marshall, the man he so greatly respects.

He decides to run for his own term in 1948, although polls predict that the Republican candidate, New York Governor Thomas Dewey, will win in a landslide. Truman is determined to take his case to the people, who have never failed to listen to common sense. He launches a unique whistle stop cross-country campaign to 'say what he means and mean what he says', the lessons learned in his youth.

The press laughs at the carnival atmosphere as he, Bess and daughter Margaret speak from the back of the train to hundreds of people at small stops along the way. He alone predicts that he will beat Dewey in a huge political upset. When he does, he enjoys watching the press greet him back in Washington with a banner, saying 'Welcome Home from Crow Eaters'.

Tough times await him for what is technically his first term. The Cold War has Republicans looking for someone to blame communist gains in China. Nor does it help those suspicious minds when the Russians finally develop their own atomic bomb.

Secretary of State, George Marshall retires, replaced by Dean Acheson, who is attacked with a smear campaign by Senator Joseph McCarthy. By then, the invasion of South Korea, by the North and its Chinese allies, makes talk of the 'Red Scare' ever more palpable for the American public.

Acheson wisely goes to the UN to gain support for a limited 'police action', rather than a war that we alone must fight. Again, the Secretary of State will be blamed for allowing this to happen. When things are at their bleakest in Korea, General Douglas MacArthur stages a brilliant move, known as the Inchon landing, trapping North Korean troops and turning the tide. But when the General oversteps his orders, Truman is forced to face huge public disapproval and fire him. Once again, this simple man from Missouri understands the lessons of history and reasserts civilian control of the military...a bedrock tenet of our democracy, no matter what the personal consequences may be.

Like Lincoln during the Civil War, he understands that wartime goals must take precedence and that a peaceful resolution of a limited war will benefit the country or in his words 'The responsibility of a great State is to serve and not dominate the world'. His sense of morality is on display even in ways the public will never appreciate. When a Native American soldier is denied a proper burial out in Iowa, Truman has his body flown East to be buried at Arlington with honors.

Truman's poll numbers are at a low point as talk of 'losing China' and a communist conspiracy within the government sweep the country. He knows that it is time to exit the stage. He has always seen himself as merely a tenant in the White House, renting the space for a brief term. A man who understands the lessons of history better than most, knows that history will one day applaud his legacy.

For this underrated man has defied the odds, crafting progressive legislation that values the common man and surrounding himself with the best talent to craft a new world order. He is content to drive back to Independence, Missouri with Bess at his side and live once more in the house his wife grew up in without pretention or fanfare.

Alexander Hamilton

THE FOX
AND THE HEDGEHOG

INTRODUCTION

In the book, 'On Strategy', John Gaddis describes the philosophy of Isaiah Berlin, the British philosopher, who acted as the 'go between', for Churchill and FDR during much of World War ll. Berlin came to the States on a regular basis to get a sense of what the country was thinking and report back to the Prime Minister prior to his own visits with FDR in the White House.

Berlin was perfect for this role as an astute observer of human behavior, who had written widely on that subject. One of his more interesting insights deals with the various methodologies used by the most effective leaders, whether in the military or in higher office, going all the way back to ancient times.

He uses the analogy of two very different animals, the fox and the hedgehog, to explain different types of behavior, one dynamic and cunning and pro-active and the other plodding, reliable and predictable. The fox, he claims, is better equipped to survive in a rapidly changing environment in which those who abandon bad ideas quickly have a distinct advantage. He sees the hedgehog as better equipped to survive in a static environment that rewards persistence with tried and true results.

Berlin claims our best leaders are those who combine the attributes of both...smart enough to use what has worked in the past and cunning enough to quickly adapt to a new set of conditions.

The author, John Gaddis, has applied these guidelines to a host of important figures in American history. But there is much more to the story. This chapter attempts to shed light on those who have succeeded and those who have failed in the use, or misuse, of these qualities.

WARTIME GENERALS

Let us start with those American generals who laid out a grand strategy that called upon the maxims of the past, while navigating a reality that created the need to constantly change tactics.

Clausewitz, whose book titled 'On War', is the definitive work on that subject, calls 'friction' that collision between theory and reality, requiring the skills of the fox in improvising.

Washington faced that dilemma early on during the Revolution in the Battle of Long Island, where he grossly miscalculated British troop strength and tactics, soon finding himself in full retreat. Had British General Howe pursued American forces, and not stopped to celebrate by dining, the war might have been over right then and there.

Washington used that opportunity to adapt to the reality of British military superiority. From then on he would use his intimate knowledge of the landscape to dodge and weave in what was called the Fabian strategy, slowly but surely wearing down his opponent's will to fight. In truth, Washington was already familiar with this strategy, one constantly used by the Indians in the French and Indian Wars. He just needed a refresher course!

Grant was the Civil War general most adept at playing the fox and revising battle plans midst the chaos of war. He outfoxed Lee, a wily opponent, many times in his Peninsula Campaign to reach the gates of Richmond.

At the height of battles in the Wilderness and at Cold Harbor, even when Confederates forces were winning, he would be up all night sketching and reimagining the landscape to find new opportunities to continue the battle the next day. He understood that the revisions need not be complex, as long as they served to keep the enemy off balance, and still expecting an easy victory.

Grant had promised Lincoln that there would be no retreat and was determined to honor that commitment, even if that meant being called a butcher for throwing his men into the meat grinder of war. Like Lincoln, he understood that preserving the Union allowed few alternatives. In warfare, sometimes morality would have to take a backseat. The cunning of the fox did not always promise an easy path.

While some military men may play the hedgehog, guilty of not modifying strategies to attain their goals, surely men without an understanding of Clausewitz and the rules of war are even more prone to make this mistake. Such was the case with President Woodrow Wilson, an academician who presided over our entry into World War l. Wilson was always prone to delivering his proclamations and theories from 'The Mount', rather than leading through the art of persuasion.

In this sense, he was a hedgehog, assuming his words would carry the day and create their own reality, without the need for a strategy to gain support. And thus, Wilson's dream of creating a new world order through a League of Nations failed.

In the end, this hedgehog was forced to engage in endless compromise with more cunning foxes in Europe, who watered down the meaning of the League, while Republicans in the U.S. Senate prevented the country from participating, thereby rendering the organization of little use in maintaining peace.

A mere ten years later, Hitler appeared on the world stage, promising to restore German honor. A functioning League of Nations, with the participation of the U.S., might have challenged his first act of aggression against Czechoslovakia if Wilson, a true hedgehog, had been more of a fox.

FOUNDING FATHERS

These characteristics of the fox and hedgehog can also be applied to our Founding Fathers, those icons throughout our history. The inability to straddle those qualities would doom some to play a lesser role. While others would reap the benefits for themselves and the nation they served through a more adept performance.

BENJAMIN FRANKLIN

Franklin played a unique role among our Founding Fathers, doing more to inspire Americans in their daily life than many equally accomplished office holders. Behind the facade of bonhomie, Franklin was a crafty and accomplished entrepreneur, having built a newspaper empire up and down the Coast.

He was a master at acting as both the fox and the hedgehog in the many roles he played throughout his life. This included his so-called 'scientific amusements' that yielded groundbreaking discoveries, where he took the everyday norms of the hedgehog and added the sly observations of the fox to create a new reality.

His mantra throughout his life was, 'What man can do individually, can better be accomplished together'. Through collectivism, he believed we could share ideas, and all be the wiser. With that in mind, he was the first to encourage the colonies to band together in their opposition to British rule, thirty years before the first Continental Congress.

Franklin was always aiming for self-improvement, putting together a list of the most desirable qualities in order to work on his faults. One was impatience, a quality he learned to curb through what he called 'persuasion through indirection' rather than through confrontation.

As our Ambassador to France at the height of the Revolution, he used this unique form of persuasion, including the wily ways of the fox, to convince the French to fund a war against their archenemy. In the process, it practically bankrupted the monarchy and led to the French Revolution.

ADAMS AND HAMILTON

These two daunting founding fathers possessed great intelligence,yet were different in far too many ways to understand and appreciate each other.

Adams was a total hedgehog, coming at you directly, without the cunning to understand when to withhold information or compromise. That worked in galvanizing support for breaking with the Mother Country at the first and second Continental Congress. But he wore out his welcome shortly thereafter with too much conversation and was 'exiled' to Europe to raise funds for the battle to come.

Even as President, he could never inspire the public with rhetoric that grabbed their imagination. Instead, he expected their praise for his intelligence and hard work.

Hamilton, by contrast, was a bundle of untamable energy, always in motion. His agile mind was that of the fox, always foreseeing the future with greater clarity than others. From the moment he arrived here from the Caribbean island of St. Croix, he understood the potential of this young nation to be a power in the world. He also foresaw the need to harness that potential through the framework of a new Constitution. He then went on to shape the interpretation of that document through his writings, including the monumental Federalist Papers.

He possessed none of the hedgehog's steadfastness, never sufficiently grounded in reality to create a political base that would yield higher office. Instead he yearned constantly for military glory through daunting feats of bravery. As a fox, Hamilton found his calling in advising a plodding realist like Washington, who at the same time was clever enough to understand the need to adopt the dreams and strategies of a brilliant fox.

His marriage to Eliza Schuyler and the birth of their children provided an opportunity to play the hedgehog. And Hamilton was in fact a devoted husband and father. But, the impulses of the fox were not to be submerged for long. There was always the need to allow danger or intrigue to play a part in his life ... as with his reckless affair with the beautiful and tempting Maria Reynolds. In fact, he was almost anxious to confess his indiscretions to those congressmen who had suspected him of misappropriating funds as Treasury Secretary.

After leaving the second Washington Administration, Hamilton attempted to live the life of the hedgehog, building a beautiful large home for his family in the bucolic upper reaches of Manhattan. But once again, he would choose to engage in the intrigue of the fox, battling with Adams for control of the Federalist party. When his rash actions helped to precipitate the demise of the Party, perhaps he needed the danger of that final fight with Aaron Burr.

It certainly could have been avoided with a letter of apology for an indiscreet remark. Yet, Hamilton chose to engage in that duel on the heights of Weehauken. Perhaps he knew that it would be better to die nobly as a fox than face a life of political oblivion as a hedgehog.

JEFFERSON

Of all the Founding Fathers, Thomas Jefferson was by far the most cunning. Contrary to the astute strategist, he often outsmarted himself with his inconsistencies. Where the true fox takes pride in developing strategies to meet unforeseen obstacles in order to attain a particular goal, Jefferson often denied culpability, hiding behind surrogates or preaching righteous indignation at the accusations of others.

His actions did not always match his high blown rhetoric, including those words, 'life, liberty and the pursuit of happiness', written in the Declaration of Independence by a slaveholder. He, more than most, embodied the contradictions within our Constitution...the desire to create a federal government to tame the diverse passions of states while at the same time leaving us distrustful of federal authority.

This fox was clever enough to exploit that flaw by founding the Republican Party to fan that distrust. Yet, once he attained the presidency, he governed from the center, acting more like the hedgehog and proving again that, as far as he was concerned, rhetoric and reality did not necessarily have to be consistent.

MADISON

James Madison possessed a brilliant mind within a sickly and slight body. He knew he could never be a man of action based on his lack of stature and weak speaking voice. He therefore devoted his life to learning and synthesizing knowledge. As he had hoped, this brought him great respect among those better able to deliver his message.

Early on, he recognized Jefferson's genius as well as his tendency to exaggerate in order to shock and keep his supporters entertained. This included Jefferson's support for the French Revolution, saying that a little rebellion from time to time 'refreshes the tree of liberty'. Madison knew that as a brilliant hedgehog, he needed Jefferson's wily fox to strategize and make things happen. He signed on to found a Republican Party because he too was concerned with a central government acquiring too much power.

Even though he and Hamilton had crafted the outlines of the Constitution, he felt that the process had yielded far too ambiguous a document...one that lacked enough checks and balances to prevent men like Hamilton from molding it to reflect their point of view.

Nor could one deny that as southern slaveholders, Jefferson and he shared a certain societal mindset that men like Hamilton could never understand. And so he was willing to break with Washington, the man he had revered and for whom he had written an inaugural address.

LINCOLN
Lincoln was perhaps the most adept at combining the qualities of both the hedgehog and the fox, possessing the ability to hold two opposing ideas in his mind at the same time without fear of contradiction. This came naturally to a man born of parents who were basically illiterate. He learned early on how to deal with a confusing landscape that befuddled a man who yearned for knowledge.

His life was full of contradictions. He constantly sought out laughter to balance a depressive nature that required quiet moments to figure out what life intended for him. From the Bible, he acquired the words and cadence that made his speeches soar. From Shakespeare, he acquired the company of others who shared lives of inner torment.

All of this played a part in constantly providing him with the lessons of life. Navigating through life with nothing but six months of education required a combination of realism and cunning. Long term goals and immediate necessities have to live side by side.

When his dreams of higher office fell apart after one term in Congress, he reconciled himself to a life as a successful attorney, despite ambitions that continued to burn within him. But when the opportunity arose to re-enter politics, the instincts of a fox resurfaced. He cleverly crafted his arguments to oppose slavery with Euclidean logic as opposed to the rants of an abolitionist. Where others offered a quick political fix, he addressed slavery as a moral issue that went to the heart of the promise of our founding documents.

Knowing that the Constitution was flawed by the 'three-fifths' clause, the fox cleverly elevated the words of the Declaration of Independence. He then created the right forums to speak these words and gain the support of those who controlled the Republican Party. This dual nature served him exceptionally well as President. When the cannons fired on Fort Sumter, he accepted the fact that political dialogue would now be replaced by a new form of communication...that of war.

His stated goal was to preserve the Union, which over time could have been accomplished as a plodding hedgehog by using the North's greater industrial might. When he sensed a war-weariness growing within the North, this fox cleverly switched tactics and decided to accelerate victory by stripping the South of a vital resource, namely the slaves that kept the economy running.

In this way, he maintained his long-term goal of preserving the Union by cleverly adding an auxiliary goal as a logical part of the process. The fox understood that once he opened the door to freeing those slaves, there could be no re-enslavement. Yet, in the end, knowing he alone could not heal the wounds of war, he ceded control of the nation's fate and placed it in the hands of the Almighty. The fox hoped to create some element of grace and forgiveness between North and South.

Had he lived, Lincoln would have continued to preach this message as 'Father Abraham', the title now bestowed upon him by the community of freed slaves. Even Lincoln would have been hard-pressed to use his skills to have the South mend its ways. Conquered territory provided few options other than ruling by fear, as the Radicals in Congress preferred.

In the end, even that failed as the South outlasted those draconian measures and invented the narrative of the 'Lost Cause' to paint themselves as the aggrieved party. As Lincoln might have learned had he lived, even the most adept of foxes occasionally has few alternatives.

FDR: THE JUGGLER

Franklin Roosevelt was the other president uniquely adept at playing both the fox and the hedgehog. Inconsistency was simply a part of life. Like Lincoln, he too came by it naturally, though born under totally different circumstances.

FDR was the scion of great wealth on both his mother and father's side. But he was also the product of a second marriage for his father, who was twice the age of his mother. Maintaining a calm and cordial atmosphere at all times for a father who suffered from a weak heart, forced FDR to play the part of a contented hedgehog.

He would wear that mask in public from an early age, no matter what his inner thoughts or feelings might be. Nevertheless, in dealing with the challenges of life outside the home, he quickly acquired the talents of the fox.

As President, he was known as 'the juggler', keeping a predictable rhythm going, while surprising his audience every so often with an unpredictable feat of manipulation. Even Eleanor, his astute wife, was never quite sure what he was thinking.

More than any other president, he would need these skills to deal with the Great Depression and a World War, the two cataclysmic events that defined his presidency. He played the fox in forging a new economic path through constant experimentation, while calming an anxious nation with Fireside Chats that spoke the reassuring words of the hedgehog.

Getting the nation to accept the burden of assisting Britain in its war against Hitler would be more difficult, but FDR had the patience of the hedgehog in waiting for the country to shed its isolationist point of view. The fox would then manipulate the country slowly into accepting our entry into the war, starting with the novel concept of Lend Lease.

But still, he needed events on the ground to work in his favor. Lincoln had Fort Sumter and FDR now received the 'gift' of Pearl Harbor. Wars in both the Atlantic and Pacific required the juggler to constantly reassess wartime goals and allocate the resources of 'the Arsenal of Democracy'. At the same time, he would have deal with Churchill and Stalin, two other wily foxes with their own agendas and wartime goals.

According to some, FDR may have been outfoxed at the last Big Three Conference at Yalta. Yet, again, he simultaneously sought to calm an anxious world by laying the groundwork for the United Nations, a plodding, inclusive hedgehog of an institution. What must not go unnoticed was the ability of the fox to conduct a war while building the machinery of peace ... a feat unmatched in the history of mankind. Some would have expected this war to curtail individual liberties. Instead, FDR expanded those collective freedoms to create a safety net that benefited the entire nation, starting with social security to guarantee a dignified retirement.

TRUMAN, EISENHOWER, JFK

After World War ll, the hopefulness of a new era of peace quickly broke apart with Soviet schemes of world domination and the descent of that 'Iron Curtain' over Eastern Europe, a phrase invented by Churchill.

The strategy to address the threat of communism, known as 'containment', was developed by the State Department's brilliant strategist, George Kennan. It emphasized the best elements of the 'hedgehog'...long-term patience guided by strategic course corrections from time to time. There was little room for the exploits of the fox.

The underrated President Truman was smart enough to understand this. He addressed the invasion of South Korea as a collaborative UN mission, drawing the line between internal subversion and an attack on territorial integrity as guaranteed under the UN charter. The plainspoken Truman did not have the dreams of being a fox. Those were left to his general, Douglas MacArthur, whom he summarily fired for overreaching and attempting to turn a limited war into a worldwide conflagration.

Eisenhower as President was also wise in staying the course, although he did allow his CIA to meddle, as somewhat of a fox, in the internal affairs of various countries to prop up congenial governments in Iran and Guatemala. He understood the changing geo-political landscape and refused to get involved in military action that had the taint of neo-colonialism. In the process, a wise hedgehog won the day through inaction... or should we call this the wisdom of the ultimate fox?

Unfortunately, JFK lacked that wisdom when he blurred the line with John Foster Dulles' unproven Domino Theory that predicted grave consequences if we did not act. This opened the door for our involvement in a civil war in Vietnam, which the next Administration under LBJ foolishly accelerated.

Both of these presidents forgot to consult established precedent, words spoken by John Quincy Adams as Secretary of State in 1819. 'America does not go abroad in search of monsters to destroy. She is the well-wisher to the freedom and independence of all. But she is the champion and vindicator only of her own.'

The lesson learned is that walls of predictability may be necessary where the hedgehog plays the major role; engaging the fox requires a precise explanation to justify those acts of unpredictability.

FUTURE CHALLENGES

Now let us fast forward to more current times. Unfortunately, there are few presidents who have possessed the skills to combine the best qualities of the fox and the hedgehog, although we were clearly in need of that on 9/11.

Had George W. Bush been a fox, he would have seized upon the international goodwill generated for our plight to set a new course. Instead, he took the most predictable path, one the hedgehog might relish. We attacked another nation to settle scores. Unfortunately, to make matters worse, it was the wrong nation, based on faulty information at the wrong moment in time. Obviously, the fox played no part in this. There was no grand strategy in mind other than retribution. If anything, this emboldened terrorists, leading to further destabilization in a region already beset with problems.

If the President had acted as the bold and unpredictable fox, he might have made better use of this moment, convening a conference on the root causes of terrorism, a subject that all industrialized nations have a stake in confronting.

The fox might have looked back to the time of the Marshall Plan during the Truman Administration when expansive communist designs threatened Greece still mired in poverty and chaos post World War ll. Instead of marching in to oppose communist sympathizers, we bolstered the economy of Greece with a huge infusion of capital...aiming for the long-term goal of economic and political stability, the best antidote in confronting the threat of communism.

If we had a Secretary of State in place like James Baker, we would have internationalized this initiative, working through organizations like the UN, GATT and the World Bank...or even creating new ones to better confront the issues at hand. For that is what Baker did when the Soviet Union was unraveling in the post-Reagan era. Baker was the ultimate fox in foreign affairs, finding new and novel ways to put together an international coalition to help convert the Russian economy to one that was compatible with the West's.

At the same time, Baker was dealing with other major issues, including putting together an international coalition to deal with the Iraqi invasion of neighboring Kuwait. But this time, the nimble Baker played the hedgehog, keeping this a limited war with limited goals. Let us not forget that it was the ultimate hedgehog, President George HW Bush who saw the fox-like talents of James Baker and the need to have him by his side.

A FUTURE FOX

Today, we face the worldwide threat of climate change, one that threatens everything from agriculture to a shrinking landmass to mass immigration that will destabilize nations. We are even more in need of another fox to chart a long-term multinational initiative that is stable and plodding enough to achieve measurable goals, yet agile enough to meet the inevitable challenges along the way.

Whether we can find the right individual with the talents of both the fox and the hedgehog to address the challenges of the 21st Century, is the prime question yet to be answered.

Abraham Lincoln

THE HALLMARKS OF DEMOCRACY

Today, when we hear our 45th President talk of delaying our elections because of the coronavirus or tampering with the means to assure a legitimate outcome, it is important to look back at some of our darkest days, and hear the words of Lincoln, as recorded by that master of 'Lincoln-ography', Carl Sandburg.

Although Lincoln was often able to use the power of his words to coax a nation toward its 'better angels', he was ultimately willing to be guided by the verdict of the people as to his performance.

In 1864, with the Civil War in its third year, Lincoln's chances for gaining a second term were looking dim, based on the negative reception for his Emancipation Proclamation of the prior year, as well as a general war-weariness in the North. When Democrats accused Lincoln of holding onto power, no matter what the verdict at the polls, his response was simple yet profound.

'I am struggling to maintain the government, rather than overthrow it.'

In those spare phrases, the astute Lincoln was making two points. He understood that anything other than accepting the verdict of the people would be treasonous. At the same time, he was reiterating the point that the Civil War was first and foremost a war to preserve the Union, rather than one to free the slaves. Yet, if he were voted out of office, the people's verdict must stand 'in maintaining government' according to the Constitution.

Lincoln's eyes were always focused on the bigger picture. The War was but a means of preserving a fragile and endangered democracy. If we were to eliminate any of the essential tools of democracy in the process of waging this Civil War, there would be nothing left worth fighting for. When his secretaries, John Hay and John Nikolay advised him not to conduct another draft until after the election, he said, ' what is the country worth to me if I have no country?'

For Lincoln, all the traditions of a nation, guided by the will of the people, were sacred. He was never one to indulge in the devious tricks of other politicians to gain an advantage. The nation deserved better. If the people saw another draft as a reminder of a war poorly waged, he would stand by that judgment.

Lincoln understood the risks he was taking. The Draft Riots in New York the previous year had ended with buildings burned to the ground and Negroes hung from telephone poles. That had been the consequence of his Emancipation Proclamation, with the Irish community feeling that they were being asked to fight a war to free the slaves. Lincoln understood, and took no action, saying that he would deal with 'one war at a time'.

As he knew from his own suffering, life was seldom fair. Those young Irish boys should be even angrier with the wealthy who were able to buy their way out of serving with a three hundred dollar payment. And so, a universal draft proceeded with all its faults, as the only fair way to gain the troops needed to fight this war.

Lincoln could be a very crafty politician when the times required. He had gained the presidency as a dark horse candidate, speaking the right words in the proper forums. If he were to win the election in November, he wanted it to be based on the faith the troops had in him. For months, he had nurtured that bond, traveling down to City Point, where Grant's troops were stationed in the final months of the war and visiting the wounded on both sides.

Winning without their support was anathema to Lincoln. And so he told Edwin Stanton, his Secretary of War, to issue furloughs so that troops could come home to vote. In the end, Lincoln's instincts were correct. The soldier vote turned out to be the determining factor in his victory.

It was never Lincoln's intent to stoke the suspicion and mistrust that filled the air. It would have been easy to do so, finding scapegoats to blame to consolidate his grip on power. Others might relish acquiring the powers of a dictator in this way, but not Lincoln. He understood that any diminution of constitutional norms would be a victory for the Confederacy, when he said, 'We cannot have free government without elections and if the rebellion could force us to forego or postpone a national election...it might already claim to have conquered and ruined us.'

And so, on that day in early November, as Carl Sandburg recorded, 'the filing of ballots went on in quiet and good order'. When Lincoln won in November, he claimed no part in the victory, saying it was the people's belief in free government that has won the day. Now he would assume the role of healer-in-chief, understanding that the road ahead in bringing the South back into the Union, would prove to be as difficult as that of waging war.

He spoke first to the South, saying, 'It gives no pleasure to me to triumph over anyone. Then he addressed the entire nation, once again united. "But I give thanks to the Almighty for the evidence of the people's resolution to stand by free government and the rights of humanity'.

It would have been easy for Lincoln to join men like Thaddeus Stevens and the powerful group of Republican senators and congressmen who planned to visit retribution on the South with trials and hangings of Confederate leaders. As history would prove, that might have been the only way to destroy the grip of the ruling class of plantation owners who had gone to war for their own greedy purposes. Now, they would outlast their victors and find a new means to enslave those newly freed slaves.

Certainly, the scene at Andersonville, that Southern camp for prisoners-of-war, where Union soldiers were starved to death, would have served nicely in developing that narrative. But Lincoln knew it would not serve his goal of reconciliation. The South could barely feed its people at this point, no less those locked up in Andersonville.

He made sure to write his Second Inaugural Address with a sense of collective guilt. There would be no gloating as General Sherman's forces ravaged the South. Instead he said, 'With malice toward none, with charity for all, let us strive to finish the work and bind up the nation's wounds.' The defeated could not be treated as enemies if there were to be any chance of reconciliation.

Only days later, Lincoln was waiting anxiously in the White House when he received word from Grant that Richmond had fallen and General Lee was about to surrender. He traveled to the city, once the capital of the Confederacy, and walked the streets without guards to watch over him. When slaves gathered around him, kneeling and calling him Father Abraham, he said,' You must kneel only to God'.

Lincoln authorized Grant to make the peace agreement; for he trusted the judgment of the only Northern General who had known how to take the fight to the Confederacy and promised never to retreat. Still, he cautioned Grant to 'let 'em up easy' and allow the troops to take their horses home for the planting season. He understood the work that lay ahead, when he said, 'Enough lives have been sacrificed. We must extinguish our resentments if we expect harmony and Union.'

The war had decimated the South in terms of dwindling manpower and economic resources. On the other hand, the North had only gained ground with a booming economy in railroads, oil, munitions and textiles. Scores of fortunes were being made that dwarfed anything comparable among the wealthiest planters in southern society. The South would have to be restored to solvency if it was ever to take its proper place in the Union.

Lincoln continued to go about the task of reconciliation in those few days left to him, addressing a crowd outside the White House from an open window. He listened to a regimental band of ex-Confederates on the White House lawn playing Dixie. His careworn face lit up. 'Once again, that tune is federal property.'

He spoke with a sense of hopefulness about molding society for durability, meaning that we would never again allow our differences to commit us to war. At the same time, he stood his ground when he said, 'I shall not attempt to retract the Emancipation Proclamation nor shall I return to slavery any person who is free by those terms of any act of Congress.'

An actor in the crowd, John Wilkes Booth, heard these words and turned to his companion, saying that he would run Lincoln through with a sword for mixing the races. But Lincoln had long since been reconciled to that possibility. He still kept at least eighty of those death threats in his desk drawer to remind him that some day someone would succeed.

Thus we see what presidential greatness is all about. It is comprised of great character and an unyielding fealty to the norms of a constitutional democracy. It is about having confidence in the people and abiding by their judgment. It is about compassion and empathy for the plight of all peoples affected by events beyond their control. And it is about not taking advantage, at vulnerable moments, to elevate personal ambition above the needs of a nation.

As the newspapers of the day said about Lincoln, in a verdict on his tenure: 'The personal character of the President is the rock upon which the opposition is wrecked. It dashes against him...but falls back baffled.'

TRUMP'S SELF-SERVING MESSAGING

As our current President has ranted about mail-in ballots in an attempt to rig an election or contest the results at the very least, it is only fitting that we describe the personal character of this President.

Donald Trump, a so-called real estate mogul, had a checkered career at best. He had been denied credit by practically every bank in New York, except for DeutscheBank, which had ties to Russian business interests that are currently being investigated by the U.S. Attorney for New York's Southern District.

His other career involved hosting 'The Apprentice', a highly rated television show where he first and foremost exploited the 'Trump brand', including writing several best seller books on the 'Art of the Deal'.

In hawking his theory of 'birtherism' and claiming that Barack Obama had been born abroad, he followed the devious 'McCarthy' script in constantly claiming to uncover relevant information, though nothing ever emerged. In the process he was able to burnish his racist credentials as someone who would try to 'make America white again'.

In his messaging from the start as President, Trump sought to divide Americans, with an inaugural address of hopelessness and fear, claiming that we were in the midst of 'American carnage'.

The Trump brand also included the art of altering reality to make highly questionable acts seem as if they were appropriate and affirmative. That required building a narrative that distorts history to dull the public's senses, including his conducting an interview with Fox News, while seated at the Lincoln Memorial. We were to assume that the huge marble statue of a seated Lincoln added the proper gravitas to give credence to his complains of the lack of appreciation from the press.

In another instance of pseudo-grandiosity, Trump walked over to Lafayette Square during riots to protest the death of a black man at the hands of an aberrant police officer, another example of a staged photo op to dull our sense of what is right. Trump then held a bible aloft in front of the church, visited almost daily by the tortured Lincoln during the Civil War, an act intended to revise history and pander mercilessly to his base.

To make matters worse, he was accompanied during this particular episode by an unwitting Joint Chief of Staff to appear to have the approval of the military. Perhaps he was thinking that this would serve as a prelude to calling out the National Guard to lock down debate should the election not go his way. Once again, the public's conscience was being dulled drip by drip, week by week, to make sure that our grip on reality is weakened.

Now, we are facing a democracy at risk, already perilously divided between the 'haves' and the 'have not's'. The art of messaging has moved from the bully pulpit of the presidency to the corporate boardrooms of America. A host of money-changers now manipulate us behind a curtain of greed and deception for their own purposes, while a feckless and damaged president serves as their leader. What could be more fitting for a man who has absolutely nothing in common with Abraham Lincoln?

WARTIME PRESIDENTS

INTRODUCTION

Starting with Washington, right up to the more recent presidency of Eisenhower, we have applauded the ability of an exalted military man to successfully transfer his talents to the executive office. There are other presidents who were forced to take the opposite track...men who knew nothing about conducting a war, but were forced to learn quickly on the job, with the help of the right advisors.

Their job was made even more difficult by the fact that they had to handle the usual presidential business of running a country as well as putting in place both the military and economic underpinnings required to wage war. Their marshaling the forces to successfully accomplish this has propelled these men into the pantheon of presidential greatness, although all of them handled that task in different ways.

Abraham Lincoln

ABRAHAM LINCOLN

Lincoln is revered as our greatest president for bringing the nation out of decades of pandering regarding issues vital to saving our democracy and ending the scourge of slavery. His speeches, both Inaugurals and of course the Gettysburg Address, are a vital part of that legacy to heal a nation's wounds and make sense of a senseless war.

We must also acknowledge that Lincoln was a wartime president and without a victory for the North, the nation would have been torn asunder. How he waged that war and fought against various factions and issues to finally defeat the South is a story unto itself.

A REBELLION

The Civil War, our only internal war, was cleverly referred to by Lincoln as a 'rebellion'. Otherwise, we would have admitted a reality we dared not face, invited England or other nations to interfere,

However, only in war could the North legally impose a blockade, which Lincoln accomplished as one of his first acts. He already knew that there would be conflicts in navigating the process, requiring numerous sleights of hand.

Lincoln was immediately faced with multiple impediments. The South was much more of a martial society, where men rode horses with great skill. Many of the best at West Point were southern boys, who sided with their neighbors and joined the Confederacy, including that brilliant warrior prince, Robert E. Lee.

In addition, the South was defending its perimeter and knew the landscape intimately, a huge asset in war. By contrast, the North, a society that was a churning commercial landscape, was mandated to invade a vast area that would require huge amounts of manpower to attack on more than one front.

Unlike the South, Lincoln would have to rely on various state militias to send their troops to Washington for training while the South was ready to fight from day one. The North would lose many battles before a real fighting force was in place. This was partially due to a series of weak generals, a process that was not helped by the need to appoint 'political generals' to keep state governors happy.

Lincoln was always resourceful. Life had long ago forced him to rely on his own instincts. He watched generals like McClellan, another West Point graduate, dither and delay, forcing him to go to the Library of Congress to read up on Clausewitz and wartime strategies on his own. That is, until Grant appeared and started winning battles on the Mississippi.

Lincoln also displayed great political savvy in maintaining the loyalty of the border states of Missouri, Kentucky, Maryland, Delaware and West Virginia. While others accused him of having the wrong priorities, he knew he could not win the war without their resources and populations, no small feat that required his triangulating constantly as to his war aims.

While others in Congress and the press would take issue with these changes, they were in fact based on the intricate game of 'save the Union' chess, one that he executed brilliantly.

CHANGING MINDS

While he personally abhorred the institution of slavery, Lincoln knew that he had to honor the fact that it was enshrined in the Constitution under the three-fifth's clause and approved of by large segments of the population in the North, known as 'Copperheads'. He had made that point clear from the start in trying to reassure the South of his intentions. Finally, with that first cannon firing on Fort Sumter, he knew he had no alternative but to return fire.

Lincoln also understood that changing minds could only be accomplished over time, which he bought by constantly saying that his primary goal was to save the Union. For that was the only way to keep the North united, especially when a war-weariness set in after losing far too many battles. Sensing that he had few options, he calculated the cost of continuing the war and offered the South the full amount to cover the cost of disbanding a slave society. When the South turned him down, Lincoln knew he had to search for other options.

Lincoln had more to contend with on the political front. Frustrated by the way he was handling the war, the Radicals in Congress constantly took issue with his tactics, setting up committees to wrest power from him and take charge of firing generals. For they saw things in black and white, while Lincoln saw things in shades of grey. It was only through his clever use of Article ll's commander-in-chief powers that he was able to thwart their efforts.

ADDRESSING SLAVERY

While Lincoln always wanted to find a way to end slavery, his first option was actually 'colonization'...having them leave the country for a safe haven in Liberia or a location in the Caribbean. It was only when men like Frederick Douglass explained that this was their country and freedom was their right as residents, that his own thinking evolved to find other alternatives.

That of course was the Emancipation Proclamation, signed on January 1,1863. Again, this was accomplished under his war powers, cleverly presented as a means of stripping the South of a vital resource that allowed its economy to function. It was more than simply a benevolent act that many in the North would take issue with, another indication that Lincoln was keenly aware of public opinion. He was also astute enough to have the Proclamation apply only to those states currently in rebellion, eliminating those slave-holding Border States from the edict, lest he lose their allegiance in fighting the South.

In the meantime, throughout the war, the Northern economy was booming as the government poured funds into various industries. By the end of the war, an industrial economy was in place to flourish in peacetime, no small legacy considering Lincoln's brief time in office.

The West was gaining population as well, lured by cheap land and land grant colleges that offered an education to those moving west, including a boom in farming and agriculture.

The need for a stable currency had the Union creating the novel 'greenback' and war bonds to fund the war and keep the Union solvent, another step on the way toward building a stronger financial system. But more than anything, it was Lincoln's genius that held the Union together in a war that was never his choice to pursue.

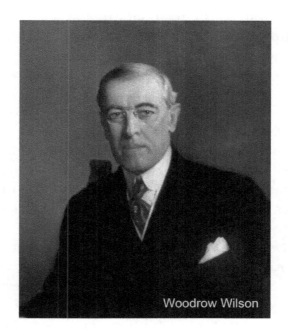

Woodrow Wilson

WOODROW WILSON

W oodrow Wilson had been the President of Princeton University and a well-respected academic, before a meteoric rise up the political ladder, achieving the governorship of New Jersey in 1910 and the presidency in 1912. As such, he had already written widely on the erosion of presidential authority and was determined to turn the office into one of idealism and ideas.

Like Andrew Jackson, he viewed the presidency as the premier organ of government closest to the people and superior to the two other branches, or in his words: 'the vital place of action in the system, the single lever to control the whole complicated machine'.

His working style was unique. Unlike most presidents and as an academic, he often worked alone in his study at his typewriter, using his meticulous shorthand. His objective was always to channel what he deemed to be the national will and seize an historic moment, something he had written about in various publications and was now free to accomplish. Wilson called this the 'prime gift of statesmanship' in crafting thoughts into stirring prose to inspire a nation. This might even be called 'Lincolnesque', as at Gettysburg, when Lincoln made sense of a senseless war as leading to a 'new birth of freedom'.

Wilson took it further, going up to Congress, almost like a Prime Minister, to sell his programs to the public. This methodology served him well in the lead-up to our entry in World War I, when he awakened a nation, still clinging to an ideology of isolationism and reluctant to face a world in chaos.

In his first term as president, Wilson's achievements were notable on the domestic front, continuing the progressive era of Theodore Roosevelt and his successor, William Howard Taft. He acted to tame monopolies, creating a more competitive marketplace and reforming the banking system by establishing the Federal Reserve.

WAR COMES TO EUROPE

In August of 1914, the assassination of Archduke Ferdinand in Bosnia lit the match that exploded into World War 1. Within a month, eighteen million men were already mobilized. Wilson pivoted to prepare for the U.S. to enter on the side of the Allies. But already the Europeans found him far too self-righteous to be listened to. They had already allowed a series of foolish interlocking agreements, later described as 'worthless pieces of paper', to drag them into a war not of their choosing. They would be sure to hold on to their colonial empires as the cost of fighting this unintended war.

For now Wilson, understanding the public's isolationist preference, opted for a policy of 'strict neutrality' even though Germany had already breached international norms by invading Belgium. It was only when Germany sank the British passenger ship, Lusitania, along with the death of one hundred twenty-eight Americans, that Wilson decided to take action. He spoke the words to awaken an isolationist nation to the threats abroad. 'The world is on fire and the sparks are liable to drop anywhere and war may be impossible to avoid'.

To his credit as a statesman, he already saw the larger picture and the need to avoid future wars. He proposed establishing a community of nations to use collective force in the future. It would be called a League of Nations, defending each member nation's sovereignty should it be threatened by outside forces.

However, in attempting to gain public support for entering the war, Wilson mis-stepped, 'wrapping' himself in the flag and hawking 'Americanism', while attacking hyphenated citizens as less than patriotic. Considering his academic credentials, it was rather alarming that he would take actions not seen since the era of those Alien and Sedition Acts that marked the demise of the Federalist Party.

GEARING UP FOR WAR

For the first time since the Monroe Doctrine was first enunciated in 1824, we were entering into the affairs of Europe, with Wilson believing that he could now act as that honest broker in crafting the inevitable peace agreement.

Again, he used elevated words to stir a nation and chart the future, saying those famous words that echo through history. 'The world must be made safe for democracy. We desire no conquest ... we seek no indemnities ... we are but champions of the rights of mankind'

PEACEMAKER: ABROAD AND AT HOME

Wilson was fortunate in Pershing's conduct of the war when the recently arrived American Expeditionary Force blew up a critical bridge at the Marne, forcing the Germans to retreat. This represented a turning point in the war, with Wilson determined to have European nations abandon dreams of continued 'spheres of influence'.

However, unlike Lincoln, who was able to convince others through patience and his mastery of logic, Wilson was never one to miss the opportunity to lecture others. He hurled far too many abstract phrases at the Allies that did not serve him well, especially when dealing with savvy politicians like Clemenceau and Lloyd George.

Wilson put his own ego first, ignoring advice to stay out of the peace process and foolishly set sail for Europe. He miscalculated by excluding Republicans from the process, even though they had just won the midterm elections and now controlled the Senate. He arrived in Paris determined to combine the Versailles Peace Agreement with his League of Nations so that neither could be challenged separately.

The process was exhausting. A young Franklin Roosevelt, invited to attend by Wilson as his Assistant Secretary of the Navy, watched Wilson's hands shake ... a sign of physical issues that would threaten his presidency shortly.

He arrived back in the U.S. with a sense of 'righteous indignation', lest anyone challenge his dreams for that new world order, cautioning Congress not to 'refuse the moral leadership that is demanded of us'. An indignant Henry Cabot Lodge, head of the vital Senate Foreign Relations Committee, responded in kind, saying: 'We too have our ideals, even if we differ from those who try to establish a monopoly on idealism.'

These might well have been the words spoken to Lincoln by the Radicals in Congress who were always eager to hijack his presidency. But Lincoln never suffered from a case of 'righteous indignation'.

If anything, he was always in search of 'common ground', eager to listen to others before making up his mind, a trait exemplified by our best presidents.

When Cabot Lodge predictably refused to sign an agreement that compromised American sovereignty, Wilson took his case to the American people, telling them, 'American soldiers saved Europe and now American citizens will save the world'.

These words might have served Wilson well at a different time, but the country was no longer interested in saving the world. We were about to elect Republican Warren G. Harding, a man who promised nothing more than a return to 'normalcy'.

The severe stroke Wilson suffered during his trip across the nation was but the physical result of a failed approach to matters that required a common touch, something that Lincoln always understood. Yet, history would prove Wilson prescient in many ways. The descent into revenge politics at Versailles would set the stage for more revenge as Hitler redeemed German honor with World War ll.

No one will ever know if the League of Nations, with the vital participation of the United States, could ever have prevented World War II. But, FDR, by Wilson's side at Versailles, must have thought so. For he insisted, from the start of his collaboration with Churchill during World War II, that a United Nations must be seen as a vital goal in establishing a new world order.

Franklin Roosevelt

FRANKLIN DELANO ROOSEVELT

FDR liked to be called 'the juggler', never letting his right hand know what his left hand was doing. He had the same effect on those who surrounded him, never leaving his aides or Cabinet members quite sure where they stood or what he was planning next. This gave him a certain flexibility to change his mind without being tethered to a specific policy and always open to new ideas when old ones were no longer working. As his wife, Eleanor said, 'The President doesn't think, he decides'.

Lincoln too was accused of dithering when it came to military matters. But he knew if he was to truly save the Union, he had to be cunning as well as honorable. FDR combined many of the best qualities of Lincoln and Wilson as he addressed an isolationist nation, reluctant to heed the darkening clouds of war that are about to engulf the entire world.

FDR'S FLEXIBLE THINKING

Unlike Lincoln and Wilson, FDR was not totally devoid of military experience, having served as Assistant Secretary of the Navy in the Wilson Administration at a time when Britain and France were already engaged in an arms race. Undoubtedly, he had learned many lessons as to what not to do while sitting beside Wilson as he crafted the Treaty of Versailles, including not selling one's ideas to the public without using easily understood concepts, rather than high blown rhetoric.

FDR's first task was to convince the country to abandon a policy of 'Neutrality' and enable him to turn the U.S. into that 'Arsenal of Democracy'. This process began with a clever ploy called 'Lend Lease', promising that in return for supplying war materiel to Britain, we would obtain a ninety-nine year lease on many of her possessions.

He then took the time to explain 'Lend Lease' to the public in simple yet highly effective terms during his Fireside Chats, comparing this to lending your neighbor a hose to put out a fire that was about to engulf your house as well.

With the attack on Pearl Harbor, FDR found himself having to fight a war in both the Atlantic and the Pacific. Fortunately, by then fighting the Depression at home had yielded a new economic philosophy called Keynesian economics. Government would now borrow and spend to offset weak consumer demand, making major investments in producing thousands of tanks, ships and aircraft.

COMPARING THREE WARTIME PRESIDENTS

Nonetheless, FDR leadership skills failed him at a time when refugees were fleeing Europe, especially those Jews who were being stripped of their rights and citizenship in Nazi Germany. If Wilson erred during the war in hawking a brand of 'Americanism' that encouraged suspicions of other citizens, FDR was equally unmoved by the plight of those from foreign lands. He allowed his State Department, rife with anti-Semitism, to find far too many reasons to deny refugee status to thousands of Jews at a time when Hitler was still allowing them to emigrate.

Perhaps the most egregious display of 'fear of the other' during World War ll took place on the West Coast, where native Americans of Japanese ancestry were rounded up under an Executive Order and placed in internment camps for the duration of the war.

With the Japanese having destroyed most of our fleet at Pearl Harbor, FDR knew it would be at least two years before we could match Japanese naval power. In the meantime, he would keep the public from despair by constantly re-asserting wartime goals with stirring phrases.

Lincoln's stated goal had been to save the Union, no matter what that required. For Wilson, the stated goal was to 'make the world safe for democracy'. For FDR, it was 'unconditional surrender', a goal he stated early in the war at his conference with Churchill at Casablanca.

Unlike Wilson, FDR was adept in taking control at those famous meetings abroad with other world leaders, starting with Churchill at the Atlantic Conference early in the war and right through his last meeting with Churchill and Stalin at Yalta.

At the same time, FDR made sure to keep discussions of a United Nations front and center, paying homage to Wilson by establishing the framework for that international organization to keep the peace and foster democratic governments in the postwar era. Remembering Wilson's failures, FDR made sure to get the Senate on board and keep the conversation bipartisan.

He was also more flexible than Wilson in dealing with men like Churchill, who still believed in 'real politik' and those 'spheres of influence' that had stymied Wilson. He understood and appreciated the need for the Anglo-American relationship to endure...and the trials the British had suffered while standing alone to fight the Nazi's.

Most of all, FDR understood the complexity and genius of Churchill, knowing when to heed his advice and when not to. His astute wife Eleanor, who knew her husband better than anyone, felt compelled to remind Churchill that her husband could not be easily conned saying, 'You know, Winston, just because my husband smiles and nods doesn't mean that he necessarily agrees with you'.

DEALING WITH THE ALLIES
Churchill was constantly delaying the Normandy invasion and trying to convince FDR to achieve lesser goals that would suit his interests in maintaining the British Empire. While Marshall and other generals vehemently disagreed, FDR understood that war objectives must give way to political considerations on occasion.

He therefore allowed Churchill to have his way in promoting an easier victory in North Africa and another in Sicily before moving on to a cross-channel landing to confront the Nazi's on their own turf. But that meant dealing with Stalin, the individual who most strenuously objected to these delays.

He would ultimately blame the Allies for allowing the Germans to focus their unchallenged military prowess on Russia, losing millions of lives in that fierce battle at Stalingrad before turning the tide during the winter of 1943.

Once again, FDR used those skills as a juggler to balance the needs of Stalin with those of Churchill, sometimes favoring one over the other at those later conferences. Still, he already knew that Russia would emerge as a great power after the war, far more important than Britain.

In the end, a clever Stalin would use his nation's suffering to extract more from the Allies in the postwar era, including control of Eastern Europe. Some would blame that on FDR's failing health during these later conferences. But Stalin and his Red Army already controlled much of that territory, and there was little FDR or his generals could do to alter the demographics.

THE WAR WITH JAPAN

Once the war in Europe was over, an ailing FDR still had to contend with a Japan, defeated militarily but not in spirit. Given the casualties we had suffered in Saipan, Iwo Jima and Okinawa, our generals were already estimating the loss of hundreds of thousands of additional lives in an invasion of the Japanese homeland.

With all of the uncertainty still surrounding the development of an atomic bomb, FDR decided to extract a commitment from the Soviets to enter the war and attack from the North. Once again, historians will speculate as to whether that allowed Stalin to reclaim much of the territory Russia had lost in the Russo-Japanese War of 1905.

FDR's death in April 1945 left those decisions to Truman who would ultimately drop that bomb on Hiroshima in early August, leading to the Japanese surrender.

THE GREATNESS OF FDR

FDR had no equal in marshaling all the means to wage a successful war... military, institutional, propagandist, diplomatic and political ... all to support the objectives of this juggler. Above all he was practical in fighting a Depression as well as in waging war, sometimes proceeding boldly and at other times cautiously.

He could spell out lofty goals like Wilson and then summon people to follow him, like Lincoln. He could also address those goals with calculated compromise when necessary, as could Lincoln when it suited his needs in holding onto those border-states.

It was only Wilson of the three who could not appreciate the art of compromise. In the process, he lost the opportunity to have us join that League of Nations and possibly avoid World War ll.

Of the three presidents, FDR alone was challenged with a war on both fronts ... a task that required multiple goals and multiple strategies involving numerous world figures, rather than the clear-cut goals that others might enjoy. As with Lincoln, FDR would not live long enough to preside over that vision of a new world order. That task would fall to his Vice President, Harry Truman, a man without any experience in foreign affairs.

CHANGING POLITICS

O ur political system is constantly changing...occasionally for the better and sometimes presenting us with new challenges. This can be the result of changes in technology, changes that alter old norms and affect that vital task of keeping that potential voter properly informed with facts rather than fiction. These changes can be inspired by an individual who arrives on the scene to offer a new and galvanizing idea.

Our federal and state governments supply a constantly churning supply of these individuals, who rise to the fore and occasionally alter the landscape of our political system.

These ideas can occasionally give birth to a new party...as they did with the birth of the Republican Party in 1856 and the emergence of Lincoln. Or they can result in the demise of a party that is no longer viable in representing the goals and hopes of a sufficient number of Americans.

PARTY POLITICS: ADDRESSING POLARIZATION

INTRODUCTION

It should come as no surprise that a political party can enter a death spiral of sorts and be replaced with other alternatives. In our two hundred thirty year history, from the time the Constitution was written, such has been the case more than a few times.

Washington's Federalist Party of the founding era preceded the two party system, until Jefferson created the Republican Party. Internal disputes destroyed the Federalist's, with only the Republicans in control between 1800-1824. Even then, there were several party factions during what was called the one-party rule of the 'Era of Good Feelings'.

Andrew Jackson then created the Democratic Party apparatus to destroy those politicians who had deprived him of the presidency in 1824 through what he referred to as the 'corrupt bargain'. The Democratic Party has been with us ever since, with obvious philosophic changes along the way and more than a taint of white supremacy at certain moments.

The Whig Party was then created by Henry Clay in 1832 over the so-called 'bank issue' and to challenge President Jackson's imperial presidency. Its demise in 1856 was primarily due to failing to confront the oncoming battle about slavery, a battle to salvage the meaning of our founding documents from being permanently damaged in a perversion of democratic and constitutional norms.

At the time, several splinter parties had evolved to tackle this issue. It was only in 1856 that the new Republican Party finally emerged as the successor to the Whigs. Even Lincoln remained a Whig until the very last minute before joining the party with his famous 'Lost Speech' at the Republican convention in Bloomington.

The Democrats, ever since the Civil War, have represented the status quo of a repressive South and the interests of the working class in the North with political bosses representing their interests.

THE MODERN DAY PRESIDENCY

It was Theodore Roosevelt (1901-1908) who added a progressive agenda to the Republican Party, seeing the presidency as the Bully Pulpit to represent the interests of all the people. The so-called Progressive Era, embraced by segments of both parties, stretched from TR through Woodrow Wilson, representing almost twenty years of rebalancing the working conditions and rights of average Americans.

During the 1920's, a country exhausted by a World War and progressive agenda reverted to the hedonism of Republican 'normalcy'. This represented what was called the 'Jazz Age' with abundant consumer goods and booming new technologies to create a better life. Add to this, a booming stock market and rampant speculation that put money in the average man's pocket.

The Great Depression, beginning in 1929, quickly changed that, leaving many jobless and in poverty. The Republican response under President Hoover (1928-1932) was to follow the traditional rules of economics and wait it out in hopes that banks would agree to start lending to business once again.

The Democrats, the party of the working man, found a president in FDR (1932-1945) who was pragmatic enough to consider groundbreaking alternatives, including Keynesian economics. This approach had the government stepping in with huge infusions of money and innovative programs until private demand and business confidence could be restored.

Over the next decades, including President Truman (1945-1952), the two parties remained fairly consistent in their underlying philosophies, one favoring business and fiscal responsibility and the other catering to the working person most affected by the Great Depression. It was the Democrats and the New Deal that began to repair a frayed safety net as a right of citizenship rather a privilege.

The Republicans regained the White House twenty years later under Eisenhower (1952-1960), a war hero and a 'uniter', whose party affiliation was in doubt right up to the moment he accepted the Republican nomination. A fiscal and social conservative, Eisenhower nonetheless left the programs and legislation of the New Deal era in place as 'valid precedent', presiding over a nation once again at peace and anxious to enjoy the 'good life' of a prosperous superpower.

Eisenhower's wise stewardship encouraged bipartisan legislation, re-building infrastructure and inadvertently unleashing a spate of liberal decisions, starting with those of the Warren Court. We cannot deny the impact of these decisions on school desegregation, Miranda rights and abortion. They in fact stoked the fires on the Right as to government intrusion in their rights and beliefs.

Lyndon Johnson's civil rights legislation, finally unleashing the meaning of constitutional amendments crafted a century before, finished the job and created a total realignment of the parties and their philosophies ... the results of which we are living with today.

The symptoms of this realignment were already apparent in 1964, when LBJ sought re-election against Republican Barry Goldwater. He and his fellow conservatives were a new breed of politicians, dramatically revising the history of the Progressive Era and challenging the liberal establishment to a war of words.

THE SLOW TRANSFORMATION OF THE REPUBLICAN PARTY

Even LBJ himself knew that he had lost the South with his civil rights legislation. Republicans now picked up votes by pandering and winking at white supremacy. This was the start of a Party addicted to 'single issue voters', not because their issues were relevant to core beliefs, but simply to build enough votes to win elections.

Reagan, a great communicator with an optimistic message of 'Morning in America', was loyal to the Republican mantra of pro-business policies and tax breaks. But even he knew enough to deliver the right message by opening his campaign in Meridian Mississippi, where three civil rights workers had been killed.

Reagan's economic policy, known as 'trickle down economics' began the process of growing income inequality. A sinking middle class barely survived by putting the wife to work for a two family income, while mortgaging the house to put the kids through college.

The evolution of the Republican Party continued throughout the next three decades. Desperate to increase its numbers in a changing society, the Party assiduously courted various interest groups that never shared core values of the old GOP. These included what might be called victims of a 'culture war', using a script that labeled the opposition as 'the other', while denying true American values.

The one common thread uniting all these groups was fear of an oncoming multi-cultural tide. This transformation of the Republican Party left it hollow at the core, without a cohesive agenda other than claiming to be fiscal conservatives and thwarting Democrats at every opportunity. This has been driven in large part by the wealthy, who pander to these groups to win elections that allow them to accumulate more wealth with greater income inequality.

THE TRUMP ERA

While some look at Donald Trump as an aberration, not at all representative of Republican values, he in fact the perfect 'poster boy' for a party without core values.

Trump's foray into politics with the 'birther issue', scurrilous and cynical as it was, more than qualified him for the presidency for those core voters. His lack of political experience on any level...local, state or federal...was another asset, considering the narrative begun under Reagan that 'government is the problem, not the solution'.

A meaningless phrase like 'drain the swamp' resonates as well, based on the inherent belief in widespread government corruption and as payback for those left wing Supreme Court decisions. The same sense of hypocrisy applies to phrases like 'build the wall' to keep out 'others' who supposedly threaten a white majority and way of life.

The lack of core values, other than demonizing and fear mongering has made it easy for Republican office holders, such as Majority Leader Mitch McConnell, to support Trump. Even an easy bipartisan issue like 'infrastructure' has been bypassed in favor of putting borrowed funds into a trillion and a half dollar tax break for corporations at a time of full employment when the economy needed no such stimulus.

Yet, despite the emptiness of the Republican agenda, the Party has been adept at creating a message that paints Democrats as the enemy of the people, exploiting all the myths of self-help and individualism that stifle a discussion of income inequality and a frayed safety net.

Democrats, on the other hand, have a real message of substantive programs to rebuild the safety net and create a life of dignity and self worth. But that is far beyond what most voters are willing to listen to. Democrats therefore need to come up with a succinct yet emotionally visceral response that captures their message in a few words. This might include the saying, 'no American should be too poor to live a life of dignity'.

This harkens back to the hopefulness of our founding documents, while playing the 'rage game' that clearly resonates with many marginalized voters.

USING THE BULLY PULPIT

With COVID-19 revealing the emptiness of years of extolling the 'majesty of markets' in giving the average American barely a living wage, it is time to come up with a detailed agenda that both parties can agree to. Any president who aspires to these goals must use that long-neglected presidential bully pulpit to create bipartisanship and invite all relevant parties to the table to chart the proper course.

This will be essential in not only preserving capitalism, but also balancing this economic model with the need to rebuild a robust middle class...including the rights, rather than the privileges, for a life with dignity and fairness for all. Yes, that so-called trend toward 'socialism' could even be rebranded as fulfilling the meaning of our founding documents.

The sooner a president builds the proper structure to discuss twenty-first century issues, the quicker we can begin to address them, including the following:

1. Dealing with the age of artificial intelligence and robotics to make sure these new technologies benefit society as a whole and not merely in financial ways.

2. Constructing a countervailing authority representing labor to thrash out work-related issues with representatives from business community in ongoing collective bargaining.

3. Developing new forms of compensation for workers in addition to a minimum wage that would be reviewed annually against various economic benchmarks.

4. Creating new versions of Teddy Roosevelt's Bureau of Corporations to establish and monitor specific benchmarks of corporate behavior with penalties for those who breach these standards.

5. Establishing a 'Fair Rules Commission' to evaluate compensation in various segments of the economy, rather than a one-size-fits-all solution.

6. Rethinking various types of higher education to meet the needs of the economy and provide twenty-first century employment opportunities with the proper incentives and benefits.

7. Rebuilding a viable safety net that honors a commitment to the health and well being of all our citizens without vilifying it as a handout or socialism

REINVENTING SOCIETY

All of this will require societal changes as well, a new mindset that will yield healthier party politics. This must start with the recognition that we are officially a multi-cultural society.

Rather than using this issue to divide us, we will need a heightened awareness of each other to learn to be comfortable with our differences rather than have them exploited for political advantage.

Some of the ways to accomplish this should start with our youth... whose formative years will define who they are.

YOUTH INITIATIVE

Past successes can help to map the future, as in the years after World War ll when programs for study abroad built a sense of internationalism, as with Fulbright scholarships and Pell grants that peaked in the 1960's.

We should now transfer that thinking to programs here at home to create a greater awareness of each other, so that we are no longer strangers, easy to be stereotyped. That might include reducing college to a three-year program in the classroom with the fourth year for service...in a totally different part of the country.

It would also have the benefit of reducing tuition by 25%, while making higher education responsive to public needs.

High school programs as well, where 60% of students end their education, can emulate these programs, starting with 'homogenizing' a multicultural society with classes on citizenship and those founding documents, along side classes to become skilled workers.

CORPORATE INITIATIVE

While we tend to vilify large corporations as dismissive of worker's rights and well being, they too must learn to practice good citizenship, supporting programs that benefit business while promoting a healthy society.

These might include sending workers to regional offices in other parts of the country to create a greater understanding of their role in a multicultural work force.

Corporate citizenship might also include lobbying for legislation that benefits them as well as society in general ... including a gas tax to build infrastructure, affirmative action programs that help to create a well educated multicultural workforce as well as broadband for left-behind rural America.

This last item is critical for areas, which have fallen further behind, with a cultural as well as an economic divide that has greatly impacted politics.

CHANGING LEGISLATIVE POLITICAL NORMS

Most importantly, the Republican Party must once again become one of shared values if we are to have a functioning democracy. This includes addressing issues, many of which are more of a constitutional and historic nature.

THE HOUSE OF REPRESENTATIVES

Certainly that includes preventing excessive partisan gerrymandering by state legislatures that enable a minority party to dominate congressional races ... an issue that the Supreme Court has dodged up to now as a political issue belonging to Congress to resolve.

Adding representatives to the House is long overdue as well, considering that some in Congress now represent almost a million voters, a number that can hardly provide proper representation to all its constituents.

This should be done in a way that carves out districts in a non-partisan way with more swing voters that create ideologically heterogeneous districts...reducing the need for Republicans to blindly follow an extremist agenda.

Building a moderate Republican constituency in the House is the only way to start the party's move to the center, if at all possible.

THE SENATE

In the Senate, this task will be more difficult, based on the Constitution's Great Compromise, assigning two senators per state, regardless of population.

However, several steps may return the Senate to a functioning bipartisan legislative body. This includes returning to state legislatures the process of selecting senators under the 17th Amendment, which calls only for those making the selection to have 'qualifications requisite for electors'.

Battles for dominating this body would then be fought on a state grass roots level removing it from the Republican hierarchy and that of large corporate donors to dispense favors in return for party loyalty.

Arguably the most outdated rule of the Senate is the filibuster, originally instituted to preserve the South's dominance through the three-fifths clause that inflated those States' population.

Removing the need for sixty votes for cloture, and closing down debate, would honor Hamilton's reasoning behind Federalist 22... that 'giving a minority a negative upon the majority is to subject the sense of the greater number to that of the lesser number'...and 'risk handing power to an insignificant and corrupt junto'.

Actually, Hamilton's prophesy is reminiscent of the Tea Party's takeover of the Republican Party.

THE ELECTORAL COLLEGE

The final consideration in changing the political landscape and one that would require a constitutional amendment is whether or not to abolish the Electoral College. This institution was intended to favor slave states, which it did quite well, considering that four out of five of our first presidents were slaveholders from Virginia.

Eliminating the Electoral College would have all candidates campaigning in all states rather than simply swing states, modifying and possibly softening their views in order to attract a wider base of voters. (On the other hand, that might simply mean more targeted advertising, with more money spent on advertising.)

Having elections decided by popular vote may also open the door to third party candidates who would win with a minority of the popular vote.

SUPREME COURT APPOINTMENTS:

Perhaps nothing would restore balance more than moving hearings to confirm Supreme Court justices to the House.

That would accomplish two things at once:

1. Confirmation by the 'people's House' will represent a clearer expression as to the will of the people.

2. Removing this from the Senate will reduce the ability of less populated rural America to have an oversized voice in critical lifetime appointments that affect all segments of the population.

This has become even more important at a time when congressional gridlock has closed down a national conversation that should be addressing matters critical to the nation with a massive amount of legislation.

This in turn has pushed the resolution of many of these questions regarding all aspects of life to the courts...and ultimately to the Supreme Court.

Their decisions will echo through the ages as either solidly based on precedent or veering wildly from the words and intent of the Constitution...and in effect legislative from the bench.

Considering the current role for the courts that may become the new norm, it is critical that those Justices represent the choice of the broadest group of legislators in Congress, speaking for a majority of Americans rather than inflating the voices of the few.

MOVING THE REPUBLICAN PARTY TO THE CENTER

It is the Republican Party of today that is a danger to democracy. Yet, that is its strength in winning elections. For it is a unified movement, rather than a party, whereas Democrats are diverse, splitting their votes among various segments, which giving Republicans a distinct advantage.

Therefore, various factions of Democrats need to moderate their views to win elections while Republicans have to harden their views... driving the Party further right. As Trump has cleverly figured out, Republicans live in fear of being 'primaried' from the Right...giving him total control of the Party apparatus.

SAVING THE REPUBLICAN PARTY

If we are to save the two party system, it will require the Republican Party to be less of a movement and more of a functioning party of diverse ideas. There is simply no alternative. For, if Democrats were to emulate Republicans and move further left to become more of a movement as well, it would spell the end of two party politics.

On the other hand, if Democrats were to splinter into four separate parties, we would likely be moving toward a parliamentary system.

To save the Party, today's typical Republicans need to fear competition from the center. That would require at least half a dozen conservative Republican centrists funded perhaps by a concerned billionaire and voting with Democrats to pass legislation.

They would then have to survive attacks from the Right for re-election, especially with Trump having weaponized ethno-national resentment of a significant portion of the Republican base.

In other words, there are no easy answers in creating a viable two-party system; but, we must try. For there is no alternative if we are to save a functioning American democracy.

POLITICS AND RELIGION

A belief in God and religion, and the ability of both to raise the human spirit, is a strain that runs deep in the American psyche. God is mentioned in the Declaration of Independence but not in the Constitution, a document crafted on the precepts of the Enlightenment that assumed we would leave a secular education up to the state and a religious education up to the individual.

Only in the Bill of Rights, enacted by popular demand in the first Congress under the Constitution, did those founding fathers officially codify this separation of church and state with Madison in control of the agenda. The Constitution now reads: 'Congress shall make no law respecting the establishment of religion or prohibiting the free exercise thereof'.

Even so, religion crept seamlessly into our lives. By the early 1800's, itinerant preachers, mostly Methodist in the North and Baptist in the South, were civilizing the most humble of log cabins with the Bible. Their work continued within local communities, building faith-based colleges, which often evolved into some of our finest secular universities.

By the 1830's, religious beliefs had inspired women to found benevolent societies and act as the moral conscience of the nation. These soon evolved into Anti-Slavery Societies, facing the wrath of a besieged South. By 1860, thanks to a persistent message spread with the help of the printing press, the North was finally convinced that slavery was an evil destined to wither and die or be eradicated.

After the Civil War, these sentiments remained, for the most part, in the home and in the church until the 1960's, when government action and Supreme Court decisions began to place opposing points of view in the public square.

It was then that the Religious Right began to mobilize and fight against what they perceived as a loss of respect for biblical values led by preachers whose eloquence and marketing skills had already built a large following. For the first time, evangelical Christians in the South joined anti-abortion Catholics in the North to build a new faith-centered national coalition, finding a congenial home within Republican Party. They called it the 'Moral Majority', a play on Nixon's 'Silent Majority' from the days of his 'Southern Strategy' that helped him to barely win the election in 1972.

All that was needed was the right candidate to lead this national movement as president. Ultimately, the Religious Right decided on Ronald Reagan.

Over time, the Moral Majority transitioned into an even bigger tent under the 'Christian Coalition'. The Party also reached out to other so-called 'values voters', including gun supporters, all railing against a government that supposedly wanted to take away their rights. What really unites these 'values voters' is the complexion of the Republican Party, white versus an increasingly multi-cultural country and their determination to keep it that way.

When the disasters of the George W. Bush administration led to an electorate ready for dramatic change, the religious right's worst fears were realized as a multicultural society now possessed the votes to elect a black man. The commitment on the part of Republicans to make Barack Obama a one-term president was based on nothing more than the fact that he was different from other presidents, despite the eloquence, intelligence and obvious grace he brought to the office.

The narrow electoral victory in 2016 by Donald Trump was in large part the result of an energized Republican base, eager to take back their country. Now the Trump era has unabashedly put this racist stance front and center.

TODAY'S UNIQUE SITUATION

As history lays out in greater detail, this is not the first time that religious groups have felt besieged and susceptible to being involved in party politics. In the lead up to the Civil War, when parties were unraveling over their stance on slavery, the anti-Catholic 'Know-Nothing' Party looked as though it would be the successor to the Whigs, now in a death spiral.

In 1960, the question as to the electability of JFK revolved primarily around his religious beliefs as a practicing Catholic. It was only after he made a speech, assuring the nation that he would keep his religion out of his decisions as president that the furor abated.

Some form of religious bigotry has always been with us. It can hide behind a different mantra, as when rural America looked at urban voters as godless minorities. However, the role played by the Christian Coalition is quite different. Without their numbers, the Republican Party cannot win elections, making this a vital component that must turn out in large numbers every year for local, state and national elections.

To keep the Religious Right actively involved in Republican politics requires a steady stream of warnings of an imminent apocalyptic event pitting good against evil and painting Democrats as destroying a Christian America ... words that deny Constitutional norms.

The Supreme Court's liberal decisions by the Warren Court of the 1950's and 60's certainly provided fuel for the fire. It was the decision in <u>Roe v. Wade</u>, legalizing abortion as a constitutional prerogative that represented the ultimate assault. Being religiously 'pro-life' became the Republican mantra, even though the Party refused to fund programs that promoted the life and well being of that unborn child.

Nevertheless, the question remains, what has made these religious groups so susceptible to this message as to bring religion so forcefully into the public square?

THE SCOURGE OF FORGOTTEN AMERICA

Perhaps the intrusion of religion is simply a manifestation of a crisis of the spirit, part and parcel of an economy that only celebrates wealth. Stagnant wages represent fifty years of a huge transfer of wealth to corporate and financial interests that has demeaned and demoralized American workers, causing them to seek self-worth elsewhere. Is it any wonder that some would turn to guns and opioids, while others turn to religion to restore their souls with the words of the metaphysical that are comforting?

In other words, this search for self-worth in religion is not entirely a higher noble pursuit. It is based on a fragility of the spirit that desperately needs constant nurturing. Like a drowning man, those in search of inner calm, will cling to it as if his life depends on it. When these beliefs are challenged by what is perceived to be godless liberal interests, it will be taken as an assault on core beliefs that must be defended at all costs.

Thus, issues like the Court's granting abortion rights, as a constitutional norm cannot be accepted as merely the right of others to act accordingly. For today's Religious Right this is a betrayal of core values that must be demolished. As a result, you have individuals standing outside abortion clinics and assaulting those trying to enter with invective and occasional gun violence that is justified in pursuit of saving the lives of the unborn.

In this battle to right the wrongs of the world they live in, the Religious Right will look for others to blame, never understanding who initiated this lack of self worth that has chipped away at their standing in society. On the contrary, those who now possess 99% of the nation's wealth will pander to these religious beliefs and deliver any message that energizes the base and keeps them in power.

There are more than enough targets to point to. The Left's embrace of globalization has not helped it to escape the wrath of the religious community. They see this as an elitist plot to destroy the fabric of America, despite the fact that those in the middle class need those savings offered by globalization to support a diminished life style.

Still, with so many to blame, it is easier to focus on the most vulnerable in sabotaging their way of life and stealing their jobs. That of course would include immigrants and people of color, pandering to a racist and xenophobic strain in the DNA of America that has always worked in troubled times.

REMOVING RELIGION FROM THE PUBLIC SQUARE

The question remains, what will end this intrusion of religion into our public square and return it to houses of worship or the home where it properly belongs? What will end an evangelical passion that affords little space for the beliefs of others and creates this cultural divide?

History tells us that systemic poverty spawns anger and violence, which is playing out in rural America. Yet, we are told by demagogues that godless immigrants are the reason for this 'American carnage' rather than a failed economic system. The verdict is yet to be decided. These are dangerous times, when we are most susceptible to despots and autocrats who promise a way forward.

This is the time when we most need a prophet to preach a new way. Perhaps it is time once again to replace the profit motive with a message that honors every individual's right to reach his or her full potential in the pursuit of life, liberty and happiness.

The value of work must once again be rewarded with an appropriate living wage to support a family, along with benefits that include a robust safety net, decent housing and a countervailing bargaining agent to represent labor in its negotiations with business. Publicly funded programs will guarantee every child a decent education, beginning in pre-kindergarten through a college curriculum that offers options in non-academic areas as well.

With these and more, another version of a 'New Deal' may restore the balance lost in decades of greed and misplaced values. Over time, that younger generation in the evangelical community will no longer be a pawn in the hands of an elite that nurtures their grievances in order to acquire their votes. Instead, a reconstituted Republican Party will have to fight for their support with real programs or lose them to Democrats who offer solutions for real problems.

REINVENTING
THE NEW NORMAL

INTRODUCTION

The coronavirus pandemic is perhaps that proverbial 'straw that breaks the camel's back'...that impactful event that leads to a significant course correction in addressing the economic ills and societal disparities that have been building for decades.

For this pandemic has made it difficult at best to go back to business as usual, considering all the social norms that have been forever changed and the economic disparities that have been laid bare. Just as the Great Depression required a rethinking of our value system as to whether we would consider the worth of every individual or only celebrate the success of the few, so the wrath of nature has brought us to the same moment.

It should not be lost on anyone that closing down an economy and limiting social interaction has most impacted the most vulnerable among us, those who do not have the means to make it week to week without a paycheck. At the same time, it is many in this 'underclass' who have been called upon to attend to the sick and maintain those vital services that keep us safe and put food on the table.

9/11 was, however, a cataclysmic event of sorts that also put those who keep us safe at great risk. We preferred to see this primarily as a wake-up call that terrorism had arrived on our doorstep ... that anger and rage abroad by the disenfranchised and forgotten could have repercussions here.

We addressed that continuing possibility by creating a Department of Homeland Security and tapping into various databases that limited the individual's right to privacy, all in the name of keeping us safe. We also went abroad in a misbegotten search for so-called evildoers at great cost in lives and treasure.

Now for the first time in decades, we are again acknowledging the disenfranchised and forgotten at home, while recognizing that the jobs many of them perform are vital in keeping our society functioning in times of great stress. Too many questions are staring us in the face to pretend that we can go back to business as usual if and when this pandemic is tamed, either through herd immunity or a vaccine.

Let's hope that we do not make the same mistakes as we did in 9/11...failing to use a national moment of great crisis to create a better world at home and abroad. Hopefully, this time we will not look for others to blame and instead ask the hard questions that are staring us in the face.

Can we continue with an economy that fails to recognize and reward the contributions of the long forgotten members of society? For that matter, can we ignore all the everyday signs, including the long lines at food banks around the nation that tell us how many of our citizens live just above the poverty line?

WHAT HISTORY TELLS US

Human nature is about survival. It is only when the day seems darkest, that we think of new and novel ways to extricate ourselves from a sense of hopelessness. Perhaps we needed a pandemic, one that cannot be manipulated by hollow rhetoric, to see the emptiness of the words of our leaders.

We have been there before, in the lead up to the Civil War, when politicians were all coming up with a compromise and a quick fix for the issue of slavery, until a moral conscience appeared in the form of Lincoln. Perhaps we needed an economy to implode...as social distancing became more important than the art of making money...to remind us that the values of family and nurturing each other still give meaning to increasingly barren lives.

We had to see the ravages of racial discrimination played out before our eyes in the death of George Floyd, finally unable to turn away and pretend it was not happening. We had to see our front line workers in hospitals and vital services, many of them people of color, their worth finally acknowledged after decades of dismissing their value as human beings.

Because of these converging themes, brought on by this pandemic and the abject failures of the Trump Administration to address it, there is now a willingness, even an eagerness, to embrace change. Suddenly, the public overwhelmingly supports a national health care plan, higher taxes on the wealthy and the goals of 'Black Lives Matter'...particularly among the younger generation that will be living with these decisions for decades.

As in the past, abject failures of government often create opportunities. Without President Hoover's failure to address the Great Depression, we never would have had FDR's bold and novel experiments to right the ship of state, including The Tennessee Valley Authority's rural electrification... the Civilian Conservation Core putting young men to work in the forests of America...employment opportunities for authors and play writes to share their talents with an impoverished nation.

Today's Herbert Hoover is Donald Trump, equally clueless as to the needs of the average American...a man who amplifies the hollowness of corporate greed and trickledown economics, while dividing us into tribes so that we prefer to dwell on petty grievances.

But change still requires the leadership of men like Lincoln or FDR to point us toward that better day and unleash the 'better angels' of our nature. The outdated myth that self-reliance and individualism are at the heart of America's core values was demolished by the Great Depression in 1929 and now once again by the coronavirus in 2020, almost a hundred years later.

The task at hand for the next president will be to elevate those core values of collectivism, the very reckoning that brought thirteen states together in 1787 to write a Constitution that elevated the needs of the entire nation above those 'residual powers' left to the states. Nor is there only one way to accomplish change. Plenty of horse-trading was required to write that Constitution, compromises that are still being worked out today in this living document. As Benjamin Franklin envisioned forty years earlier, only banding together would save a fragile democracy.

A MORE HOPEFUL FUTURE
After decades of starving the government of the funds to do its job properly, we will need to restore that level playing field envisioned by Madison as essential to a vital and vibrant democracy. This must start with taxing policies that address egregious income inequality and re-establishing the countervailing authority of labor to tamp down the worst of corporate greed.

Again, an activist president should follow the lead of FDR, who sought to put money in the hands of the average citizen at the height of the Great Depression, rather than giving funds to banks and corporations to fix their balance sheets. Today, that would mean rebuilding a frayed safety net, from the cradle to the grave, currently the most meager among industrialized nations. That alone would give the most vulnerable a sense of security and well-being, once and for all dispelling the myth that this is a handout rather than a right.

By investing in people, rather than stocks and bonds, that president will set the record straight as to our priorities, no matter what the color of one's skin. But this chief executive will also have to reverse the corrupting effect of today's Gilded Age on our institutions.

Restoring faith in government must include reining in corporate greed with re-engaged government oversight. Clearly, Senate Republicans have not done their job when it comes to preserving the guardrails of democracy, putting their grip on power above their principles. Will a drubbing at the polls in November have those 'Never-Trumpers' retaking control of the party and reasserting traditional Republican values? The opportunity to honor the wealth creation of capitalism while tamping down its excesses is up for grabs for either party.

REIGNING IN CORPORATE GREED

If we are to finally rein in corporate greed, we can look to our history, where Theodore Roosevelt stepped in at the turn of the century to thwart its excesses. Today that would include those promoting fossil fuels with dollars that overwhelm other voices, and at a time when the effects of climate change are already threatening the health of the planet.

Nor will these corporate voices be easily dismissed until there are limits on the ability of corporations to fund lobbyists, who in turn fund members of Congress. FDR railed many times against those 'money changers who had fled the temple of wealth' at the height of the Depression, only to return during his second term to attempt to reverse much of the New Deal legislation.

An activist government will need to create government agencies to monitor corporate behavior on an ongoing basis. This may include reactivating anti-trust legislation as well as putting new benchmarks in place to deal with new types of monopolistic practices. For today's titans of industry now include those entrepreneurs who have built mammoth tech companies in this digital age with the ability to affect much of our personal behavior and influence our national dialogue.

This includes Facebook and its influence in shaping the information received by millions of Americans. New standards must be established through government oversight as the younger generation migrates to social media and abandon traditional newspapers as their source of information.

The pandemic has also accelerated the demise of small business throughout the country, a vital source for our domestic economy. This includes the role of e-commerce in replacing traditional retail, as companies like Amazon decimate 'bricks and mortar' retail. If 'bigness' and 'predatory practices', the ability to dominate a particular industry, was the standard used in the past to break up corporations, today's tech behemoths more than meet that standard.

A TIME FOR DRAMATIC CHANGE

As with FDR when he entered the Oval Office in January of 1933 at the height of the Depression, there will be a long list waiting on the next president's desk come January 2021. FDR's 'First Hundred Days' should be replicated with a flurry of activity to calm a nervous nation and address critical issues that have been festering for decades.

But now, the pandemic has added unforeseen consequences that will require a new vision to rework the landscape of America, starting with those thirty million who have been laid off and are not likely to be rehired.

For these millions and more, health care can no longer be attached to employment, an archaic system foisted on the average worker to appease those who have long thought it a sinful perversion of capitalism. Ultimately, with Congress locked in perpetual gridlock, a bipartisan commission will have to address this with healthcare-for-all that finally untethers 'a right rather than a privilege' from one's employment.

The changes in the future urban landscape must be acknowledged and addressed as well. Large corporations and financial institutions, currently functioning with a dispersed workforce, will continue to emphasize the 'new normal'... today's ability to work from home in an interconnected virtual office. Employees will in turn benefit with less commuting, including air travel, less corporate dining out, more time to spend with family and the ability to pursue personal interests. Altogether, perhaps a better balance of work and leisure.

Yet, this puts massive changes in place as huge swaths of prime real estate in cities like New York or Chicago go begging for tenants, creating a new market for visionaries who foresee a different urban landscape. Perhaps housing opportunities for the real middle class will finally begin to equalize the income disparities that have plagued our cities in this latest Gilded Age. With that may come a resurgence of 'mom and pop' retail to satisfy the everyday needs of smaller and more intimate urban communities.

With those venues where people gathered in large numbers... theater, stadiums and the like...compromised for the time being, the urban landscape will favor a smaller more intimate setting. The arts, fostered by government programs as in the 1930's with the Federal Theater and Writers Projects, may find a more congenial home in these neighborhoods to replace or live side by side with larger venues. Workshops in theater, dance, writing and the visual arts will nurture talent and permanently expand the footprint of the arts in American culture.

EDUCATION AND R&D

In the field of education, the pandemic has only accelerated the trend of declining college enrollment, given today's demographics as well as a less hospitable environment for attracting students from overseas. This is another area where an activist president can make his mark, empowering experts to address questions that have been swirling about for decades...including the cost of higher education and the burden of student debt.

College students, having been furloughed at home for months, have become increasingly comfortable in an interactive setting. Whether this proves to be a satisfactory alternative for learning in the classroom is yet to be determined. Undoubtedly, improvements in on-line college curriculum raises the possibility of alternative forms of learning to obtain that valuable degree at a greatly reduced cost to enhance one's future employment and earnings opportunities.

In the process, colleges and universities will have to think about survivability in a world where students have additional options for off-campus learning. Will this ultimately reduce the number of private colleges and favor those state funded institutions? Or will the valuable plant and equipment at these institutions be put to better use as research centers, based on various existing expertise?

In effect, this is what we once accomplished in converting a consumer driven economy to one that won World War ll as the 'The Arsenal of Democracy'. We managed to have government and industry work together to put plant and equipment to better use at a critical moment, including transforming the enormous Ford automobile plant at River Rouge into one turning out B-17 bombers. We enlisted the help of major industrialists like Henry Kaiser, who transformed his factories on the West Coast into cost-effective manufacturers of ships to win the war in the Pacific...a job he performed so well as to be dubbed 'Sir Launch-A lot' by the nation's press.

Big projects have always brought out the best in American ingenuity, where we once believed in the government's ability to accomplish great things. That included building the NASA space center in Houston to explore the cosmos, starting with that lunar landing.

Today's changes in the academic landscape may actually be a godsend, given the urgency to address issues like climate change with new technologies in energy, agriculture and encroaching sea levels to name a few. Again, government and academia will work together to address lagging investment in science and R&D, with the goal of maintaining life, as we know it on our threatened planet. And in the process, we will dispel the anti-science bias that has afflicted much of our thinking for far too long.

A CHANGING SOCIETY

What the pandemic has altered most is our perceptions of society, and the deficits to be addressed as well the opportunities to be pursued. This returns us to that comparison with other events in the past that have created a 'tipping point' of sorts.

Both World Wars forced us to come together to face some harsh realities as to the place in society of women and minorities, long excluded from equal rights as to pay and dignity in the workplace. The social upheavals of the pandemic may be even more far-reaching. The new normal may require a minimum guaranteed income, long before artificial intelligence hollows out more opportunities in the workplace.

We have only to heed the words of FDR when we faced that picture of two America's at the height of the Depression. We were told by the wealthy and entitled to be suspicious and fearful of change. But FDR reassured an anxious nation that change was a good thing.

We are not likely to hear those words from our current president, a man who has made this pandemic infinitely worse by ignoring all the warning signs that it would be coming to our shores. Instead, he worried about a negative effect on a rising stock market, as though saving an economic indicator was more important than saving lives.

President Trump represents the culmination of trends that have been allowed to flourish for far too long, but they did not start with him. An aberrant strain of anti-intellectualism and individualism has long been part of the 'majesty of the marketplace', where only profits and preserving individual rights are the measure of success.

REDEEMING OUR INSTITUTIONS

Unfortunately, the extension of these theories are now embedded in legal precedent, thanks to recent Supreme Court decisions. These include the <u>Heller Case</u> regarding unlimited access to guns and the <u>Citizens United</u> decision, granting corporations the dominant voice in our national dialogue that drowns out others. These will ultimately be seen as outliers that elevate individual rights far above constitutional norms, while ignoring the threat posed to the rights of the body politic.

Changing the composition of the current Court to accomplish this is not unknown in our history. Nor is mandate for collectivism, fairness to all segments of society in their right to a life of dignity and opportunity. This will once again become the standard for constitutionality. That Madisonian vision of a level playing field among various interest groups will once again tame our worst instincts that have encouraged an epidemic of gun violence and the intrusion of religion in our daily life. If, from the ashes of this horrific pandemic, we can once again rise to create a better society and objectively face our failings, we will have given voice to the best in America.

EVALUATING BIDEN

Up to now, we have only referred to an 'activist' president in dealing with the multiple challenges precipitated by COVID 19. At present, that individual appears to be Joe Biden, the Democratic candidate. There have been many rumors swirling about as to his 'diminished capacity', much of it based his tendency to misspeak and have to issue an explanation or an apology.

History tells us to concentrate on more important matters. This includes Biden's very able service, both in the Senate where he headed the Judiciary Committee and as Obama's Vice President, handling many important initiatives with great competence.

Many able presidents were not particularly noteworthy in their speaking style. This included Washington, who possessed what Abigail Adams preferred to call ' his gift of taciturnity'...while others blamed this on a painful set of false teeth.

Dwight Eisenhower was known for his mangled syntax, leaving many befuddled as to what he meant to say. Some called this his sly way of avoiding answering reporters' questions. Others thought he was simply too old for the job, compared to the incoming youthful

President Kennedy. History has applauded Eisenhower for his solid judgment in addressing Soviet ambitions while presiding over a prosperous nation.

What Biden does seem to possess, in addition to competence in the field of government service, is good character and an exceptional empathy for the plight of others, based on his having experienced a great deal of human tragedy in his own life. These are the qualities that can turn the electorate into believers, even as he advocates groundbreaking legislation to throw off the shackles of the past.

Ironically, if Donald Trump has left us yearning for anything other than competence, it is decency and a sense of morality. Perhaps Supreme Court Justice Oliver Wendell Holmes said it best when he described then candidate FDR in 1932 as possessed of 'a second rate intellect, but a first rate temperament'.

FDR was accused by many progressives of being too much of a conventional politician without deeply held beliefs. History tells us that the times often make the man, even a conventional one who sees both sides of the issue. Like FDR, Joe Biden's being a so-called conventional politician may well be an asset, uniting all the people with a deep-seated belief in the goodness and fairness of America while he goes about the business of transforming the nation to meet the challenges of that more perfect Union.

LEADERSHIP IN
UNEXPECTED PLACES

PROLOGUE

In the summer of 1775, George Washington was hard at work, attempting to craft a functioning army out of a ragtag assortment of state militias. For in truth, that was at the heart of the task to build our nationhood ... to make one out of many.

When an epidemic of smallpox broke out, Washington immediately followed the science of the times, creating a quarantine and forbidding any of his troops to go down to the stagnant ponds that were thought to be the breeding grounds for the disease. Nor should that be surprising. It was during the Age of Enlightenment, the age of Newton and scientific experiments that the American Revolution was fought and our Constitution conceived.

Madison's handiwork itself was a scientific experiment of sorts, a finely crafted machinery of checks and balances to collectively thrash out the issues of good governance. For our founding era, and crafting those founding documents, was always about protecting individual liberty through well-organized, collective action.

Not that those documents were always perfect. In fact, it was assumed early on that interpreting the Constitution would require some elasticity under the mandate to 'create a more perfect Union' in order to meet the needs of the times. This assumption was at the heart of the groundbreaking decisions of the Marshall Court of our founding era.

When and if the Constitution was found wanting... as under the 'three-fifth's clause'...men like Lincoln were clever enough to look to other founding documents, such as the Declaration of Independence and its promise of 'life, liberty and the pursuit of happiness' to renew the promise of America for all its citizens.

TODAY'S CONTRARY APPROACH

Given this history, it is ironic that today we have a government that has faced the coronavirus pandemic with a sense of skepticism and resentment for allowing scientific information to control the conversation. Instead, the federal government under President Trump has proven inadequate to the task of marshaling the nation's resources, both scientific and economic, to address an issue that requires the coordinated national response that has always served us in our darkest hour.

Per his playbook, Trump prefers to divide and conquer, playing one group of states against the other in order to reign over manufactured chaos that 'he alone can fix'. Of course, the only 'fix' in the this playbook will be more chaos in order to prove that democratic government does not work; and we must now trust him to reign supreme without the guardrails of a workable Constitution.

THE ANTIDOTE

Fortunately, however, in our federal system there are those at the state level who can fill the vacuum and lead the way to viable alternatives. These are the individuals who will now provide case studies in leadership to guide the future. Nor is this something new in our history. Were it not for the 'Great Depression' of 1929, which lingered with us right through the 1930's, we would never have elected Franklin D. Roosevelt, then Governor of New York.

For while President Hoover was treating an economic pandemic of hopelessness as nothing more than an economic downturn that would soon pass, FDR was in Albany addressing the consequences for the average American with a host of experimental programs. In effect, he was searching for the right 'vaccines' to inoculate the people from the effects of this economic scourge.

Today, New York's current Governor, Andrew Cuomo, seems to be playing that role, as do a host of other governors who have been left to fill the void in federal leadership.

THE ROLE OF STATE GOVERNERS

Interestingly enough, Cuomo is an unlikely candidate, called to greatness only recently. Up to now, he has looked like more of a political fixer...adept at manipulating the levers of power and constantly at odds with New York's mayor over who controls the city's failing schools and subway system. Nor did he immediately rise to the occasion. Like the rest of the nation, he had been lulled into ignoring the consequences of the oncoming tsunami ... the predictable result of a nation that has been living in the 'alternate universe' constructed over the past three years by Donald Trump.

Yet once the true intentions of this pandemic became obvious, and while the President dithered and denied reality in hopes that it would simply miraculously vanish, governors like Cuomo commandeered that unused 'bully pulpit' and spoke to their constituents as well as the nation.

They were in effect acting like FDR in a prior era, self assured and factual, using their skills on the public's behalf. Like FDR in those 'Fireside Chats', who used the power of that new invention called radio to calm a weary nation, Cuomo personalized the effects of self-isolating, letting us know we were not alone. Instead, he noted the many ways it had affected his family as well, inviting us into his life and his personal space.

Most of all, he stuck to the science as enunciated by the experts to chart the course. Again like FDR, who surrounded himself with a group of academics known as 'The Brain Trust', Cuomo honored the statistics that foreshadowed a stunning rise in deaths unless we stayed the course. He used his significant managerial and political skills, acting more like a military quartermaster to beg, borrow or steal the necessary resources to meet the challenge of the data about hospitalizations and deaths.

Governors like Cuomo have also been resourceful, as a chief executive should be, in identifying various untapped resources, including empowering qualified medical students to start practicing as physicians. At the same time, they understood the need to deal with the federal government and a President who demanded fealty and flattery, despite his obvious ineptitude.

FDR ultimately forced then President Hoover to enact a large stimulus package.

Likewise, governors finally convinced the Trump Administration to allow states to do their own testing on those showing symptoms of the virus. When the results indicated a dire situation unfolding, they urged the President to invoke the Defense Production Act to mobilize industry with government oversight.

Like Hoover, Trump has been a victim of his own shortsightedness and failed theories. Having railed against government, with his constant chant to 'drain the swamp', he has been powerless to effectively mobilize the government. Instead he has preferred to leave it to the states to find their own solutions and have someone to blame if and when things went wrong.

INDIVIDUALISM VS. COLLECTIVISM

Nor could either Hoover or Trump escape a seeming lack of compassion for the plight of ordinary Americans. For Hoover that meant stressing the cure of American individualism and self-reliance, despite the fact that many could not even find a job to feed their families. Likewise, Trump's message, as opposed to the science of self-isolating, has been to say that wearing a mask should be optional and that we can't have a cure be worse than the problem ... implying that collective action must take a backseat to the needs of the individual.

Actually, this is a narrative that contradicts our founding creed that we should always stand together in the face of adversity.

Unfortunately, the President has added a racist tinge, believing that the lives of the poor, the aged and the vulnerable are less worthy then those of the rich. Like those immigrants who are infecting our society and need to be kept out with a wall, he sees these elements of society as equally unworthy and dispensable in a world that celebrates only 'winners'.

By contrast, governors like Cuomo have been quick to act as the nation's cheerleaders, encouraging the people to stay the course. They celebrate 'flattening the curve', applauding the people for having 'reached the top of the mountain' and begun to 'tame the beast'. Compare this with the daily briefings from the White House that have dispensed with the science and turned into an endless campaign rally with the President insulting reporters who dare to question his judgment.

Ironically, the coronavirus may have inadvertently and convincingly re-written the script for America. Perhaps we are finally ready to question theories that are so antithetical to our past...those accusations that the 'deep state' and 'fake news' have corrupted the nation's ability to function.

Could it be that those who have told us that our most precious birthright is our personal liberty, that 'live free or die' is the true American mantra, have finally been challenged to confront today's reality?

Will they be ready to honor our common humanity as worthy of a minimum level of human dignity and rebuild a meager safety net for all rather than celebrate financial success as the only barometer of self-worth? Or has the promise of America been demeaned and forgotten for too long to have much meaning? Will we follow Donald Trump's revisionist version of history and choose to believe that this pandemic is merely another display of the chaos that envelops us when we allow immigrants and other unworthy souls to corrupt society?

Has our descent in questioning those values enshrined in our founding documents proceeded for too long to turn back? We can only hope that those so-called deep state technocrats and highly competent state governors will now find that national audience to chart the way...a point that should not be lost on an electorate prepared to vote in November.

CONCLUSION

It is ironic that the phrase 'states rights' has usually stood for preventive the nation for moving toward that 'more perfect Union'... starting with ending the scourge of slavery.

Many of the great men and women in our history have made their mark in opposing various iterations of 'states rights'...that warping of the Constitution to elevate the voices of the few through word play as to phrases like 'residual rights'.

This includes the same opponents elevating words such as 'individualism' and 'religious liberty' and 'First Amendment freedoms' to make their point.

However, in times of gridlock or abuse of power, when our Legislative Branch or our Chief Executive do not do their jobs, we can applaud the vision of our founding fathers in carving out that roadmap toward statehood, including state constitutions that include certain benchmarks.

Those functioning state governments move the nation forward with their programs for infrastructure, scientific research, new and innovative programs in education...just a few programs where congressional gridlock has taken a toll on an effective government in Washington.

And now we can add, developing the talent at the state level that can learn on the job and replace those who are not doing their jobs properly at the national level.

Thomas Jefferson

FUNDRAISING:
A FULL TIME JOB

AN HISTORIC PERSPECTIVE

Politics in this country has always been a nasty business to one degree or another. Getting the message out to voters to build a constituency often requires tackling hot-button issues that get the attention of a particular audience. That was certainly the case in the late 1790's when Thomas Jefferson decided to build a second party to challenge a one-party system presided over by the Federalists.

He went about this in a very clever, if somewhat devious and underhanded manner. This included his rather duplicitous act of starting his own newspaper within the confines of State Department, where he presided as Washington's Secretary of State.

It also included his lining up a number of very competent surrogates to challenge Federalist office holders with a consistent and highly salable message ... one that insisted that the country had betrayed our founding ideals and needed to find our way back to them. Jefferson's behavior should tell us that the worst of human nature will usually play a part in politics.

Lest one think that Mr. Jefferson was simply selling 'snake oil', those surrogates included James Madison, also known as 'Father of the Constitution', who was second-in-command of the operation. In fact, Madison, who had been Washington's key ally in the House of Representatives, was happy to use his talents to convert other members of Congress to espouse this new Republican agenda.

That included a smaller, less intrusive federal government than the one being promoted by Washington's Treasury Secretary, Alexander Hamilton. It also favored giving more powers to the states, along with a subtle tinge of racism in embracing the institution of slavery where it currently resided.

MOTIVATING THE MASSES

Finally, this message was then cleverly distilled by Jefferson to reach the masses. To accomplish this, he invented a number of clever buzzwords to hawk a sense of indignation, accusing Federalists of being 'monocrats' or 'anglophiles' and assailing those who embraced the British rather than showing the proper gratitude to France for funding the Revolution.

When it came to Hamilton's brainchild of creating a National Bank to pay off the nation's debts, Jefferson preferred to ignore the fundamental benefits in making us a credit-worthy nation. Instead, he concentrated his fire on the inevitable greed of insiders with 'get-rich' schemes in buying bank stock. Hence, the additional invented epithets of 'scrippomania' and 'bankomania'.

There are other iterations of this same pattern of messaging to incite the wrath of the masses, but the point should be clear. We have always been a highly literate society, soaking up the latest news as well as salacious accusations, like a sponge. Now that these outlets of today have exploded in an era of a growing social network, messaging a sense of righteous indignation has been transformed into a quasi art form to further complicate the matters.

CHANGING MEDIA

Again, let us compare this with our founding era to highlight both similarities and differences, starting with Benjamin Franklin, our first media czar and the Rupert Murdock of his day. Franklin, who owned a franchised network of newspapers up and down the East Coast. He made sure to boost circulation by cleverly peppering his news with salacious gossip to keep his readers happy.

Today's tools of the trade would no doubt have fascinated Doctor Franklin, a man who loved to tinker, whether with his media outlets or those scientific experiments that brought him great fame. There is little doubt, however, that he would have used his daunting messaging skills to promote division, rather than bring us together as Americans, united in a common creed.

MESSAGING AS PURE FUNDRAISING

While Dr. Franklin grew wealthy as a media czar, there is nothing to compare with what has been added to the 'messaging' equation... anger and money, tons of it!

Politicians have discovered that the best way to unlock the wallets of constituents is to recognize that people are far more motivated by anger, fear and grievance than by positive emotion. Today's technology allows politicians to test and harness the right message to the right database to reach the right voter, who will react in a visceral way. And the explosion of various apps and platforms to accomplish that, without the costs of 'paper and postage', has turned this into a vast money-making proposition!

Even that return envelope or postcard has been eliminated as you receive email and contact information instantaneously, along with the ability to make that donation, courtesy of PayPal or a credit card...giving the politician's house list even greater resale value.

While Supreme Court decisions like 'Citizens United' have unlocked corporate wallets from the likes of the Koch Brothers and the Mercers to promote their own message, congressmen have learned the art of a more intimate one-on-one form of fundraising to fill their coffers.

Every step of the recent impeachment hearings was seen as a fundraising opportunity for politicians like Devin Nunes, senior Republican on the House Intelligence Committee. Even though House Republicans could not dispute the facts presented at these hearings, they were free to express their indignation regarding procedural matters to their cadre of 'true believers'. Nunes reportedly received more than twenty million dollars from small donors by offering items like a post-impeachment T-shirt to skewer the 'Deep State'.

'Performative fundraising' has become a new term of art to explain the current gridlock that has diminished the role of Congress in crafting legislation. Now posturing to activate the base and fundraise is the preeminent goal without the need to provide some achievable alternative.

It is only natural that these techniques would find their way to the Oval Office as the present Chief Executive preferred to preach grievance over a legislative initiative in order to keep the base loyal and satisfied. Certainly, no one has monetized the art of fundraising with greater skill than Donald Trump. He currently has the largest small donor list ever created by a GOP presidential candidate and has used it as a cudgel to keep the party in line, whether during primary season or for that vote on impeachment.

Unlike prior presidents, who have used the bully pulpit primarily to sell important 'policy' issues, Trump, bereft of any clear cut policies, prefers to use his rallies to demean so-called evil-doers from the press to political opponents in order to keep his voters invested, personally and financially.

THE CAMPAIGN OF 2016

With few legal restrictions and few moral constraints, Facebook provided the perfect platform in which to test various degrees of racism and 'truthiness'.

Trump's head of Digital Marketing took advantage of this capability, constantly modeling ads based on immediate response rates and tailoring them to the needs of specific markets.

Today, in anticipation of the upcoming presidential election, the Trump team is exploring Facebook campaigns that can suppress the vote among idealistic white liberals, young women and African Americans...three key constituencies the Democrats need to win.

It should not be surprising that Trump, primarily a marketer, is planning for his own future as well. While he now tests his messages at rallies to maximize turnout and fundraising, the list he is building will likely provide the underpinning of a vast media empire.

SUMMARY

Today's forms of political messaging most resemble those of the past in their continued visceral appeal to emotion over reason. But where men like Jefferson used these techniques to build a Republican Party, once in office he followed through on his stated agenda to reduce the size of government and pay off the national debt.

He also made sure that his Inaugural Address included perhaps its most important phrase, 'We are all Republicans...we are all Federalists', indicating that, other than party differences, we all come together as Americans to celebrate our democracy.

Nor did he destroy federal institutions and legislation indiscriminately based on petty resentments. When his Treasury Secretary affirmed Hamilton's Bank of the U.S. as a necessary and highly desirable institution, he left it as is, along with other policies the Federalists had put in place.

On the contrary, Trump agenda is focused on demolishing the Obama legacy, even when it serves the interests of the nation. Could it be that the mania to collect money in order to game the political system with highly targeting rhetorical hot buttons has become an end in itself? Could it be that stripping the government of competence and appointing toadies and sycophants is a goal unto itself?

What is new in today's fundraising is the lack of any intention to use those funds for the betterment of the nation...another symptom of the current Gilded Age, which values gaming the system for the few above all else.

In the process, the current explosion of traditional, cable and streaming media has provided the means to take nihilism to new heights, leaving much of the electorate clinging to its guns, fears and frustration, further preventing us from restoring good governance.

Ronald Reagan

A CHANGING
POLITICAL LANDSCAPE

INTRODUCTION

The nation is currently at a pivotal point in deciding its future,
which raises a number of questions:

1. Do we continue down the path of greater income inequality with a shrinking share of the nation's wealth in the hands of everyone but the super-rich?

2. Do we continue to allow that 1% of the population to have the dominant voice in our national discourse along with the ability to lobby Congress to write legislation that favors its interests?

3. Do we allow our courts to be populated with right wing judges who take an oath, not to the Constitution, but to an agenda written by the Federalist Society?

We have been here before. In 1932, with a country deep in the Great Depression, Franklin Roosevelt charted a new economic policy that tamed the rampant excesses of capitalism...despite great opposition from a class he defined as 'those money changers who had fled the Temple' of their own greed and self- importance'.

To chart a future course, it may be instructive to better understand how we reached this point in our national conversation, based on a series of seemingly benign decisions that have corrupted the hopefulness of our founding documents.

IN BETTER TIMES
The 1950's was a time of great prosperity, presided over by President Eisenhower, an avowed Republican centrist who always preferred to chart 'the middle way' between the extremes. Although a man educated in the ways of the military throughout his life, he purposefully cut military expenditures and dedicated those funds to building infrastructure to propel commerce and benefit the growth of Main Street America's middle class.

It was a time when, for many Americans, one income from the family breadwinner provided all the funds necessary to live a comfortable life. Many employees were happy to spend their lives working for one company, while the CEO was often a member of the same community. He had usually worked his way up the executive ladder, earning a higher salary that was perfectly in line with greater responsibilities.

Eisenhower disappointed those Republicans who wanted him to overthrow the legislation of FDR's New Deal. As far as he was concerned, it was established precedent and heartily approved of by the public. Nevertheless, those naysayers fought back, inventing new economic and social theories to cloak the old conservatism in shiny new garb. Their spokesperson at the time was young William Buckley, a Yale graduate and member of a wealthy Connecticut patrician family.

His rhetoric resonated with fellow patricians in the East; but more interestingly, it found a home in the West, the land of that mythical cowboy, with those who embraced individualism as a pre-eminent American creed. This new conservative ideology was the basis of a best selling book, 'Conscience of a Conservative', written in the late 1960's by Arizona Senator, Barry Goldwater, a member of another wealthy family.

THE FIRST STEPS TOWARD A NEW PARTY

It would eventually open the door for another messenger, Ronald Reagan, with a more compelling message. Still, Goldwater being drafted as the Republican candidate in 1968 was clearly an omen of things to come. The Party knew that the current president, Lyndon Johnson was unbeatable. Yet it was willing to gamble on modifying the brand to reach out to a new constituency.

Johnson's impressive civil rights legislation had already offered an opportunity in that regard, with the ability to move the 'solid South' into the Republican column to rebuild the Party's numbers. The Republican Party had always been run as a rich, white man's club. It would still remain mostly white, but with the taint of white supremacy and racism added to the mix.

There was also an unspoken libertarian streak in this iteration of so-called conservative values that set it apart from previous versions. That included a passionate call to be free from the encumbrances of a meddlesome and corrupt government that coddled the needy and impeded the mission of wealth creation.

Again, it is interesting to note that individuals enjoying the benefits of great wealth, with little reason to be dissatisfied, were hawking this dissatisfaction with the status quo. Like most revolutions, this one would be ignited from the top down by the privileged who would harness the vague dissatisfactions of the masses to suit their interests.

BUILDING A LIST OF GRIEVANCES

Among these universal dissatisfactions was the obligation to pay taxes, another idea ignited in the West with a proposal to cut property taxes. Thus began the second theme of this new Republican creed. In order to limit government intrusion in our daily lives, simply 'starve the beast'! There were additional issues to help define this re-envisioned party, including those increasing number of families coming from Central America and crossing those areas in the southwest, namely the Rio Grande and Southern California.

Bipartisan support for immigration had prevailed throughout the 1950's. Now this began to look more and more like a 'liberal issue', with legislation to allow immigrants to petition to bring family members here under a policy of 'family reunification'. The Supreme Court added to this narrative in its decision in Plyer v. Doe, where it ruled that children of illegals were entitled to the same education opportunities as native-born children, giving birth to another Right wing narrative about 'anchor babies'.

The Party hierarchy, that wealthy privileged class that controlled the levers of power, recognized that reducing taxes and limiting immigration could only go so far in bringing the average American on board. What was needed were visceral issues that created an emotional bond, all those so-called liberal issues that could be painted as an abdication of American values.

One obvious target was the large cities in the East during the 1970's where many immigrants and citizens of color lived in an era of welfare payments to cushion endemic poverty. This would present the perfect story to target government programs as giveaways to the less worthy, further expanding the narrative for reducing taxes. More important, it would create an 'us versus them' narrative for voters viewing cities beset with rising crime and wanton liberalism.

WRITING A SCRIPT

While the leaders of this wing of the Republican Party were adept at harnessing these issues, they recognized that grasping the levers of power from traditional conservatives required an impressive narrative. Up to now, ever since the era of the New Deal, a belief in a liberal ethos under the Constitution had prevailed in the courts and in Congress. To counteract that, the precepts of less government and more unbridled capitalism would have to be presented as a superior intellectual endeavor to honor the nation's founding documents.

Well known economists like Milton Friedman helped the cause with concepts such as 'monetarism', claiming that the Federal Reserve could properly control the money supply that would allow the economy to self regulate. Other economists invented the theory of 'supply side' economics, hypothesizing that reducing taxes would unleash supply, while ignoring the more traditional concept that supply follows demand.

Again, the wealthiest members of corporate America, seeing their opportunity to turn back the clock, stepped in to fund conservative think tanks, including the American Enterprise Institute, Cato Institute and Heritage Foundation. These institutions would create an alternative historic narrative while serving as a training ground for future leaders in Congress and state government.

Seizing control of the courts was important enough to require a separate think tank. The Federalist Society would be mandated to transform a judiciary, populated by centrist or liberal judges perverting the message of America with so-called 'judicial activism'. A new judicial theory was created and branded as 'originalism', limiting constitutional interpretation to the precise words and intent of those individuals who drafted this sacred document in 1787.

The Federalist Society's disciples would form law firms throughout the major cities to challenge liberal institutions that impeded the goal of unbridled capitalism, including unions and unionism. The time was ripe for this, as unions had already compromised their standing with the public through obvious corruption among top officials, overreaching on workers' benefits, overly generous pensions and far too many strikes that offended the public.

There was already enough unease throughout the country for people to be looking for new product in the financial market, known as 'money market accounts' that put no limits on interest charges.

GREED IS GOOD

The answer seemed to be the words of Ronald Reagan, saying 'that government is the problem, not the solution'. We were told to celebrate individualism while corporations were to pursue profits, even at the expense of the well-being of employees. We were to be a consumer driven economy, satisfying the luxury fever of the super rich and less affluent wannabes under the mantra of 'greed is good'.

We learned to celebrate the genius and greed of corporate raiders, executing leveraged buyouts with junk bonds or a few upfront dollars. The goal was to sell off the assets piece by piece, even when this included long-term employees losing their pensions. Gone were the days of the halcyon 1950's when major corporations like Sears, Proctor & Gamble and US Steel were proud to initiate profit sharing plans to reward workers. Those companies were now looked upon as easy targets by those raiders, ripe for lots of cost cutting.

The concept of profit sharing, along with stock options, would only be used to hold onto talent at the top, those whose value was constantly being overrated. Maintaining the value of those options and keeping the stock prices high was more important than workers' salaries, which would continue to be at the mercy of the marketplace.

'Trickle down' economics would start the march toward vast income inequality as wages at the top ballooned by one hundred fifty percent while middle class wages grew by fifteen percent on average. Crumbs would occasionally be thrown their way as long as business benefited in the process, as when the Reagan Administration deregulated small regional savings banks in order to promote easier terms in financing a home.

With stagnant wages, living well for the average American required the accumulation of debt. This was made easier through a new financial device, the credit card, with nationally chartered banks free to set interest rates under the Supreme Court's decision in <u>Marquette Case</u>. The 'magic of the market' would now set salaries, escalating reimbursement for Wall Street executives or CEO's of major corporations. Titans of industry and finance had been making thirty times a worker's salary. Thirty years later, that would increase to three hundred times a worker's stagnating salary.

Salaries would no longer to be measured against increased output per worker. In a prior era, that would have been the job of those representing labor at the bargaining table, as would the additional benefits covered by nearly every other industrialized nation, such as health care, sick leave or paid time off to care for a baby. However, those representatives were no longer at the table as union representation shrank to cover a mere fifteen percent of the nation's workforce.

All of these trends are pushed into high gear under Reaganomics, an era of heightened 'Social Darwinism' with wealth and success defining winners versus losers. Rather than negotiating a wage increase, Unions are forced to agree to concessions and givebacks. Perhaps the most long-term damage to wage prospects occurs when Reagan undoes New Deal legislation and allows corporations to use profits to buy back stock.

This now inflates stockholder value while giving rise to stock-based compensation, all at the expense of workers' wages. Additional guardrails of government oversight are removed by deregulating trucking and airlines, opening the way to mergers and acquisitions. Corporate raiders are free to buy airlines and sell off various routes to competitors as retirees lose their pensions.

INFECTING POLITICS

It is only a matter of time before the 'greed cycle' infects politics, this time with Supreme Court decisions in <u>Buckley v. Valero</u>, allowing so-called 'independent groups' to spend freely with total anonymity.

Campaign costs skyrocket as congressmen scramble for funds and donors hire a host of lobbyists to keep their interests front and center. To manage the process, congressmen hire a new class of 'political consultants' to identify those causes must worthy of being pandered to.

By now, the Republican Party has added the evangelical community and the supporters of unrestrained gun ownership to their cause, with the approval and validation by the Supreme Court. All segments of the Party have now been aggrieved in one way or another by the policies of liberal democracy.

In 1994, more than a decade after the start of the Reagan Revolution, a highly ambitious Congressman named Newt Gingrich is elected Speaker of the House. He supplies the Party with the ultimate mission to match these grievances...all out war to take the country back from the liberal evildoers. From now on, the Republican Party would be seen as an ideological movement, a permanent insurgency, unwilling to compromise in its assault on corrupt liberalism and big government.

Inherent in this message is abjuring the need to pledge fealty to the Constitution. Unlike those Right Wing judges, who invent a theory for interpreting the Constitution to serve the cause of 'less government', Republican politicians have merely to wage a war in the name of God and country.

DISSEMINATING THE MESSAGE

The next demon to be dealt with in the march toward ideological purity is the media, long seen as having a liberal bias. Even if it did not, the Party needs a loyal ally to support their views without question. A number of fortuitous events change that landscape as well, aided by insider influence or outright bribery.

The Federal Communications Commission once required parties to reserve a certain amount of airtime to discuss 'public issues' and opposing points of view. With the proliferation of cable and other outlets, this stipulation is removed as an unconstitutional limit on free speech.

Two events now fill the void when conservative media czar Rupert Murdock founds Fox News as the official headquarters of the Far Right messaging machine. The Supreme Court's decision in <u>Citizens United</u>, giving corporations the right to free speech, allows corporations like the Koch Brothers to create 'Americans For Prosperity' to spread the message of the glories of fossil fuel, low taxes and less government. Eventually, more than half of all House Republicans will sign a pledge for 'no climate tax'.

A NEW BEGINNING

Today's corporate mindset is the result of decades of building a false narrative that elevates profits at the cost of the well-being of workers. Stagnating wages have represented a huge transfer of wealth from workers to stockholders and corporate executives, estimated by some at more than fifty billion dollars a year.

The words and actions of FDR at the height of the Depression still ring true, when he described an 'industrial covenant' as a commitment to 'provide a living wage and sustained employment'. Today that requires a realistic minimum wage and benefits enacted by Congress for every worker to enjoy ' the fruits of one's labor' along with revitalized government institutions to monitor those guidelines.

This also includes eliminating those clever tricks winked at by Congress in hiring part timers or classifying employees as 'independent contractors' to avoid the obligation to pay a living wage...as well as corporate devices that limit an employees' ability to change jobs through non-compete agreements.

As FDR discovered upon proclaiming the guidelines of the 'New Deal', business will fight this tooth and nail, claiming that increased benefits and higher salaries will force layoffs, while threatening competitiveness at home and abroad. These claims will always be made despite the fact that history has disproved them. More important will be keeping corporate malfeasance in check through oversight and re-imagining a countervailing authority that unions once represented.

Breaking the stranglehold of corporate governance will have many additional benefits beyond that of more equitable workers' rights. In the process, burgeoning new industries in areas like 'green technology' will spring up to challenge the fossil fuel industry of yesterday, especially now that much of this is already cost affective

The opportunities for renewed economic vitality, a new birth of freedom, await a nation awash in profits.

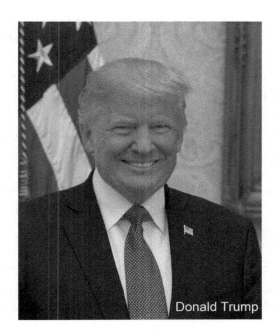
Donald Trump

TRUMP'S WAR AGAINST
THE GOVERNMENT

Donald Trump is the president who has done the most to take the Republican mantra of perpetual war against government to its logical conclusion. Much of this has been catalogued by Michael Lewis in 'The Fifth Risk'.

Ironically this has less to do with ideology ... as Trump is devoid of that concept...than his lifelong need to be free of guardrails or impediments that interfere with his preference for impulsive and unpredictable behavior. For the first time, Trump is being held accountable for his words and deeds, something he could skirt in New York as a wheeler-dealer in real estate. That is one reason why he rails constantly against the 'fake news', an organization he once courted assiduously.

His claims that he could run his business and the presidency at the same time is reflective of seeing his job, not as President of the United States, but as the CEO of 'corporate America' ... something to be dismantled and monetized to serve his personal ends and reward cronies.

For that reason, he will appoint these individuals to his Cabinet and other positions to open the floodgates of self- serving ... trashing the Emoluments Clause without consequence thanks to a complicit Republican Senate.

That is minor compared to the damage he is doing to the various government departments under his jurisdiction, paid for by the taxpayer and mandated to operate for their benefit. That includes Immigration and Customs Enforcement (ICE), and his campaign pledge to stop hordes of Mexican rapists from entering the country.

As Lewis describes in vivid detail, he has encouraged and promoted lawless behavior among its most willing officers, turning the Department into an anti-immigrant strike force of rogue vigilantes, untethered from traditional norms. That same scenario has now played out in Portland, where the President has sent in another rogue strike force to maraud among protesters while dressed in fatigues and without proper identification.

Many of these acts breach constitutional norms, including:

1. His claims to be acting under the National Emergencies Act of 1976, without defining the particular emergency.

2. His actions under the Posse Comitatus Act of 1878, one that generally prohibits the use of military force for domestic law enforcement.

3. Based on precedent, exceptional and seldom used executive powers such as this have primarily been used under the International Emergency Powers Act of 1977, covering economic measures outside the U.S. related to an international emergency, often involving terrorist groups.

PROVOKING A CONSTITUTIONAL CRISIS

When other presidents have activated seldom used powers, it has always been based on important matters such as Andrew Jackson's use of the military, under the Force Act of 1832, when he addressed threats of nullification on the part of the South. One could hardly compare Trump's creating a border crisis to satisfy his base to Jackson's actions. Or is he trying to expand emergency powers without a suitable crisis on the horizon.

His overreach represents rampant executive authority and an egregious distortion of presidential power under Article ll, another impeachable offense by a Congress willing to put the interests of the country over those of party.

Equally alarming is the President's relationship with Fox News, practically a plot to destabilize our democracy and stoke the fires of division. This relationship has also emboldened Trump to cross the line in threatening a free press, with the approval of a privately owned news outlet operating as a quasi-member of the Trump Administration.

If we are accusing the Russians of hacking social media and distorting the conversations that pit Americans against each other, how much different is it for a domestic news organization to be involved in doing the same thing?

A GOVERNMENT OF ONE

Perhaps nothing illustrates the contempt in which Trump holds the various departments of the federal government more than Chris

Christie's descriptions in his book titled 'Let Me Finish'. Christie was assigned the task of putting together a thirty-volume transition plan, initiated by the Obama Administration.

What Governor Christie failed to appreciate, when he undertook this task is that those thirty binders threatened what Trump values most in his presidency … unpredictability and impulsive volatility. For Trump's ideal is a government that values personal loyalty far above competence. He can then boast of putting his gut instinct above intellect to justify the constant contradictions.

Taking all of this into consideration, it should not be surprising that his inaugural paints an apocalyptic vision of American carnage, for which he says 'I alone can fix it'.

He follows the same pattern in international relations, where predictability in honoring treaty obligations was once assigned to a functioning State Department. Trump, on the other hand, prefers unpredictability and chaos to keep partners or foes off base...as though he is still operating as that real estate mogul and withholding payments from contractors.

Where our word was once the gold standard, it is no longer trusted around the world as other countries make their own arrangements without us. The gut and personal animus against those who are intellectually and morally superior have him overturning treaties with abandon, hoping to put his name on new arrangements that he will undoubtedly then try to renegotiate.

In the past, tariffs were often nothing more than a political ploy that could go awry. Presidents were more often victims of this process rather than perpetrators. Even highly capable Presidents, like Teddy Roosevelt, shuddered whenever the subject was brought up in Congress, freely admitting ignorance.

Originally tariffs were intended to help domestic industry flourish and reduce imports … with the consumer caught in the middle and paying higher prices. It is essentially a shortsighted nationalist policy designed to 'beggar thy neighbor' and gain the advantage to enrich oneself. In the process, the opposing country would feel and inevitably put up trade barriers of its own. Thus the whole world would become poorer.

That is precisely what happened in the lead up to the Great Depression during the 1930's and why it became an international calamity far more damaging than a domestic one. The distrust and bitterness generated by tariffs were central to the rise of fascism and the lead-up to World War II. It gave men like Hitler the opportunity to blame others for leaving Germany hungry for answers and for food on their table, blaming all of this on vulnerable targets, including so-called Jewish bankers and moneylenders.

One can only guess at the consequences of Trump's fixation on so-called 'winning' as these tariffs inevitably threatens world order. This may simply be something he welcomes in his apparent thirst for creating chaos and using bludgeoning in order to win on completely different issues, such as immigration. Ironically, these tariffs will do more damage to those embattled blue-collar constituents he has courted so assiduously in his attempt to 'Make America Great Again'.

Based on this brief review of the Trump era, no nation will stand idly by and be embarrassed or demeaned by these policies. Even if the United States has the strongest economy, these nations will ultimately strike back, individually or perhaps in unison. This in turn will only elevate the stakes and diminish the prosperity that has flourished worldwide under a globalized economy.

So much for underestimating the ability of a failed billionaire, bereft of appreciation for the workings of government or the Constitution, to reshape the government in his image. If this is the antithesis of presidential greatness, the ultimate accolade for a chief executive, it still is 'consequential' even in the eyes of history.

TROUBLING
TRENDS

Often times, things do not go smoothly for the nation. These can include economic or social unrest of various sorts that affect a national audience.

The symptoms are multifold, including a proliferation of 'hate groups', as in Charlottesville. We may be prone to blame outside forces and retreat from the rest of the world. This is of course a form of isolationism, a long-term strain in the American psyche.

Actually, any crises of spirit may benefit certain segments of society. In a democracy, those groups or individuals also have the right to promote their point of view. That may include corporate interests that possess the biggest 'megaphone' to drown out others in shaping public opinion, another crisis of sorts.

With all these roiling issues, we must from time to time look to those founding documents promising all citizens 'life, liberty and the pursuit of happiness'. For as troubling as these trends may be, they are in fact part of the democratic process and that ongoing conversation foreseen in a Constitution's march toward that 'more perfect Union'.

WHITE NATIONALISM

INTRODUCTION

The current rise of white supremacists and neo-Nazi groups is of course alarming and a tribute to the President's ability to appeal to our worst instincts so that he can continue to dominate the conversation. In truth, 'white-nationalism' is part of our founding DNA. From our earliest days, we callously destroyed the lives and culture of Native Americans in our quest to turn the country into our vision of 'white America'.

That was made easy by our assuming the inferiority of their culture and explaining ours as a noble mission to 'elevate and civilize'. Never mind that between exposing this population to smallpox and introducing liquor, we decimated these Native Americans, making the task of 'civilizing' that much easier.

That particular viewpoint was never simply ours. It was the underlying assumption in justifying the 'white man's burden' in building the British Empire and for that matter, all of European colonialism nor should we ignore the mineral wealth that was extracted in the bargain. We can even assume that those Japanese internment camps during World War ll were made easier by slanted Asian eyes, since we never performed the same ritual with German Americans. Although some would explain that the Germans never directly bombed our country as the Japanese did at Pearl Harbor.

THE BLACK EXPERIENCE

The black experience was somewhat different. The color of their skin and originally importing them into American culture as slave labor branded them as outsiders who were inferior from the start and not worthy of 'educating and elevating'. The narrative to explain slavery as a paternalistic system to tame wild impulses and deal with intellectual inferiority helped justify the South's so-called 'peculiar institution'. It was not only men like John Calhoun who perpetuated this theory in the lead up to the Civil War.

Even men like Jefferson and Lincoln were certain that there could never be a mixing of the races and that exporting the problem to Haiti or Liberia would be the best way to solve the problem and ease the 'white man's burden'. It was only after educated blacks like Frederick Douglass visited with Lincoln at the White House he abandoned this cause.

SELLING THE THEORY

It should not therefore be surprising that the books spelling out the case for white nationalism were usually written by well-educated men from the upper classes of society, who freely espoused such theories. One of these was patrician Madison Grant, one of the founders of the conservation movement that helped to save the American buffalo. (His other good works included helping to found the Bronx Zoo and the Museum of Natural History, along with Teddy Roosevelt's father, a member of the same class.)

Grant had another side to him. Just as he feared the extinction of the buffalo, he felt the same way about a white population of Nordic descent. His theories are described in detail in his book 'The Passing of the Great Race', one of the most famous racist books ever published. Interestingly, this book and similar white supremacist tomes at the time were published by Charles Scribner's and Sons, the same house that published distinguished authors such as Hemingway and Fitzgerald. It was said to even have been read by Adolf Hitler, who wrote a fan letter, calling it 'My Bible'.

According to Grant's theories, all of Western civilization was created by a race of tall, blond, warlike Nordic peoples, which he calls the 'master race'. They supposedly ventured down from Northern Europe every so often to start great cultures with their unique 'germ plasm' (in addition to normal body plasm), which possessed special qualities, as opposed to the fluids of inferior races. According to Grant, over time these special fluids would be 'mongrelized' by mixing with inferior races.

For men like Grant, the most devastating event of recent times had been the defeat of a white nation such as Russia at the hands of Japan in 1905. Ironically, a man of Grant's social class named Theodore Roosevelt would have disagreed. He had mediated the peace agreement in the Russo-Japanese War and had been much more impressed by the Japanese diplomats than the tiresome and clearly outfoxed Russians.

Grant predicted that this type of event would ultimately lead to a worldwide uprising against the Nordic Race, a theory promoted by Hitler himself in his rise to power. Perhaps Grant knew more than we are willing to concede. For he also correctly predicted that Japan would expand its influence in the Pacific, leading to a confrontation with the U.S and that India would ultimately throw out the British.

It was only later that political correctness of another era turned these authors like Grant into pariahs among the better educated and into heroes among today's white supremacists.

TODAY'S WHITE NATIONALISM

The rise of white nationalism today is being played out in different era, namely that of the post Obama presidency. For those who believe in white nationalism, the fears given voice by men like Madison Grant as to 'mongrelization' of a so-called superior race have now become a reality. Trump's claim of 'good people on both sides' at

Charlottesville is all they need to hear in order to know that they have a sympathetic ear in the White House.

Thuggish groups like Patriot Prayer and Proud Boys, often sporting Trump's MAGA hats are encouraged by social media posts to dress for combat and bring guns to provoke those seeking social justice, easily caricatured by Trump and his Attorney General as an anti-fascist movement.

A similar foray was supposedly launched to restore order in Seattle, again portraying Americans marching for social justice as anarchists. It has allowed the President to claim that a violent Left is preparing for an insurrection to grab illegitimate power, requiring 'real Americans' to protect themselves from those being incited by the fake media. Could this be a practice run at activating the President's supporters if he were to lose the upcoming election in November?

All of this contributes to talk of a conspiratorial Deep State, determined to run out the clock on the presidency of Donald Trump... another way to justify his building that border wall to keep illegal immigrants from destroying the fabric of America.

Which returns us to the prior conversation as to the roots of white supremacy, and the claims that whites are being systematically displaced from their homeland by violent low IQ 'third worlders' or, in Trump's words those coming 'from shithole nations'.

The central theme of white nationalist propaganda has always been 'white genocide' and those dark forces conspiring to encourage mass immigration, low fertility rates, miscegenation and abortion. Donald Trump is seen as the first President to openly support this cause, one of the major reasons he was elected by a minority of voters in strategic locations.

THE UNMASKING OF UNFORSEEN EVENTS

The Trump Administration's handling of the human and economic toll due to the coronavirus has laid bare its ineptitude in all areas of governance. For the past five months, we have watched the stark reality of economic and social injustice, with people of color continuing to work overtime as our first line of defense in hospitals and in other vital services to keep the economy going, while they expose themselves daily to COVID-19.

As if that were not enough to honor their role in society, we were then exposed to the blatant murder of George Floyd, a middle aged black man, arrested for a questionable petty crime in Minneapolis. Watching a police officer, with a foot on his neck, squeezing the life out of him second by second, created a hard-to-forget moment for many...exposing the falsehood of the usual explanation that 'he had it coming to him'.

When this latest display of racial injustice led to demonstrations in the streets of major cities, in support of 'Black Lives Matter', the Trump Administration preferred to play to the fears of the public by branding all the participants with the broad brush of treason and lack of patriotism. The President then went to Lafayette Square where protesters had gathered where he opted for a photo op, holding a bible upside down as a symbol of his being on the side of godliness.

The reaction was not what the President expected, with several of those accompanying him later apologizing for being there, particularly those in the military who were sending the wrong message to those peacefully protesting.

Perhaps the President's actions and his inept response to COVID-19 have had their affect and we are ready for a new narrative that speaks to the value and self-worth of every individual who participates in this democracy.

Barack Obama

ISOLATIONISM VERSUS GLOBALISM

WHAT HISTORY TELLS US

Some of our finest moments have been in overcoming that founding tendency to separate ourselves from world affairs with the assumption that we could live happily in splendid isolation.

From the beginning, our continent, separated from the battles of Europe by two huge oceans, has given us a sense of security. The

Monroe Doctrine was our official notice to the world that we would not meddle in Europe's affairs and they would not meddle in ours.

Teddy Roosevelt was the first president to openly advocate globalism, celebrating our push to gain new markets abroad while embracing the role of civilizing these nations. We had already wrested control of the Philippines, Cuba and Puerto Rico from Spain in the Spanish American War. Now, Roosevelt would enter into high stakes statecraft, grabbing Panama from Colombia by staging a phony rebellion and building the canal without partnering with the British, as originally planned.

He saw this as necessary to make us a player on the world stage in both the Pacific and the Atlantic. Only the Panama Canal could give us access to trade East and West and allow our growing naval presence to easily move from one ocean to the other.

Woodrow Wilson won the presidency by promising that we would never enter World War 1, fought for empire and power in far off Europe. Like many future presidents, he had to take back those words when the outbreak of World War I threatened democracies overseas and was likely to affect us as well at some point.

Wilson became an internationalist at that point and a visionary, foreseeing the need for a new world order, to be named a League of Nations, removing decision-making from individual countries as to confronting aggression.

FDR would not have an easier time when it came to involving us World War ll, even though Britain's Prime Minister, Winston Churchill was begging us for arms to deter a Nazi invasion. Only FDR's superb messaging and patience allowed the public to accept his proposal of Lend Lease, with Britain giving us control of her ports in the Caribbean in exchange for our 'lending' her armaments and ships.

Truth be told, without the Japanese attack on Pearl Harbor, FDR might never have changed public opinion. Making this a battle to 'save democracy' was just what was needed to elevate the struggle beyond simply helping the British.

It was our place in the post-war world that finally broke the back of isolationism. For we were no longer talking about engaging in war, but rather engaging in a lasting peace and using our unique power and moral authority to do so. The Marshall Plan became a high point in international diplomacy with the U.S. rebuilding war-torn nations at our own expense. In the end, it created credit worthy nations with which to trade, while preventing the spread of communism.

The invasion of South Korea by the North and its Chinese Communist allies could easily have been pursued unilaterally, but thanks to a superb act of statesmanship by Secretary of State, Dean Acheson, Truman chose to work through the UN.

The next President, Dwight Eisenhower, maintained our moral authority abroad, viewing the attack on the Suez Canal and French involvement in Vietnam as nothing more than rampant colonialism

JFK, after a shaky start with the 'Bay of Pigs' fiasco, another foolish attempt at quasi-colonialism, reasserted the Monroe Doctrine in confronting the Soviets during the Cuban Missile Crisis.

Unfortunately LBJ, a neophyte when it came to foreign affairs, was hoodwinked by a bogus Domino Theory and a military eager to precipitate the Vietnam War. As Eisenhower knew, the odds of winning were never good when we were opposing a bona fide national hero in Ho Chi Minh.

Nixon redeemed himself as an internationalist, after foolishly expanding our presence in the Vietnam War, with his opening relations with China, a brilliant move by this American Machiavelli.

Reagan, that Cold War hawk, was smart enough to negotiate both arms reductions and a potential path to winning the Cold War in his negotiations with Soviet leader Mikhail Gorbachev.

George HW Bush, was adept in using American soft power through his Secretary of State, James Baker, who negotiated a soft landing as the Soviet Union was in the throes of setting satellite nations free to make their own choices.

After having stood by without stopping the genocide in the African nation of Rwanda, the Clinton Administration adeptly crafted the Dayton Accord, ending the carnage and racial holocaust in the former Yugoslavia, another display of patience and the use of soft power.

The 21st century dawned with a new president, virtually elected by the Supreme Court. Unfortunately, George W. Bush squandered the opportunity for worldwide solidarity after a terrorist attack and the destruction of New York's Twin Towers.

Instead of mobilizing the world with our 'soft power' to deal with the root causes of terrorism, we launched an attack on Iraq, based on false intelligence regarding the existence of 'weapons of mass destruction'. In the process, we destabilized the entire region for more than a generation, perhaps the greatest geopolitical blunder in American history.

OBAMA ON THE WORLD STAGE

The election of Barack Obama in 2008 was in large part a rejection of old solutions and a chance to regain our moral authority in the world with the nation's first black president. Obama followed the path forged by George Marshall and built strong coalitions for various multilateral institutions, including the G-7 and NATO, while adding to this legacy and increasing U.S. prestige with leaders around the world.

However, no one can deny the successful use of American soft power and prestige under Obama with various multilateral agreements, including:

1. Paris Accords, an attempt to galvanize the industrial world to structure a long-term project to tame the affects of global warming with measurable benchmarks in place.

2. The Iran deal, gaining Iran's consent to delay the development of a nuclear capability over the next ten years with consistent monitoring by UN and other authorized personal in exchange for certain benefits including the reduction of sanctions and releasing Iranian funds held by the U.S. government.

3. The Trans-Pacific Partnership, a multi-lateral agreement among all the nations in the Pacific Rim to thwart China's military and economic ambitions in the Pacific.

However, all of these were executed under Executive Authority, due to consistent congressional gridlock. These can therefore be overturned by another president...particularly one with an animus toward multilateralism and the president executing this.

THE PARIS ACCORD

The Trump Administration has replaced a globalist approach with ultra-nationalism and an America first agenda that confront allies and adversaries alike with the antithesis of cooperation, including our withdrawal from the Paris Accords. This at a time when only an international alliance can save the world from impending doom... not from a nuclear war on the horizon, but from nature's wrath at our abusing the health of the planet for far too long.

Allied on the side of isolationism is a daunting force of empowered interests, including the fossil fuel industry that has vast resources in lobbying and messaging to lull the public into allowing us to pour more hydro-carbons into the atmosphere.

Their allies include a complicit Supreme Court that has allowed them to dominate the conversation by calling money the equivalent of free speech and a renegade Republican Party under Trumpism that controls at least two branches of government and currently operates outside of constitutional norms.

THE CHALLENGE OF CLIMATE CHANGE

This brings us to the issue of 'climate change', perhaps the most daunting threat ever to be faced by our country, our planet and the future of mankind. The statistics already confirmed by the vast majority of experts on the subject are daunting indeed. We are told that the process is accelerating at an unforeseen pace, and that we have only twelve years at best to cut the use of fossil fuels in half to avert a global catastrophe.

If carbon levels continue to increase at the present rate, we could be approaching a two-degree increase in world temperature within a few decades, a level which scientists now consider as calamitous, with over one hundred fifty million people dying of air pollution.

This, despite the fact that technology is on our side in dispensing with fossil fuels. Even in Africa, which lacks a robust infrastructure, inexpensive solar panels are lighting villages, running hospitals, starting businesses and marketing and manufacturing products, all without drilling or building networks involving power poles and miles of copper wiring. (Cell phone technology also mirrors the same pattern of less infrastructure with greater use.)

Our grossly diminished response to the crisis of climate change is simply another byproduct of years and decades of denigrating the role of our federal government.

Ironically, this may be the moment for Trump or some future president with his autocratic inclinations to move toward the autocracy he so admires in other countries. For a large segment of the American public might well be ready to embrace that alternative, having been worn down over the past decade with congressional gridlock.

The President could then have ordered our borders sealed, immune from dealing with those hordes of invading immigrants. For in truth, there would be an invasion as climate change destroys millions of acres of fertile land in Central America. Of course, that issue could be dealt with by a consortium of nations, but by that time a dialogue would have broken down as each country pursues its national interests.

Nor would we share our still bountiful supply of food, augmented by a trade agreement with Canada, where global warming would actually increase agriculture in the Hudson Bay region. At that point, deprived of the right to immigrate and enough food to support the populace, wars are likely to break out among those nations of Central America to gain what little is left to support a meager way of life. Hordes of desperate immigrants might then head to South America, destabilizing those countries as well.

Having survived the worst of global warming, at least for the moment, our government could then claim success of sorts and be rewarded by a vote of confidence, if that were even necessary at that point. In the process, we would have avoided dealing with those thorny issues of science in converting to a 'green' economy that would have destroyed much of our current energy suppliers.

Europe might try to maintain its democratic norms and continue to develop green technologies that are now cost effective. But their populations might prefer our solution as hordes from African nations reach the shores of the Mediterranean and enter through any available route.

If there is any truth to this possible scenario, it speaks to a crisis in both our constitutional process and our national will. The most damaging contributing factor by far is the outsized 'political voice' bought by the fossil fuel industry and big business in general, to control the national dialogue.

COVID-19 AND THE PERFECT STORM
At the same time, a pandemic has awakened the nation to the consequences of a two-tiered society that has been rewarding the wealthy over the past four decades while systematically starving the lower and middle class of a decent income and safety net to cushion the impact.

We now have the people allied on one side and wealthy corporate interests on the other, the makings of the perfect storm that will determine our future ... whether we restore the promise of America or move toward an authoritarian regime to preserve the status quo.

The pandemic has already smoothed the way in lulling us into accepting new governmental norms. It has already decimated small businesses that could not survive the long lockdown and elevated the standing and dominance of large corporations in hi-tech, finance, energy, media, telecommunications and retail. Their ability to dominate Congress and the Executive Branch with their lobbyists and payoffs allows them to skirt regulation to curb monopolistic practices, ending any opportunity for smaller competitors to flourish.

Government will continue to transfer tax dollars to big business in the form of tax breaks and other incentives rather than fund programs that benefit the public, further reducing funds for a frayed safety net.

This way of life will not be challenged. On the contrary, with their control of a national conversation, the usual suspects will blame others for a faltering economy. Isolationism has always found the right scapegoats, including minorities, immigrants and godless liberals who are perverting the message of America.

The President will promise to return the country to national greatness by keeping these forces in line. Marches and sporadic violence will be used to furnish an excuse to impose martial law and limit constitutional rights.

THE THREAT TO GLOBALISM

Ironically, isolationism will foster the creation of a more threatening world as we withdraw from international collaboration with nations that share our values while using tariffs to bludgeon rather than negotiate with adversaries.

A diminished State Department that no longer possesses the skills to use diplomacy as a viable alternative will only exacerbate the process. A president will use the ensuing chaos to justify greater control of foreign affairs in a dangerous world, diminishing the role of the CIA and the NSA in keeping us safe and avoiding reckless decisions.

OBAMA ON THE WORLD STAGE

Thus far, we have withdrawn from several of those multilateral agreements noted above and crafted by the Obama Administration. We are going it alone with unexpected consequences as to the Iran Deal.

Other signatories, including the major powers in the European Community, China, Russia and Turkey, have remained committed to this arrangement.

They have already developed alternative methods of payment to avoid U.S. sanctions...leading the way to remaking current methods of finance, without the dollar as the international standard.

This is already adding unforeseen consequences, potentially affecting our position in international trade, for China and Russia have long advocated limiting their reliance on the dollar in their dealings with the E.C.

In addition, our unreliability regarding our commitment to NATO is creating the possibility of an independent European strike force...further destabilizing world order.

This resembles the situation in the lead up to World War 1, where various alliances became highly questionable, allowing certain nations to test the limits. The ramifications our actions inadvertently put in place will be hard to reverse once certain decisions are made.

The embrace of our responsibility as the leader of the free world was the underlying premise behind the major initiatives undertaken by President Obama.

Each of these, crafted in large part by Secretary of State John Kerry, represented the results of intensive negotiation among many nations to craft multilateral, binding agreements that established ongoing dialogue with allies and adversaries, believing that changing minds and monitoring behaviors would best be served by this process.

THE TRUMP ERA

The extensive narrative above serves to demonstrate several points, including the relationship between domestic policy and our ability to project soft power abroad. This power does not require military action, but rather the involvement of the United States to lead and support a stable world order.

For now our soft power is severely diminished, with a transactional president at the helm, and intent on destroying norms that have existed since the days of Marshall Plan. We now face an uncertain, isolationist future, having turned friends into skeptics at best, based merely on the latest financial transaction.

'Winning' on the international stage is now based on an erratic and unreliable standard, known only to a particular president. Other nations will make their self interest the standard as well in a more chaotic world of continuous uncertainty.

With this pervasive atmosphere worldwide, nations will withdraw into themselves and promote their own selfish agendas without regard to the international consequences. The power vacuum left by our withdrawal from the world stage will likely be filled by China, seizing the opportunity to make new alliances that may be difficult to alter, even after we come to our senses with a new administration.

In the meantime, every economy will suffer, those of weaker nations even more so, leading to political unrest that can easily spread. With economic uncertainty, trade barriers and trade wars, we encourage the possibility of actual wars based on miscalculations without verifiable multilateral agreements to keep the conversation going.

THE HISTORY OF INCOME INEQUALITY

THE CHECKERED HISTORY OF FINANCE

When Alexander Hamilton, a financial genius, arrived in this country from the Caribbean island of St. Croix, he saw a nation possessing endless wealth in land and natural resources. In 1789, as the first Treasury Secretary, he set out to use all the mercantile skills he had acquired at a trading house in the West Indies to utilize those resources and make this country credit worthy and respected.

With Washington as president, he had the richest man in America in the White House to support that policy of national 'wealth management'. Starting with his creation of a National Bank of the U.S., approved under the Constitution's implied powers clause and later validated by the Marshall Court ... Hamilton had the government assume all the state and federal debt accumulated during the war. In the process he made the financial community rich by assuming previously worthless debt.

In the process, he also set off a debate that we still face today ... how much to favor the rich and entitled over the common man, a conversation that gave birth to Jefferson's Republican Party. For, in America, while we value the ability to rise in our economic and social station, we still have suspicions regarding the wealthy 'gaming the system'.

That in fact was the imperative behind Andrew Jackson's challenging the Bank of the U.S. back in 1832. Once again, there was a fear and suspicion of federal institutions lining the pockets of the elites, while the common man was denied credit to build a business. To be sure, there was also the tendency for local banks to issue worthless currency that was not backed by gold or specie, especially those banks in the West that had been starved for credit.

The issue was often 'hard money', favored by the rich and backed by a limited supply of gold versus 'easy money', backed by a larger supply of gold, silver and other metals, favored by the average man.

Even Jackson, a man who espoused white supremacy and states rights for the common man, knew where to draw the line. With an overheated economy, with too much easy money, creating rampant speculation, he pulled the plug on land sales that were not backed by gold. Unfortunately, this pushed the country into a severe economic downturn that lasted for years.

Lincoln was a President who freely admitted his ignorance when it came to financial matters. He left it up to his Treasury Secretary to devise a currency that replaced gold and called it 'the greenback'. It managed to fund the Civil War and satisfy the needs of a booming economy in the North.

The rural areas of America were constantly clamoring for a currency backed by more plentiful silver, but lost that battle when the populist of the day, William Jennings Bryan, was defeated for the presidency by William McKinley in 1900. The absence of proper financing for rural America has been with us to this day.

To expand currency, still tethered to a gold standard, Woodrow Wilson gifted the captains of industry in 1913 with the Federal Reserve System, a new version of the Bank of the U.S., but with more flexibility in lending to federally chartered regional banks around the nation.

That was the beginning of the so-called modern era of finance with the addition of congressional fiscal policy, spending bills and tax legislation added to the mix over time. It was the addition of

Keynesian economics in the midst of the Great Depression that added an essential element, the federal government's injecting huge sums of money at times of flagging consumer spending.

THE MODERN ERA

Today, the world uses the dollar as long as the standard in all international transactions. This allows the United States to print as much currency as we need without restrictions other than the possibility of initiating inflation. The gold stored in Fort Knox is not the measure of the stability of our currency. That depends on how credit-worthy we are in the eyes of the rest of the world that funds our national debt.

Truth be told, the United States is judged by a different standard than the usual balance sheet. To the rest of the world, the U.S. is a supermarket of investment opportunity, open and ready for business without government restraint. We are also at present the most politically stable country for long-term investment, regardless of the politics of the moment.

GROWING INCOME INEQUALITY

Today's issues with the flow of capital within the United States have less to do with a weakened dollar and foreign investment than with the migration of money into the hands of a smaller percent of the population and their ability to dictate laws that favor the rich at the expense of the average American.

Wall Street, always a bastion of capitalism, has become a bastion of entitlement and greed, with a relative few living in their ivory tower, totally out of touch with the rest of the country in their 'let them eat cake' moment.

Ironically, it was Jefferson who predicted this moment in his heated discussion with Hamilton. In truth, Hamilton would not be been happy as well with an economic system that stifled competition.

Certainly, Supreme Court decisions have not helped in labeling corporations as 'individuals' worthy of the right to 'free speech', particularly at a time when fading Unions no longer represent a countervailing power base.

Imagine the concerns of Madison as well, whose Constitution is based on the workings of a vibrant democracy premised on a level playing field with a host of regional interest groups.

Perhaps the opportunity is ripe for another Lincoln to educate the public once again on the hopefulness of the Declaration of Independence that everyone should be entitled to the fruits of his labor, including a safety net of benefits to guarantee a life of human dignity.

Just as Teddy Roosevelt put an end to the Gilded Age of robber barons, by enforcing regulations that tamed the excesses of industry, today we need a man to tame the excesses of capitalism. That includes the enormous sums of money made by manipulating markets, stripping companies of their assets in order to gorge on the profits. This also includes hedge funds betting against the financial health of America and making billions in the process.

The solution today might include a tax policy to cap these transactions at a reasonable sum while returning the balance of the profits to the public coffers to fund important government programs that continue to level the playing field and help re-establish a vibrant middle class.

The president who can accomplish this will be credited with getting America through another crisis, one that elevates the making of money far above other values.

MONEY AND THE MEDIA

Any discussion of the increasing power of the 1% must also include their power over today's messaging. There was a time decades ago when the major networks supplied most Americans with their news, marginalizing radical views from both sides of the aisle and fostering a bipartisan viewpoint in general.

Exposing the over-reach of a president in Watergate brought luster to a newspaper for getting at the truth with the end result supported by most of the public and the Supreme Court. Today, it is more likely that a large portion of the public would doubt the validity of such a story, including various findings of the Mueller Report.

With journalism no longer a lucrative industry, what sells is not necessarily truth, but rather controversy. No one has taken greater advantage of this decline in the standards of journalism than the Far Right where even major news organizations do not observe truth-seeking norms.

Mainstream media cannot be exonerated from some responsibility in their quest for so-called journalistic balance. During the campaign of 2016, hard-hitting stories on Trump were seen as requiring equivalent stories on his opponent, Hillary Clinton. At the same time, the much larger story of Russian hacking and the involvement of many running the Trump campaign was suppressed on the assumption that Trump would attack that as media bias.

If we are to address the overwhelming corrosive effect of income inequality in our nation's long term health, we need to be properly educated on the data and facts, a questionable feat at best in today's journalistic landscape where 'truth' has been replaced by 'profits'.

The stakes are high. Rising incomes distributed to a growing middle class have always been the hallmark of a vibrant democracy. Income inequality will conversely cause democracy to be in retreat, despite the world becoming richer over the past century.

In the 1930's, when the world faced the Great Depression and the results of a fragile peace after World War 1, the solution was either a trend toward fascism, based on a so-called nation under siege from 'the other', or another form of more inclusive capitalism. Change will not be easy, given the highly polarized society of today that talks past each other on the social and political issues that comprise their major concerns.

Much of the Left/Right divide concerns how far government should go to equalize opportunity for those in the workplace and children in the next generation born into unequal circumstances. Without vilifying any participants in the conversation, this should be discussed under what is called 'humanity identity politics', an open dialogue as to those marginalized by the color of their skin rather than the content of the character ... the same rationale that drove the civil rights movement under Martin Luther King Jr. That is, not forcing white Americans to accept a new concept of justice, but rather embracing the founding ethos of 'life, liberty and the pursuit of happiness'.

MILITARY SPENDING AND NATIONAL PRIORITIES

INTRODUCTION

When you hear that a trillion and a half tax break for the wealthy has just used up any funds for infrastructure and entitlements, you know where the priorities lie for the Trump Administration. Naturally, we are tempted to look elsewhere, and no slush fund is larger than the current military budget, confirmation of what President Eisenhower branded as the vast 'military industrial complex' in his outstanding farewell address.

Today, only a bona fide war hero like Eisenhower could have made that statement without having his patriotism questioned. And conversely, the only one whose image is elevated by increased spending is a president whose avoidance of military service is well known.

Our military budget currently dwarfs that of any other government expenditure. With the support of both parties in Congress, it is not likely to change in the foreseeable future. The only question asked in that annual congressional review is how much to increase the budget, never how much to cut.

It is rarely about military strategy, the likely battles to be waged, or the alternative weaponry that has transformed warfare dramatically over the past decades. Nor are these costs weighed against the needs of a society mired in declining incomes and unable to meet basic daily needs, including the right to free health care.

Military budgets can sound eminently reasonable and defensible when one plays the 'percentage game'. After all, these expenditures currently represent as small percentage of GDP. Instead, defense spending should be measured against all discretionary expenditures, where it currently dwarfs all others.

A congressman with a military base, weapons supplier or back office in his district would be unlikely to challenge this expense. Thus, obsolete tanks are still being built along with aircraft carriers that are increasingly vulnerable to advanced missile technology.

Even with these excesses, the Trump Administration can in fact make one realistic boast. It has doubled down on huge increases in spending despite no rationale to do so, leading to starving all other Cabinet agencies with far more worthy programs. This, despite the fact that current cyber technology favors the development of a multitude of cheap unmanned weapons controlled by networked satellites and artificial intelligence, and requiring a leaner fighting force and lower expenditures.

Compare the current process to that of a prior era when men like General George Marshall and his military aide, Dwight Eisenhower, were plotting the long term needs of a military fighting a war on two fronts during World War ll. The mission was to give our forces in Europe and Asia all the weaponry and air and naval support required to win the war... and not a penny more. Of course they had a highly competent staff feeding them the information, but still, ultimately it was their decision to make.

When Hitler launched his last desperate attempt to defeat the Allies at the Battle of the Bulge, there were many who questioned Marshall's judgment and whether our forces were at a disadvantage. Nevertheless, FDR stood firm and confident in Marshall's judgment, which was ultimately vindicated. This is what leadership is all about when it comes to military matters, appointing the right people to do the job correctly.

Today's bloated military tells us that currently this is not the case. There are therefore questions that must be asked:

1. Has today's military industrial complex gamed the system as Eisenhower warned, in putting its financial interests above that of the country's?

   • That was a question that was also front and center in World War ll when Senator Truman convened a committee to look into wartime waste and fraud, ultimately saving the country billions of dollars.

2. Are we making zero sum decisions in calculating the minimal dollars for long term military needs?

   • The end result of an intensive investigation by the Truman Administration at the end of World War II was to merge all three branches of government under a Joint Chiefs of Staff, avoiding disputes among the Army, Air Force and Navy, all fighting for dollars in an unending turf war.

   • The need for disinterested, competent voices...those loyal civil servants who toil endlessly and know the subject matter intimately...is probably the place to start in evaluating current programs with absolute objectivity.

3. Are we properly evaluating new technologies that can transform our needs vis a vis the traditional weaponry?

   • Again, let us look back to World War ll and FDR's allocating two billion dollars to fund the top secret Manhattan Project to build an atomic bomb before the Nazi's beat us to the punch.

- This project was initiated based simply on a letter FDR received from Albert Einstein, perhaps the most eminent physicist of the day. Even so and despite the huge expense, we could not be sure that it would perform as expected until it exploded over Hiroshima, causing the Japanese to surrender shortly thereafter.

With today's technology constantly spawning new options, this requires another team of experts, the Einstein's of today, again with total objectivity to constantly evaluate these options. These should then 'bubble up' to decision makers at the top...as with Marshall and Eisenhower, who performed with distinction during World War ll.

Otherwise, evaluating military needs requires long term planning, without micromanaging by a Chief Executive. Eisenhower, despite his military credentials, left that to his Joint Chiefs, who reported to him at weekly meetings of his National Security Council.

A NEW ARMS RACE

A president's job, in his constitutionally mandated oversight of foreign affairs, is to work with the assistance of his Secretary of State to negotiate and sustain agreements that obviate the need for military action.

Unfortunately such is not the case today, as we seem to be discarding the wisdom of the past thirty years and creeping toward an expanded arms race.

This inadvertently began to take shape when the Obama Administration negotiated a new start arms limitation agreement with Putin. At the time, both sides mandated to cut nuclear warheads from 30,000 to 6,000, including upgrading their aging nuclear capabilities.

When President Trump entered the White House, he naturally saw this as a sign of weakness, especially when negotiated by

Obama, and demanded building back to the 30,000 level and basically trashed this agreement.

After forty years of arms agreements reducing a nuclear threat, these activities along with Chinese nuclear ambitions, are again accelerating the potential for a new arms race. The question becomes how much is enough deterrence power and what does Trump's obsession with 'winning' look like in another era of assured nuclear destruction?

An astute military man like Eisenhower was not interested in wasting our economy on foolish little wars, nuclear or otherwise. For he understood that other nations could play that game, and suddenly the entire world would be subject to the whims of nuclear blackmail or other misunderstandings.

Clearly, this is not a strategy our current president would understand, according to Trump's 'art of the deal'. Unfortunately, much of the public will applaud this as looking tough, without understanding the ramifications. After all, we have been bombarded for years regarding dangers abroad that only the military can address and demagogues will be sure to surface, accusing such a president of selling us out and diminishing our place in the world with 'effete diplomacy'.

Nevertheless, the benefits will be impressive if we switch from relying too often on bluster and so-called 'hard power' to the type of 'soft power' that gathers talented diplomats around the table with a sense of mutual respect to build and sustain international institutions that are capable of crafting feasible solutions.

We are not talking about eliminating military preparedness, should the need arise. Scarcer dollars to fund those needs will inevitably lead to wiser choices that are both cost effective and suited to the needs of current times.

If Congressmen are concerned that their districts will lose funds that spark employment, the hundreds of billions of dollars saved should be devoted to programs long neglected within their districts, including infrastructure and a more robust safety net that favors the needs of the average citizen.

DISPELLING THE MYTHS

Ironically, the coronavirus has only revealed many of the fallacies embedded in the narrative that has led to a gross misallocation of our resources. Excessive military budgets have now limited our ability to fund more worthy programs, including protecting the American public against death and disease rather than a fantasized series of military threats.

The open door Trump has provided the military for more funds has been a long-standing policy over the past four years. The Center for Disease Control and Prevention may not have been on our radar, at that time, but based on today's anti-science animus, it was already compromised with budget cuts long before the pandemic reached our shores.

While we applaud our military, presidents like Eisenhower, an exalted military man, understood that business interests were always at play in negotiating contracts. He would not have been surprised to know that CEO's of these companies in the military industrial complex put profits ahead of national security, more interested in their balance sheets than the efficacy of their production timelines. As statistics reveal, over one hundred billion dollars have been spent over the past decade repurchasing corporate stock to boost its value for stockholders and corporate officers.

Some of the more egregious examples of unwarranted purchases that will neither add nor subtract from our military capabilities include a new generation of intercontinental ballistic missiles. This has already been identified as redundant and vulnerable to being fired without the proper systems to validate the need, as well as opening the way to the possibility of an accidental nuclear holocaust.

Added to this list is the military's Indo-Pacific Command. Not wanting to be left out of the feeding frenzy, it seized the opportunity to use fear mongering about China's growing military capability to be rewarded with another twenty billion dollars for a dubious 'Pacific Deterrence Initiative'.

Perhaps this is the wake-up call we have been waiting for. Will Congress continue to fund a bloated military without proper restraints while they dither regarding funding for the twenty million workers who are waiting for those unemployment checks to stay afloat during the Pandemic?

A TALE OF
FORGOTTEN LABOR

I s today's age of gross income inequality, and labor's sinking to an all time low in terms of its share of the national income, more of an aberration than the norm? The answer requires an in-depth look at the past, that is from the time we became an industrialized nation, to better understand when this was not the case.

A BRIEF HISTORY

The aftermath of the Civil War turned us into an industrial power. The era between 1870 and 1900 was known as the Gilded Age, when presidents were happy to let business run the country and workers marched to their tune. If they happened to rebel, there was a price to be paid.

The first leader to appear in the battle for workers' rights was Samuel Gompers, originally from England, who formed the American Federation of Labor (AFL) in the 1870's to represent the more skilled segment of labor. But for those with lesser skills, the going was tough when it came to organizing, for a number of reasons.

First, we as a nation have always applauded the ingenuity of the entrepreneur and the more successful, the higher his standing in a world of 'Social Darwinism' where survival of the fittest entitled him to a larger voice. Therefore, men like Andrew Carnegie were not likely to be challenged by workers. And if they dared to strike, the government was likely to grant an injunction and send in forces to restore order.

Such was the case with several important events, starting with the Haymarket Massacre in Chicago that ended in bloodshed on both sides. This was followed by The Pullman Workers Strike of the 1880's and the strike against U.S. Steel at the turn of the century, both of which set back the rights of workers for another two decades.

IMMIGRATION AND LABOR

Another factor adding to the pre-eminence of business interests was the continuous flow of immigrants. This allowed disgruntled workers to be readily replaced with a fresh supply of those eager to take their place. For the most part, that was seen and celebrated as part of the capitalist system. Certainly that was the case for the Irish fleeing the potato famine of the 1840's. They arrived on the East coast and settled in major cities, assisted by local political bosses in exchange for voting Democratic.

Many then found employment in the sweatshops of local manufacturing. Others became firefighters or policemen on the beat, again with the help of those political machines led by men like Boss Tweed in New York.

But when the color of their skin and features were different from the norm, those immigrants caused a vehement reaction. That was the case with the Chinese on the West Coast, accused of taking jobs at low wages to build a transcontinental railroad system. The Chinese Exclusion Act of the 1890's banned their entry for the next three decades and was expanded to include Japanese with what was called the Gentlemen's Agreement under Teddy Roosevelt.

Skin color counted as well for native-born Americans, seen as 'invaders' of sorts. That was the case with the Great Migration, as blacks fled the Jim Crow South that re-imposed a new form of second-class citizenship. They too migrated to the big East Coast cities of Chicago and New York, only to be excluded from good paying by both unions and business.

ENTER TEDDY ROOSEVELT

Teddy Roosevelt was the first President to take issue with the treatment of workers. He had already received an education prior to the presidency when he visited the slums of lower Manhattan with journalist Jacob Riis and saw the wretched living and working conditions first hand. As President, during a major coal strike that threatened the economy, he was appalled by the arrogance of the coal barons in dealing with Union representatives. He then demanded that they arbitrate issues, finding for labor on many of the key issues.

This led eventually to the founding of the United Mine Workers under the leadership of the charismatic John L. Lewis, who would become a political force in his own right.

LABOR AND THE CONSUMER ECONOMY

The advent of mass production in the early years of the 20th century, starting with Ford's Black Tin Lizzie, represented a major change in the relationship between labor and management. Suddenly, huge numbers of workers were being employed on massive assembly lines, doing repetitive work that did not require traditional apprenticeships.

Ford was smart enough to offer decent pay so that workers could afford to purchase his cars. But, it was only a matter of time before many workers would find common ground in creating unions to fight for additional benefits, including job security, decent pay and an eight hour day. (The vehemently anti-Union Henry Ford was known for strong-arming anyone suspected of trying to unionize workers.)

REWORKING CAPITALISM

It was not until FDR arrived on the scene to deal with the Great Depression that we began to question the myths of capitalism, including the assumption of the permanent dominance of business over labor.

During the 1930's, after finding business still set in its ways and unable to compromise, FDR shook things up with the groundbreaking National Labor Relations Act (drafted by New York's Senator Robert Wagner). This created the National Labor Relations Board (NLRB), to monitor disputes between management and labor, along with the right of labor unions to engage in collective bargaining with management.

Labor's organizing methods became bolder and more strategic under men like Walter Reuther, who headed the United Auto Workers (UAW). FDR stayed on the sidelines when Reuther staged the first sit down strike inside General Motors Fisher plant, bringing production to a halt.

GM, more interested in getting production going than prolonging a strike, quickly settled, as did Chrysler. But Ford, the last of the Big Three, held out until the government withheld vital contracts in the lead up to World War ll. A beaten Henry Ford watched his son Edsel give the UAW everything it demanded.

Having conquered the automobile industry, an emboldened Labor then went on to organize other major industries.

WORLD WAR LL

World War ll gave labor and the labor movement higher standing among the public and with the Administration. Where industry was reluctant to give up the profitability of a consumer driven economy, labor was far more willing to adapt to a wartime economy. In fact, it was Walter Reuther who first suggested transforming the auto industry into one that manufactured aircraft, which finally came to pass after Pearl Harbor. Unfortunately by then, we had already lost two years worth of precious production time and were now fighting a war on two fronts.

In addition, labor made sure that there were few if any strikes as industry geared up to become the 'Arsenal of Democracy', producing tens of thousands of battleships, tanks and planes in the fight against the Axis Powers.

By now, the labor movement also included women, as they entered the work place in large numbers for the first time to replace the men going overseas to fight. Eleanor Roosevelt, taking a personal interest in their wartime role, made sure to fight for additional benefits, including child day care.

She was also adept at seizing this opportunity to seek employment for those in the black community, both in industry and in the military. If we look at the eventual integration of our military, beginning with President Truman, we must give credit to Eleanor for beginning this process.

POST WAR LABOR

When the war ended, many women opted to remain on the job, rather than return to their prior life. The war also transformed the lives of many returning veterans. While many resumed their former jobs, a significant number elevated their standing in both the labor and the business community, thanks to the bipartisan GI Bill of Rights. This domestic piece of legislation was akin to the Marshall Plan overseas in unlocking human potential far beyond the dollars expended. This offered generous benefits, including a low cost college education and easy financing for housing. That in turn led to communities like Levittown and the migration of many growing middle class families to the suburbs.

In addition, the rationing of the war years had created tremendous pent up demand and spending power, making it easy to convert from a wartime economy to one that was hugely consumer driven. Throughout the next twenty years, the 50's and the 60's, middle class

Main Street America thrived on one income, with powerful unions negotiating a working wage in our factories along with benefits that offered a dignified retirement.

A GROWING DISTRUST OF GOVERNMENT

The politics of the times was bipartisan as well, with both Democrats and Republicans agreeing on much centrist legislation until the war in Vietnam and the Civil Rights legislation of LBJ fractured various coalitions. This led to a distrust of government among both liberals and conservatives for very different reasons.

A new Conservative ideology had been building in the West for some time, personified by Arizona Senator, Barry Goldwater preaching self-sufficiency and a return to so-called American values. It found its true messenger in former California Governor Ronald Reagan, who swept into the presidency in 1980 in a landslide with his optimistic message of 'morning in America'.

It was 'trickle-down economics' that was at the heart of the Reagan economy meaning that so-called prosperity would start with those job creators at the top and trickle down to the less worthy average worker. By then, the labor movement had lost much of its promise. Big city bosses were colluding with the day's less-than-stellar labor leaders to offer huge giveaways with oversized pension benefits that were bankrupting major cities like New York, Philadelphia and Chicago. This in turn provided an ideal target in the supposed fight against government excess and the need to restore fiscal sanity.

The answer at that moment was less government and a greater reliance on the majesty of the market place. As with all such movements, this provided excesses of its own. Over the next four decades, as the economy continued to grow, a new Gilded Age emerged with huge income inequality, in part due to a dramatic decline in union representation for the average worker and its ability to negotiate a living wage with significant benefits.

AN ALTERED AMERICAN LANDSCAPE

Often forgotten in this 'tale of labor' are the social consequences of this diminution of labor's value that permanently scars the landscape of America.

More money in the hands of corporate management or stockholders tend to be spent on a luxury item rather than a necessity. On the other hand, workers are inclined to spend their salaries immediately within the local community, giving rise to what is called the 'multiplier effect'. That in turn gave life to those stores along Main Street, providing additional layers of income that make a town thrive as the center of life for small town America.

Eisenhower, a product of Abilene Kansas, understood this when he cut a bloated military budget, saying that one more battle ship was the equivalent of building a hundred new schools.

In an era of trickle down economics, stagnating wages forced many to abandon Main Street, shopping instead at that new mall built along a stretch of highway. In short order, that local butcher or grocer was gone, along with a way of life etched in the drawings of Norman Rockwell. In the process, those roots that tied generations of families to a town, worshipping together and subscribing to a local newspaper, are gone as well.

The next generation has been affected as well. Local roots, providing a sense of security and predictability, have been replaced by faceless malls, where teenagers were dropped to spend time aimlessly wandering around and introduced to smoking pot to ease the emptiness.

Unfortunately, those consequences don't make headlines, especially when compared with the statistics that celebrate a booming economy. What will be required is a change of mindset ... one that values the lives of ordinary Americans over a system that coarsens our national dialogue and focuses only on a short term goals while ignoring the long-term consequences.

For the financial health of the country is based far more on the physical, mental and emotional health of all the people than the 'monies piled high by the bondsman', in the words of Lincoln.

A LOSING LEGACY

America's workers have been losing out for decades with labor's share of the national income declining to its lowest levels in seven decades. Along with globalization, much of the resultant wage stagnation, corporate downsizing and moving business off shore has been due to the decline in unions and their ability to negotiate on behalf of workers.

This includes a stark difference in the dollars spent by business and labor in terms of lobbying to get their interests represented in Congress ... where unions spent approximately fifty million dollars, while corporate America spent three billion dollars, merely sixty times that amount.

It should therefore come as no surprise that the U.S. is currently the only advanced industrial nation that does not have laws guaranteeing the most fundamental of benefits, including paid maternity leave, vacation time or paid sick days. Why should it, when the lack of unions or some other mechanism to challenge corporate malfeasance, allows the hiring of temps, trainees and part-timers to avoid paying the most basic benefits?

To put this in perspective, we now have the lowest minimum wage as a percentage of the median wage, currently at 34%, versus 62% in France and 54% in Britain.

GUIDED BY THE PAST

The fight for workers' rights has always faced strong headwinds, mainly because of a misplaced belief that hard work and self-reliance are part of America's heritage, rather than relying on help from either Unions or the government.

To combat this misplaced belief, we need a president who can explain and educate the public as to these long held beliefs that inhibit the right of workers to participate equitably and fairly in the economy. This of course would include a host of alternatives, much the way FDR experimented with new programs to cushion the impact of the Great Depression on ordinary Americans.

It was Lincoln who explained to a war-weary nation that slavery contradicted the basic premise of America, as laid out in the Declaration of Independence. That mandated that everyone was entitled to 'life, liberty and the pursuit of happiness'.

He then defined 'happiness' as including the right to the fruits of one's labor. Surely, a competent president could explain how today's workers are also entitled to the fruits of their labor...including fair pay, fair working conditions and a fair and dignified retirement. Anything less would be a bondage of sorts, with someone else exploiting your labor for their own benefit.

Our history, as previously laid out, illustrates that a bipartisan agreement as to this core belief in our Founding Documents will yield the best result, rather than a winner-take-all approach. While some will call this solution a move toward socialism, in truth, it will only make the wealth creation of capitalism more widely accepted.

To phrase the issue in a more constitutional manner, the lack of a level playing field of countervailing interests is at work in denying labor's advocates the most basic rights accorded elsewhere. Nor has globalization helped this process, with jobs moving overseas and sapping the strength of this domestic constituency. Ironically, in this era, unions or another viable alternative are needed more than ever to negotiate a fair severance package for workers who desperately need retraining to remain in the workplace.

LOOKING FOR SOLUTIONS

Then what are the options available to restore the worth of labor in the public square, especially with the possibility of Artificial

Intelligence and robotics poised to further diminishing employment opportunities?

The answer may lie with that activist president who can emulate a Teddy Roosevelt when he had Congress create a Bureau of Corporations to monitor corporate behavior, including the imposition of certain standard as to the rights of labor'.

This legislation should enshrine another type of 'civil rights', one not based on race, but representing a color blind standard for basic, workers' rights ... including a specific package of benefits that finally has the U.S. achieving parity with those of other industrialized nations.

While the amount of these benefits may vary according to various benchmarks to be spelled out by the appropriate mandated agency, these will no longer be subject to negotiations by unions or business and will apply to all workers, whether temporary, freelance or some other classification.

In line with finally putting an end to the so-called 'majesty of the market', perhaps it is time to address the myth that those at the top of the corporate ladder are the 'job creators, deserving huge salaries and bonuses. Again, we should let the proper agency monitor management's salary as an acceptable multiple of the average worker's salary.

Over time, additional benefits may be granted, including mandatory retraining programs and profit-sharing programs, currently restricted for the most part to reward management rather than the workers who contribute directly to that success.

A workers' Bill of Rights will represent a new era, leaving the failed policies of trickle-down economics behind and opening the way to a level playing field that balance the rights and privileges of business and labor.

If so-called American ingenuity is put to the task at hand, there are myriad ways to achieve this and restore the promise of America for all citizens.

THE NON-GROWTH ECONOMY OF THE FUTURE

THE PROMISE OF AMERICA

Whether it was business in the driver's seat or the president, neither power center could survive for long without delivering the steady growth that promised each successive generation a better life. For that was the essence of the promise of America and its marketplace of ideas and innovation.

That in turn required a revolution of sorts every so often regarding the methods of production. The Civil War ended in 1865 by creating an enhanced industrial machine in the North, with the growth of railroads leading the way. The post Civil War era then transitioned into the Gilded Age, where business and corruption reigned supreme right up to the dawn of the 20th Century.

That was followed by the advent of mass production, starting with Henry Ford's ingenious assembly line for automobiles, while Thomas Edison transformed the lives of ordinary Americans, building the consumer economy that fueled the Roaring 20's.

World War ll and the battle to defeat fascist Germany and Japan turned the country into the 'Arsenal of Democracy' under FDR. By the end of the war, we had created a new type of industrial behemoth along with a military machine such as the world had never seen. At the end of the war, this was converted to a consumer-driven economy on steroids, with the assumption that bigger was always better.

The war also brought a greater regard for science, particularly atomic energy, starting with the Manhattan Project conducted in complete secrecy in Los Alamos, New Mexico. The Project had been initiated by FDR based on a letter from the brilliant physicist, Albert Einstein. In that letter, he warned that Hitler might well be the first to unleash the awesome power of the atomic bomb, capable of destructive power such that the world had never seen. Thus began the first atomic arms race, one that we fortunately won to end the war against Japan in the Pacific.

We entered the 'atomic age' after the war, under the wise stewardship of President Dwight Eisenhower. He adeptly used the threat of atomic weaponry to keep the Soviets at bay under a policy of mutually assured destruction. In the process, he cut other military expenditures using these funds for worthy infrastructure programs, such as the Federal Interstate Highway Initiative and the St. Lawrence Seaway, which opened up the industrial base of the Midwest to the entire world.

These initiatives benefited all Americans; they also spurred significant economic growth. For Eisenhower, perhaps more than any other president of the modern era, understood his priorities and those he would preach to the American public.

With his appreciation for scientific research, he surrounded himself with an advisory committee that would lead us into space exploration and subsequently a moon landing under his successor, John F. Kennedy.

The next industrial revolution would be of another sort, one based on the inventive genius of a new breed of 'tinkerers' like Bill Gates, Steve Jobs and Elon Musk. These visionaries helped create the current age of technology that has vastly expanded an interconnected world, the astounding benefits and liabilities of which we are still sorting out today.

Unlike any other transformative moment, it incorporated novel miniaturization. Suddenly, bigger wasn't necessarily better. Neither was there a need for a vast manufacturing base that extracted mineral wealth and pollutants or the machinery to accomplish this. It all felt different, empowering individuals to access information once reserved to the elite in order to make financial and life decisions as to career opportunities. This now included even women in a third world country trying to escape a life of poverty and marital abuse.

But this technology did not replace those that are threatening the health of the planet.

CHANGING PERCEPTIONS

In the past, while change included the destruction of old ways of doing business, the drawbacks were usually far outweighed by the promise of expanded employment opportunities and increased productivity to be shared by everyone in forging a better life. This may not be true when it comes to the next cycle of economic change, known as 'the green revolution', responsible for converting the economy from one based on fossil fuel to one based on sustainable forms of energy, such as wind and solar.

In addressing this ground-breaking initiative, a future president will have to explain for the first time why increased productivity will now take a backseat to a higher goal, that of saving the planet for the greater good of humanity. To tackle these issues, a president will need to dispel long held beliefs as to the benefits of an ever-expanding world of productivity and technology. Perhaps, climate change is where this conversation should begin as the first manifestation that technology has its limits when compared with the destruction of our planet and way of life.

There may be no net employment gains in this transition. Change to sustainable sources of energy from one based on fossil fuels will require demolishing one infrastructure to be replace by another much leaner one. This will simply incur job loses in one area while adding more in another. Those dislocations will have to be dealt with, including long term unemployment benefits and job retraining programs...something we ignored for far too long in the transition to a global economy.

There will be a significant push back from a chorus of well financed lobbyists that will sound entirely reasonable and muddy the waters, once again requiring presidential leadership. But the reward will be there if we can muster the political will.

REDISTRIBUTING WEALTH

Ironically, as the world as a whole has grown richer through globalization and technology, the distribution of wealth has been increasingly skewed to favor the few. Perhaps, the next step among industrialized countries is not increased productivity, but rather a redistribution of wealth and re-prioritizing its use for the greater good of society.

As with Teddy Roosevelt, we need another president to impose government into the equation as the arbiter between corporate interests and the needs of society. But salesmanship must be part of the process. When Jimmy Carter tried to explain the concept of doing more with less, during the Oil Crisis of the 1970's, he used the unfortunate word 'malaise' to describe the spirit of America at the time. Ronald Reagan then followed with the message 'morning in America' and won the hearts of Americans.

Ironically, Reagan's message was actually a siren song of self-indulgence, corporate greed and less government that destroyed the middle class over the next four decades. If a Lincoln could explain the immorality of human enslavement, today's Lincoln must explain the immorality of 'old energy', enslaving us to a system that will destroy our planet if we do not take action now.

Like Lincoln, that individual must elevate the conversation beyond dollars and cents to one of moral authority. Redefining growth as a diminished goal among industrialized nations will not be easy.

Actually, the demographics of the world today will favor a non-growth economy. For, the slowdown in growth throughout the world may well be beyond the control of any one nation, based on a shrinking labor force in many countries.

By 2040, projections indicate that China's working age population will fall by over one hundred million along with negative growth. Yet, that may not preclude higher per capita growth in many countries as long as the economy shrinks less quickly than the population. In fact, this has been the case in Japan for some time, where slight economic growth has meant significantly higher per capita income. This also explains why unemployment remains relatively low in many industrialized countries, despite meager growth rates.

DEALING WITH NEW NORMS

Accepting these new norms will lessen the need to exaggerate the importance of continuous growth that threatens the viability of the planet. Still this requires a change in mindset that only a president with great moral authority and messaging skills can deliver.

If the planet is to survive, as we know it, the concept of 'growth for growth's sake' needs to be replaced by the concept of an economy that works for 'the common good of mankind'. That will require squelching any tendencies toward nationalism, a philosophy easy to exploit by those opposed to change who will encourage that isolationist strain and blame a corrupt world abroad for infringing on our freedoms.

The pathway to change will not be easy. The fossil fuel and petrochemical industries must be part of this conversation, dealt with by a 'carrot and stick' strategy, promising something of value in following 'acceptable norms in corporate behavior' with severe penalties for non-compliance.

Teddy Roosevelt accomplished some of this in taming corporate greed at the dawn of the Twentieth Century, including a newly empowered and enforced Sherman Anti-Trust Act. Even with this buy-in, the repercussions of a 'green revolution' will be mammoth, affecting the economies of various nations in different ways. It must begin with those industrialized nations that are the prime polluters and possess the wealth, infrastructure and institutions to weather the impact of change on their economies.

Initially, those cost-effective technologies of sustainable energy will foster a huge export market with sufficient funds generated to cushion the effects on those segments of society and industry that are negatively impacted. If globalization has taught us anything, it is that benefiting the many still comes with a cost in disrupting the lives of the most disaffected.

'Thinking big' on a global level through a reinvigorated Paris Accord does not mean arbitrarily imposing benchmarks from the top down. The nitty-gritty must be implemented at the grass root level. Change is difficult and those with an interest in maintaining the status quo could easily demagogue this transition as another plot by the liberal elite to take away our liberties.

The mantle of presidential greatness awaits that Chief Executive who will galvanize this country to abandon nationalist self-interest and the myth of capitalism's need for constant growth in order to focus on the greater good of humanity and the survival of our planet.

MAKING
THE RIGHT
APPOINTMENTS

N o president can do it all, unless he wants to fail miserably. Those who surround him include members of the Cabinet and the National Security Committee, as well as the Joint Chiefs of Staff.

There are also others who create the right environment for a president to do his job ... the gatekeepers, the confidantes, often with a special relationship.

These might include a Vice President with that personal chemistry or a chief-of-staff who guards the door to the Oval Office and prioritizes the agenda. It might even include that First Lady, who can provide that shoulder to lean on for comfort, and more than occasionally, some good advice.

And if the President were to turn to a Cabinet member, it would likely be the Secretary of State, that first among equals who is his emissary abroad in maintaining world order.

The only individual a president will not be dealing with once he makes that vital appointment is a Supreme Court justice, perhaps the most significant in determining his legacy.

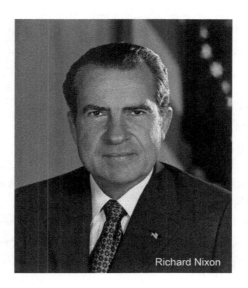

Richard Nixon

THE MAKING OF A VICE PRESIDENT

INTRODUCTION

J oe Biden's decision to select Kamala Harris as his Vice President was groundbreaking, and not just because of her gender! His current age makes it fairly likely that he will not seek a second term, leaving it quite possible that a woman of color may then seek the presidency.

While our nation's list of Vice Presidents has often been forgettable, especially prior to the modern era of greater executive authority, nevertheless it has always been a logical steppingstone to the presidency.

Let us delve into the history of our vice presidents, particularly those who then ascended to the presidency, in one way or another. Perhaps this can help to define those qualities that might yield the best results for that individual and for the public as well.

THE FOUNDING ERA

In the early years of our democracy, the vice-presidency was basically a concession prize for the individual who garnered the second most electoral votes, regardless of party affiliation. Certainly that was the case with John Adams' selection as Washington's Vice President in 1789.

For Adams, it was a dead end job right from the start. The only task clearly defined in the Constitution was his presiding over the Senate and casting that critical tie-breaking vote, when required. In fact, that is about all Adams did for eight years, even though, with the Constitution not specifying much else, he might have expanded that job and set precedents for the future.

That might have included acting as the president's liaison in promoting the Administration's agenda within the halls of Congress. Actually, that job fell to his archrival, Alexander Hamilton.

Adams' winning the presidency in 1796 was more of recognition of the vital role he had played in the nation's founding. However, many of the qualities he displayed as vice-president, his tendency toward distemper, his inability to connect with the people and his lack of political savvy, haunted his presidency as well.

Therefore, we should note that the vice presidency might well be considered a 'testing grounds' of sorts to evaluate the man (or woman) when and if he or she were to run for that higher office.

GAMING THE SYSTEM

There are a few vice presidents who viewed the office solely as a means to reach the presidency. This included John Calhoun, who served as Vice President for both John Quincy Adams and his successor, Andrew Jackson. Calhoun was the southern politician most responsible for writing the script for secession and the lead up to the Civil War. He, better than most, understood that a southerner could never be elected on his own, especially with the growing antipathy for slavery in both the North and the West.

He simply played the odds and hoped for the death of the incumbent. In fact, he continued with this tactic into the 1840's, without success.

Henry Clay, the Great Compromiser, and master of the Senate throughout three decades in the first half of the nineteenth century, refused to play this game.

Instead, he ran for president four times, narrowly losing in 1844 to James Polk. However, had he accepted the vice presidency that was offered in both 1840 and 1848, he would have been president upon the death of either of the two Whig presidents.

THE ISSUE OF COMPATIBILITY

An essential ingredient for a successful vice president, who aspires to higher office, is often based on his rapport with the President. Incompatibility has been the case more often than not for many vice presidents, who found themselves side-lined from the start.

Adams and Washington, though both great patriots, were certainly incompatible in many ways...one tall, regal and awe inspiring as well as slow to speak his mind and the other, short, stout and overly loquacious. In part, this is due to the fact that vice presidents have often been selected for unrelated reasons, including geographical balance and/or to ensure winning a critical state.

It can also be due to the expediency of the moment, by putting two political rivals on the ticket at the convention in a 'feel good moment' despite the vast differences in their personalities. Such was the case in 1960, when LBJ agreed to serve as Vice President in the Kennedy Administration. Until JFK's assassination, Johnson was mocked and excluded from decision making by the Kennedy family.

Perhaps the best case for compatibility 'gone astray' is that of Teddy Roosevelt and William Howard Taft. TR was a huge fan of his Vice President, so much so that he basically groomed Taft as his successor. But once out of office, he regretted not running for another term and began second guessing Taft's every move. He even went so far as to start a third party, The Bull Moose Party, to challenge Taft's re-election.

When factoring in the question of 'compatibility', we must also acknowledge that politicians who aspire to the highest office often have huge egos, which can lead to unpredictability. Finding the right 'partner' can be difficult at best for a. president, even when it appears to be a perfect match.

Occasionally, that presidential ego gets put aside. Such seems to have been the case with Bill Clinton and Al Gore, policy wonks in their own way, intellectually curious to a high degree and steeped in policy.

Gore's loss to George W. Bush in 2000, due to a highly partisan and questionable Supreme Court decision, may have represented one of the greatest losses to the nation in terms of competence. The nation may have avoided the disastrous war in Iraq, the effects of which are still with us today. The possible benefits of an early start in America's leadership role in addressing climate change are incalculable.

The lesson to be learned is that the qualities to be evaluated in a presidential contest often reside in the vice-presidency.

VICE PRESIDENTIAL DYSFUNCTION

The problems of incompatibility are minor when compared with the dysfunction that it can create when a president dies in office.

Such was the case with John Tyler and Andrew Johnson, both of whom ascended to the presidency and barely dodged impeachment.

To this day, no one understands the choice of Tyler, the running mate of the first Whig President, William Henry Harrison in 1840. But the chaos engendered by Harrison's death should have alerted all future presidents to select more wisely.

Tyler was, in fact, the first vice president to settle the question of whether he was to be considered the 'President' or merely a 'place holder' for the next duly elected president. This point had never been defined in the Constitution, but Tyler made sure to act presidential from the minute he assumed the office and settled that issue for future vice presidents.

John Tyler was not just a poor choice. He basically disavowed the Whig party's agenda and moved to annex Texas, thereby unleashing the spread of slavery... the very issue that Whigs, such as Henry Clay had fought against.

Andrew Johnson, a U.S. Senator from Tennessee, was Lincoln's unfortunate choice as Vice President for his second term, based on his loyalty to the Union and Lincoln's desire to heal the nation after the Civil War. Johnson's sympathies for slavery and slaveholders soon surfaced after Lincoln's assassination, beginning a political war of sorts with Congress that ended in an impeachment trial.

The lesson to be learned is that a potential vice president's core beliefs need to be more thoroughly vetted before he is selected.

FORTUITOUS CHOICES

Several Vice Presidents, also selected for the wrong reasons, have turned out to be excellent presidents upon the death of a President. These include Theodore Roosevelt and Harry Truman.

Roosevelt was seen as an iconoclast within the Republican Party and banished, so to speak, to the vice presidency to keep him out of mischief. Ironically, President William McKinley was assassinated within the first year of his second term, leaving Roosevelt free to unleash a progressive agenda that finally put an end to a Gilded Age of gross income inequality and corporate greed.

Senator Harry Truman, selected as FDR's running mate in 1944, when the President's health was rapidly deteriorating, was looked on disparagingly by many as the pawn of a political boss back in Kansas City. FDR basically kept him in the dark regarding major decisions being made to establish a new world order at the end of World War ll. When Roosevelt died only months into his fourth term, Truman surprised everyone with his take charge, decisive manner. He made it his business to learn quickly on the job, surrounding himself with a first rate team.

The lesson here is to look deep into what has formed a man's character and plumb, not just the deficits, but also those unique and positive qualities that can yield a first rate Chief Executive.

Theodore Roosevelt was a child of great wealth who overcame severe asthma. The process included developing an unquenchable thirst for knowledge as a housebound youth as well as harnessing an indomitable will to transform himself from a sickly child into a relentless outdoorsman.

Truman, a man of limited education, came from a family of farmers. He too overcame adversity in the form of extremely poor eyesight. This kept him housebound as well for much of his early years, where he read voraciously, particularly books on the great men of American history. His disability could easily have excluded him from serving in World War l. Yet, he yearned to serve, memorizing the eye chart in order to qualify and garnering a distinguished military record overseas in leading an artillery battery during a critical battle to win the war.

The lesson here is that character counts far beyond a superficial resume, starting with one's earliest years.

IDENTIFYING THE NEGATIVES

Some Vice Presidents are selected based on their merit in promoting a party's agenda. They are to connect with the party's base, while the president takes the high road and stays clear of party politics.

One might look at Richard Nixon as an example. On paper, he looked like a worthy candidate for Vice President, but he had built his career pursuing various witch-hunts of the McCarthy era, including smearing his opponent in a Senate race. There were always telltale signs of character flaws, noted by Eisenhower himself, including his tendency to be sanctimonious, manipulative and feeling looked down upon by the Eastern establishment.

By the time he attained the presidency, these character flaws had been glossed over with a slick public relations campaign that defined him as 'the new Nixon'. However, Watergate might be seen as the logical outcome for a man who felt besieged by his so-called 'enemies'.

The lesson learned is that a vice president who serves as a political 'hatchet man' may not have the character to represent the best interests of all the people.

STRENGTHS VERSUS WEAKNESSES

There are also Vice Presidents who have already had a long, distinguished career in government. Here, the assumption is that they will perform admirably as vice president, and ultimately, as president. Even then, there can be surprises, as with LBJ, a master at crafting legislation as Majority Leader in the Senate in the 1950's and '60's.

When he ascended to the presidency upon the assassination of JFK, he performed with exceptional ability in enacting the civil rights legislation that could never have been accomplished by his predecessor. However, as a neophyte in foreign affairs, LBJ was gamed mercilessly by his generals when it came to his handling the war in Vietnam.

Perhaps he simply lacked the intellectual curiosity to learn more on a subject that would be critical to his presidency. Truman, who also came to the presidency without experience in foreign affairs, took the time to read all the briefing books he could get his hands on, in preparation for his meeting with Stalin at Potsdam.

Let us add 'intellectual curiosity' to the list of qualifications that are needed in a Vice President, no matter how distinguished his prior role in government may appear to be, particularly when the presidency is thrust upon him.

A 'THIRD TERM' PRESIDENT

There are vice presidents who serve for two terms in a successful presidency and are seen as the heir apparent to continue that president's success with what is called 'his third term'.

That was certainly the case with George HW Bush and Ronald Reagan. Of course, they were totally different personalities. Reagan, the Great Communicator, selling highly questionable economics with an extremely sincere and convincing approach versus Bush, a centrist Republican from a patrician family, without the theatrical 'chops' of his predecessor.

Bush's first term went well, but he knew that Republicans were already suspicious of his party loyalty...having once called Reagan's economic policy 'voodoo economics'.

During Bush's first campaign, he tried to assuage those doubts by promising, 'read my lips, no new taxes!'

When Bush realized that Reaganomics had dug a huge hole in the federal budget, he did what any sensible person in that position would do...betrayed that promise and raised taxes. Unfortunately, his betrayal cost him his re-election bid, losing to Clinton. The lesson learned is that the mantle of a successful president can lay uneasily on the shoulders of his successor.

FILLING IN THE BLANKS

There are certain Vice Presidents who are specifically selected to make up for perceived deficits in the president's resume, to supposedly 'strengthen the ticket'.

Such was the case with George W. Bush, who was perceived as weak in the area of foreign affairs. He therefore tapped Dick Cheney for the job, a major player as Chief of Staff under Gerald Ford and Defense Secretary under George HW Bush.

Rather than support the President, Cheney built his own separate power structure within the White House. He then convinced the President to appoint his political ally, Donald Rumsfeld as Defense Secretary. The two then usurped the authority of the Secretary of State, Colin Powell, who might have prevented an ill-conceived rush to war with Iraq as our response to 9/11.

The lesson here may well be that a President should not look for a Vice President to 'fill in the blanks' in his resume. Or, said another way, he should look for a vice president who not only promotes the president's agenda, but argues his case internally.

SEALING A LEGACY

The next vice president to seek the presidency is Joe Biden, who seems to have had a close working relationship with President Barack Obama. The question will be whether the Obama mantle can be transferred to Biden, in a turbulent era of breaking constitutional norms by the current President, Donald Trump with more than a tinge of racism and white supremacy in his first term.

Actually, Biden's role in being perceived as Obama's 'third term' seems to have less to do with following his predecessor's policies, than being seen as a healer of sorts and calming the nation after a highly controversial and disruptive presidency.

And that supplies the last component to be discussed here in a vice president's attaining the presidency. The public already assumes a certain level of competence. Beyond competence, the public must view him as being possessed of a winning and calming personality.

This will make the election more about whether the country is more interested in restoring old norms of governance or remaining with a chaotic presidency that seems to have the support of enough voters to possibly win a second term.

SELECTING THE RIGHT CHIEF-OF-STAFF

A VITAL CHIEF-OF-STAFF

As Chris Whipple reminds us in his book, 'The Gatekeepers', perhaps one of the least heralded positions in government, and specifically in the Executive Branch, is that of Chief-of-Staff.

It would only be natural that President Eisenhower would formalize this job, a military man who appreciated echelon in a reporting structure that left him free to make those major decisions. That task would now be delegated to a Chief-of-Staff within the Executive Branch, an individual who intuitively understood the needs of a president, and acted as the gatekeeper in screening him from unnecessary distractions.

IN PRIOR TIMES

If we look back at our history, we can see others who operated in that capacity, without the title, and helped some of our most effective presidents succeed in accomplishing their agenda. The first would be Alexander Hamilton, whose objective was to 'make us a credit worthy and respected nation'. Washington agreed with concentrating on domestic issues and avoiding foreign entanglements in order to give the country room to grow.

Washington's favoring Hamilton over Jefferson in internal Cabinet debates was based on this point and the fact that Jefferson's competent performance at State was simply not as important as setting the nations course. Maintaining domestic tranquility and room to grow was the objective of the much-maligned Jay Treaty that was written to finally settle all those issues left unresolved with the British after the revolution. In fact, Hamilton, as Washington's alter ego, crafted many of the negotiating points to be hammered out by John Jay.

Washington gave Hamilton broad latitude in financial and other matters, recognizing his genius in writing overwhelmingly cogent arguments to 'sell' the Administration's policies. In fact, it was Hamilton who greatly expanded the powers of the Chief Executive, enumerated in little detail in the Constitution. It was his expanding the Constitution's 'implied powers' and 'necessary and proper' clauses that gave the document the adaptability to meet the times, for which Washington gets full credit.

Washington's faith in Hamilton and gratitude for his performance was illustrated often, perhaps most tellingly when a man who rarely expressed his emotions sent Hamilton a sterling silver wine cooler, along with a note saying, 'with gratitude and affection'. This takes on even greater meaning as it took place in the midst of the revelations of an affair he was conducting with the seductive Maria Reynolds. This scandal compromised Hamilton considerably in the eyes of his fellow Federalists and diminished his chances for ever seeking higher office.

Other earlier presidents, who used various individuals as surrogate chiefs-of-staff include Andrew Jackson who used the political skills of Martin Van Buren, better known as the Little Magician for inventing back room politics in Albany. When Jackson created political chaos by firing his entire cabinet, it was Van Buren who stepped in and smoothed over those damaged egos. His actions were ultimately rewarded with the vice presidency.

The list of surrogate chiefs of staff also includes Lincoln and his relationship with William Seward, the former governor and senator from New York. Seward had many contacts in government, leading to Lincoln naming him as his Secretary of State, a job he handled with great skill, particularly in keeping the British from interfering in the Civil War.

It was his interpersonal relationship with Lincoln most of all that elevated him to that higher rank. Without Seward by his side, Lincoln could never have withstood the pressures of the office, knowing how much he needed laughter and male companionship.

There were also men outside of the Cabinet who became invaluable advisors to some presidents, especially in setting wartime policy. Such was the case with Woodrow Wilson and Colonel Edward House, his political operative who spent much of his time in Europe during World War I. It was Colonel House who coordinated with both Clemenceau and Lloyd George in the lead up to our entry into the war on the side of the Allies.

A similar task was performed for FDR by Harry Hopkins, acting as his surrogate chief-of-staff as well in the lead up to World War II. Hopkins had actually been a former social worker who'd been put in charge of domestic initiatives such as the WPA, but FDR was smart enough to see his talents in building one-on-one relationships, which he did with remarkable results with Winston Churchill.

JAMES BAKER AND RONALD REAGAN

James Baker is generally recognized as the 'gold standard' for others to follow in his work as Chief of Staff for Ronald Reagan.

Baker, a long-term best friend of George HW Bush, was an improbable yet fortuitous choice, one that the astute Nancy Reagan supported. His personal attributes were on full display in keeping Reagan's old pals on the Far Right at bay and charming the press corps with his availability, while adeptly giving them context without spin. Nor did it hurt that Reagan was following a weak president in Jimmy Carter who was far less skilled at messaging.

Baker also acted like a top rate quarterback, empowering the White House staff to accomplish all the necessary grunt work in freeing the President to sell his agenda to the American public. He established a Legislative Strategy Group to make sure that Reagan's policies received a favorable reading in Congress.

By contrast, when Baker handed the job over to former Treasury Secretary Don Regan, all of that fell apart with a chief-of-staff more interested in his image than the president's well being. This allowed a dysfunctional group within the National Security Council to hatch a plan known as 'Iran-gate', trading weapons for hostages and transferring monies to anti-Sandinistas in Central America. This almost cost Reagan the presidency.

A review of other chief's-of-staff reveals their critical role in either aiding or containing the worst instincts of a president.

RICHARD NIXON (1968-1974)

The Watergate scandal occurred in large part because a paranoid president set up a second tier of operatives that did not report through Nixon's chief-of-staff, HR Haldeman.

While Nixon's ramblings were not taken seriously by Haldeman, there were others with a history of rogue behavior as CIA operatives, including Howard Hunt and Charles Colson, who were only too happy to act on the President's behalf. They planned a break-in at the office of Daniel Ellsberg, a psychiatrist in Los Angeles as an act of revenge for his passing the Pentagon Papers, indicting the rationale behind Vietnam War, to the New York Times.

That in turn led to a fatal break-in at the headquarters of the Democratic National Committee in the Watergate to steal information that might be useful in the upcoming presidential campaign. All of this took place simply to satisfy the paranoia of a president who was headed for an easy win for a second term.

JIMMY CARTER

When a President thinks he is the smartest person in the room, he is usually on his way to a doomed presidency. Such was the case with Jimmy Carter, a one time Governor from Georgia. Carter made the cardinal sin of surrounding himself with friends known as the 'Georgia Mafia', none of whom knew their way around the power brokers in Washington. This included young Hamilton Jordan, as his Chief-of-Staff, a man who prided himself on having run an un-conventional campaign, by portraying Carter as an unconventional political outsider.

Carter needed an insider's skills to deal with a hostile Congress.

Without that qualified gatekeeper, he became the most overbur-dened president in modern history, supposedly even overseeing the sign up list at the White House tennis court.

Where the American people needed a president who would use the 'bully pulpit' to project confidence, Carter preached 'malaise' of the American spirit, something any experienced chief-of-staff would have cautioned against.

BILL CLINTON (1992-2000)

Clinton's first term started on the wrong foot, naming a well-meaning friend from Arkansas as his chief of staff, rather than a Washington insider. Fortunately, by the second half of his first term, he was replaced by Leon Panetta, an experienced nine-term congressman from California.

Panetta enforced a disciplined chain of command as well as selective access to the Oval Office. His years in Congress helped Clinton face down a new breed of Republicans in Congress, led by Speaker Newt Gingrich, and armed with a new mantra that labeled Democrats as the enemy. Eventually, Gingrich overplayed his hand with the American public by initiating a government shutdown and Clinton regained the initiative to promote his agenda.

Unfortunately, no one could discipline the President when it came to his personal failings, not even a superb chief-of-staff. The Lewinsky Affair almost brought Clinton down, and forever tainted his presidency. Republicans again went too far in starting impeachment proceedings on grounds having nothing to do with his performance in office.

GEORGE W. BUSH (2000-2008)

George W. Bush appointed Andy Card as his Chief-of-Staff, a competent player in the Bush family circle. Previously Governor of Texas, Bush lacked foreign policy experience, a situation remedied by naming Dick Cheney as his Vice President, a man who had served as Defense Secretary in his father's administration.

No one could have foreseen the consequences a two-tiered reporting system that Cheney had carved out as a co-president of sorts. After 9/11, when President Bush needed to be in control of his National Security Council in determining critical issues abroad, the drumbeat toward war with Iraq was already emanating from Cheney's command central.

As a result, Chief-of-Staff Andy Card was effectively neutered as 'gatekeeper' in bringing all the players together, including the Secretary of State, to challenge various premises. There was no attempt to thrash out the major issues, including a search for a diplomatic solution. Such diplomacy would probably have thwarted the hubris that permeated the recommendations of an alternate Cheney/Rumsfeld universe.

The lesson learned is that even a competent Chief-of-Staff can be sidelined by political in fighting with a fragmented White House reporting system.

OBAMA (2008-2016)

When President Obama took office in January 2009, he and his chief-of- staff, Rahm Emanuel, a competent congressman from Chicago, faced an economy that was cratering, and a hostile Republican Party, focused on avoiding deficit spending. Nevertheless, the administration managed to pass a massive stimulus package, saving the auto industry from bankruptcy, and righting a crumbling economy.

The President was clear about his major initiatives starting with health care, the most consequential issue facing Americans. Fortunately Emanuel knew the pitfalls on this subject, having been burned trying to implement a similar plan for the Clinton administration. Although no Republican would vote for the bill, a sign of the growing culture wars that had closed the door on bi-partisanship, Democrats managed to get the legislation passed as a landmark achievement.

An exhausted Rahm Emanuel was replaced as chief-of-staff in Obama's second term by Denis McDonough, who turned out to be a perfect fit. He established clear lines of responsibility and accountability in tackling big issues such as immigration reform, climate change, and gun control.

With Republicans still committed to not working with the White House, the President implemented the idea of executive orders, which did not require the approval of a Republican controlled Congress.

McDonough went about forming small teams of professionals dedicated to big ideas, including a climate accord, an Iran nuclear deal and the diplomatic opening of Cuba. Suddenly, Obama's job approval ratings were on the rise. The issue would ultimately be the 'survivability' of these programs. Could executive actions be easily overturned by a successor with a different agenda, one who controlled Congress.

TRUMP (2016-)

President Donald Trump has replaced more than half a dozen chiefs-of-staff thus far, a verdict of sorts on his agenda and temperament. Incompetence and confusion have been elevated as the gold standard for a gatekeeper to this President, including the need to support a man who blatantly misrepresents the truth and damages a chief-of-staff's credibility in dealing with the press, a main function of the job.

THE EVOLVING ROLE OF
THE SECRETARY OF STATE

INTRODUCTION

B eing Secretary of State was once the steppingstone to the presidency, for men like Jefferson, Madison and Monroe. As the modern presidency evolved, many presidents took matters into their own hands, sometimes preferring to work through ex-officio surrogates. Such was the case with Woodrow Wilson in the lead up to World War l and his sending Colonel Edward House abroad to confer with the Allies before we entered the war.

FDR used Harry Hopkins in much the same way in World War ll, when he was not conducting foreign policy on his own with Churchill and Stalin. His death at the end of the war changed everything. A new President, inexperienced in foreign affairs entered the Oval Office. Suddenly, with an Iron Curtain descending over Eastern Europe, we were required to build a world order with the right individual as Secretary of State.

THE TRUMAN YEARS

Harry Truman was decisive, as well as a quick study. He also had a knack for surrounding himself with the right people, including George Marshall as his Secretary of State. Truman called the former

Army Chief of Staff, 'one of the great ones of the age', and the country readily agreed.

A policy of 'containment', the brainchild of the State Department's George Kennan, became the long-term policy to address a hostile Soviet Union and its ambitions to spread communism in Western Europe and elsewhere. The West would create various multilateral alliances, with the U.S. in the lead to thwart Soviet ambitions. This included the North Atlantic Treaty Organization (NATO), a mutual defense pact among the nations of Western Europe. General Eisenhower, the hero of the Normandy invasion, gave it great credibility when he was named as its first Commander-in-Chief.

Rebuilding the economies of those countries threatened by communism was the most urgent priority particularly with Britain no longer able to afford the cost of her former Empire. To fill this vacuum that might well nurture Soviet ambitions, Marshall developed the plan that bore his name.

The 'Marshall Plan' would have us spending huge sums to rebuild the economies of counties like Greece and Turkey. With this program, a country that often preferred isolationism at times of crisis became the official leader of the free world.

Marshall's tenure was followed by that of Dean Acheson as Secretary of State, another excellent choice for the Truman cabinet. He too would have to deal with communist aggression in novel ways, including the Berlin airlift to save a city deep in the Russian sector of a divided Germany.

However, he could not stop the people of China from preferring communism over the corrupt regime of the Nationalists under Chiang Kai shek. Nor could he stop the Russians from developing an atomic bomb of their own. A 'blame game' swept over Washington with men like Acheson accused of being 'soft on communism', as 'McCarthyism' entered the national vocabulary.

THE EISENHOWER YEARS

The Eisenhower era continued the policy of containment; but the President, based on his military background, added the advice of his National Security Council to his weekly agenda.

Eisenhower acted as his own Secretary of State on occasion, especially when he wisely refused to get involved in overseas adventurism that had the taint of colonialism. This included the Suez Crisis and France's plea for help to hold onto its colonial empire in Vietnam.

Over the next decades, an array of Secretaries of State assisted presidents in addressing Soviet aggression, as in the Cuban Middle Crisis during the Kennedy presidency. There were other moments when the State Department was overwhelmed by other power centers, including its failure to limit our involvement in Vietnam's internal war.

A NEW ERA

The end of the Cold War during the Reagan Administration represented another transformative moment, akin to our developing that 'containment' strategy that brought us to this moment. Once again, we would have to develop a long-term policy to address a new world order.

The Soviets had lost the Cold War, that battle between two economic systems and two different worldviews as to the fundamentals of a free society. We would now be dealing with the disintegration of the Soviet Union, which in itself would create many collateral issues to threaten an orderly world. Could we assist in this process or would this be seen as interference in their internal affairs?

At a time when the State Department's authority was being challenged by other power centers within the government, we desperately needed a Secretary of State with the vision and prestige of George Marshall to craft this new world order. Fortunately, Reagan's successor, George HW Bush assigned that role to the right individual.

ENTER JAMES BAKER III

James Baker was already known in Washington for his adept performance in the prior Reagan Administration as both Chief-of-Staff and Treasury Secretary. His courtly manner and daunting interpersonal skills already made his connections with members of Congress rock solid. More importantly, his deep friendship with President George HW Bush allowed him to speak for the nation with total credibility.

In his biography, The Politics of Diplomacy, Baker describes his novel yet highly efficient approach to managing The State Department. This vast institution consists of a sprawling presence in Washington, often referred to as 'Foggy Bottom', and vast overseas network of embassies, consulates and other institutions staffed by dedicated civil servants.

Baker's first job is to streamline an entrenched culture. He immediately changes the ground rules by appointing four highly competent and well-regarded under-secretaries who will report directly to him and oftentimes accompany him overseas.

Baker and the President agree that each initiative in international affairs needs to address three issues in transforming ideas into action:

* How each would play domestically

* How each would affect both allies and adversaries abroad

* How each would impact world order

GORBACHEV AND PERESTROIKA

His first major initiative centers on a rapidly disintegrating Soviet Union under a policy of 'perestroika', initiated by the transformative Mikhail Gorbachev. Baker goes to Congress to gain support for a major change in American foreign policy. For the first time in nearly forty years, we will be abandoning the highly successful policy of 'containment' enunciated under the Truman Administration in 1949. Instead, we will now attempt to engage a reconstructed Russia and guide it toward a productive economic model in collaboration with the West.

Baker cannot ignore the collateral damage that is already affecting those diverse nations that had been part of a sprawling Soviet Empire. These include a new set of transnational issues...such as terrorism, narcotics and access to weapons of mass destruction, all spawned by an inevitable power vacuum.

Baker and his undersecretaries travel to Moscow to forge a strong working relationship with Gorbachev's second-in-command, Edouard Shevardnadze. They listen to his concerns regarding the pace of change in Eastern Europe and Russia's fears of a unified, resurgent Germany. He addresses this by having German Chancellor Helmut Kohl commit to what he calls a more gradual 'prudent evolution', while smoothing the way for future talks between Kohl and Gorbachev.

He knows that addressing these issues in a timely manner will require modifying the existing cumbersome reporting structure at NATO, and make sure to streamline the process to what he calls '2 plus 4th'... eliminating all but four member nations from discussions. Now the two Germanys are permitted to craft the internal details of reunification while the four powers, Britain, France, the U.S. and Russia, who had presided over a divided Germany, continue to deal with external issues.

Still the Russians are uneasy about a unified Germany joining NATO at a time when they will be facing free elections in the Baltic States. Knowing that he can initiate some horse-trading to satisfy these concerns, Baker arranges for Kohl and Gorbachev to meet in Moscow. They sign an historic agreement, formally approving German reunification in exchange for billions of ransom money for a cash-starved Soviet economy.

Baker again follows the ground rules he and the President have established as critical to the success of any initiative. He shares all of this with Congress and those vital organizations within the Executive Branch, including the National Security Council and the Joint Chiefs of Staff.

ADDRESSING A HOSTILE IRAQ

Another crisis looms on the horizon when Iraq's dictator Saddam Hussein suddenly turns belligerent, accusing Kuwait of colluding with the U.S. and Israel to exceed OPEC limits on oil exports. When he invades his neighbor, Baker goes to work, putting together an alliance under UN Article 51, the same one used by the Truman Administration in 1951 to address the North Korean invasion of South Korea.

This allows member nations to enforce the right of self-defense while imposing non-military sanctions. However, Baker knows it is meaningless without Soviet support for any military action. He and his undersecretaries employ some shuttle diplomacy to have those who are still threatened by Iraq to share the financial burden. (Saudi Arabia contributes fifteen billion dollars to express its gratitude.)

When Saddam Hussein refuses to withdraw, Baker coordinates with the NSC's Brent Scowcroft and The Joint Chief's Colin Powell. They agree to force Iraq's hand with a UN resolution using phrases like 'all means necessary'. For now, Baker omits words like 'military force' to allay concerns within the Security Council. Still, he knows that in order to get that vital multinational military participation, he must go before the Security Council to plead his case.

Understanding the importance of the moment in the eyes of history, he insists that each nation's foreign minister be present. He speaks the words of history's lessons, saying, 'We must not let the UN go the way of the League of Nations. We must fulfill our common vision of a peaceful and just post Cold War world.'

His words have their desired affect, especially in alluding to Russia's role in a new world order. Gorbachev stands with the majority, adding a caveat that Saddam Hussein be given more opportunity to withdraw. Even though UN Article 51 covers military action, Baker again makes sure to seek the approval of Congress...a wise move considering that the vote of 52-47 in favor indicates great skepticism as to the wisdom of undertaking this war.

A battle plan is already in the works, with coalition troops training in the desert in Saudi Arabia. The President wisely cautions that only Arab forces are to liberate Kuwait City to avoid the taint of colonialism.

A devious Saddam Hussein tries to fracture the coalition by raining Scud missiles down on Israel to provoke a counterattack. Baker immediately sends his undersecretaries convince Israeli Prime Minister Shamir to hold his fire in exchange for Patriot Missiles to appease Israeli hawks in the Knesset, the Israeli parliament.

After one more futile attempt at peace, we launch Operation Desert Storm on February 24, 1991. Contrary to our estimates Iraqi resistance crumbles within forty-eight hours. However, Saddam Hussein manages to cling to power, negating the opportunity for Baker to forge a new way forward in the region.

A DESTABIZED RUSSIA

Baker parlays the moment to arrange a conference, with Gorbachev and President Bush as hosts, between Israel and her neighbors. He undertakes another round of shuttle diplomacy and uses what he calls 'creative ambiguity' to hype the possibilities, telling each side that the other is suddenly willing to reach a compromise. He gets the Israelis to end building settlements in exchange for a promise to table the UN Zionism Resolution. Hopes are high as the Palestinians finally agree to attend a Mideast Peace Conference in Madrid in the Fall of 1991.

Gorbachev's position is soon undermined by a coup to replace him. Baker loses an important ally when the military wavers in its support and Boris Yeltsin steps in to restore order, forcing Gorbachev into retirement. Ukraine, Belarus and others seize the moment to declare their independence. Yeltsin accepts this as the end of the Soviet Union and tries to establish an alternative Commonwealth of Independent States that can now enter NATO.

Baker is disappointed, but seizes this moment of uncertainty to use the resources of the international community (the IMF, the World Bank and GATT) to try to convert Russia from a command economy to one that is market driven. He also acts on the domestic front to have Congress repeal outdated Cold War legislation that will impede economic cooperation.

The chaos in Russia creates additional problems with those weaker breakaway republics, some embracing Christianity and others embracing Muslim Fundamentalism. Long suppressed strains of ethnic antagonism and latent nationalism surface throughout the region. For Baker, the big question remains: who will control the launch codes of nuclear missiles in an unstable region?

This same scenario now plays out in Yugoslavia as it fractures along ethic and nationalist lines. Slovenia, Croatia and Muslim Bosnia now break away as Christian Serbia threatens ethic cleansing and sets the stage for the siege to Sarajevo. Once again, Baker turns to the UN, this time acting under Resolution 757 to airlift humanitarian aid and send in peacekeepers while enacting an economic embargo on Serbia. His assistant secretaries, known as 'Team Baker', move an aircraft carrier into the region to impose a naval blockade, while cutting off the oil pipeline.

NEW CHALLENGES

Baker's term is almost at an end, yet his active mind sees new challenges ahead, as he quotes John Hay, the masterful Secretary of State under Teddy Roosevelt, who prophesied: 'The Mediterranean is the ocean of the past, the Atlantic the ocean of the present, and the Pacific the ocean of the future', a theme that will be exploited in the Obama presidency, two decades later.

As a confirmed internationalist, Baker is equally supportive of NAFTA, creating a free trade zone within the hemisphere to bring increased prosperity to Mexico and lower prices for the American consumer. He knows that a middle class, sinking under the weight of 'trickledown' economics, will need these lower prices to maintain its standard of living. However, he does not foresee those jobs moving overseas that will ultimately hollow out our manufacturing base in the Midwest, soon to be labeled 'The Rust Belt'.

Undoubtedly, had he remained at State, James Baker would have created another partnership, perhaps with the Commerce Department, to counter this with retraining programs and extended benefits.

Baker remains someone who sees strength in partnerships and alliances, rather than allowing obstacles to have us retreat from our goal. For him, the world must remain interconnected, with rising incomes and prosperity in poorer nations acting as the best antidote in fighting terrorism.

He continues to see the tenure of Acheson and Marshall as our most successful Secretaries of State, forging a new world order at a time of great uncertainty. Their confidence in our possessing a superior economic system, along with proper individual freedoms, has been redeemed.

But Baker's hopes are not realized. With the Clinton presidency in 1992, the Bush mantra of 'not gloating' over our success is foolishly set aside. Rather than including Russia in a new framework of cooperation on everything from economics to arms control, we invite the countries of Eastern Europe to join NATO, leaving Russia with an increased sense of isolation.

It will not be surprising to see the rise of a Putin, promising to restore the Soviet Union to its prior greatness. Nor will we have

Secretaries of State that can match the skills of a Marshall, Acheson or Baker.

A WORLD IN DISORDER

The loss of men such as these is particularly noteworthy in the lead-up to the second Iraqi War, when a President, lacking experience in foreign affairs, bypasses his Secretary of State and allows his Vice President to lead us into an ill-conceived war.

We are still dealing with the aftermath of this blunder almost twenty years later with the rise of terrorism. Instead of crafting a new Marshall Plan to deal with the worldwide poverty, we engage in decades of senseless nation building in cultures that cling to their own value system.

Americans are right to be skeptical of these policies and the reckless cost in blood and treasure. Unfortunately, skepticism breeds a loss of confidence in government, leaving us vulnerable to those who seek to trash those institutions. This has made us turn inward at a time when we need to address major issues that affect the global community. We have now retreated to a policy of ultra-nationalism and 'winning' according to the playbook of the current President, Donald Trump. Will we be able to dispel the doubts shared by much of the world as to our willingness to resume that leadership role? Only time will tell...

THOSE VITAL SUPREME COURT APPOINTMENTS

I n today's hyper-partisan world of politics, perhaps no presidential appointment will be as anticipated or scrutinized more than that of a Supreme Court Justice.

With lifetime tenure, that individual, one of nine on the current court, can have a significant impact on almost every aspect of our daily life. Hot button issues like the right to an abortion and the future of Obamacare may well be determined by that new voice on the Court.

If we look to the earliest years of our democracy right up to the current era, politics has always been at play when a President makes that vitally important appointment.

THE FOUNDING ERA OF JOHN MARSHALL
The Judiciary under Article lll of the Constitution was the least defined of the three branches of government. The Judiciary Act of 1789 called for a Chief Justice and five associate justices on the Supreme Court. Its lack of prestige was such that most of Washington's appointees over his eight years in office resigned at one time or another.

The tenure of Chief Justice Oliver Ellsworth of Connecticut had carried over into the presidency of John Adams. In December of 1800, he resigned, just as Adams term was coming to an end. The timing could not have been worse. The Federalist Party had just lost the election and was about to be succeeded by Thomas Jefferson, our first Republican President. Adams knew that if he did not replace Ellsworth with another Federalist before Jefferson took office in March of 1801, the Supreme Court would fall into Republican hands and much would be lost.

Adams went immediately to his Secretary of State, John Marshall, a man whom he regarded highly for his exceptional intelligence and loyalty, to discuss this urgent matter. Both men were concerned about a Jefferson presidency and the changes in government that would be made. After all, the Republicans had called their election 'The Revolution of 1800', promising to restore the principles of the American Revolution that they claimed to have been betrayed by Washington and his Federalists.

Adams determined then and there to draft a new Judiciary Act to replace that written into 1789, expanding the judiciary. It would enable the Federalists to appoint a raft of judges before Jefferson took office. But Adams still needed to find a new Chief Justice to replace Ellsworth, having already been turned down by several would-be candidates. Almost in desperation, he decided to offer the position to his Secretary of State, knowing Marshall's qualifications as a highly talented attorney. Much to his surprise, John Marshall accepted the position. Now a highly political appointment would build the judiciary into a formidable, independent third branch of government.

Over the next three decades, until his death in 1836, Marshall and his Supreme Court would craft over four hundred unanimous decisions that would change the face of the nation, heralding the supremacy of federal law over that of states that would be left with so called 'residual powers'.

He would codify the Court's power to review the constitutionality of both the legislation of Congress and the actions of the Chief Executive in the landmark case of <u>Marbury v. Madison</u>. Marshall would expansively interpret various phrases in the Constitution, such as the 'commerce clause', to build that commercially viable nation Alexander Hamilton envisioned.

His decisions would often enrage presidents such as Thomas Jefferson, who would call many of them 'twistifications' for defying so-called 'Republican principles'. Nevertheless, they were masterpieces of judicial logic and unassailable in building a body of precedent that would more than equal that of British common law.

Marshall would set other precedents, including having his Court dress in simple black robes and boarding together when the Court was in session to create a bond that would defy politics. Even when three successive Republican presidents appointed eight associate justices to the Court over the next twenty four years, Marshall was able to bend them to his will in yielding unanimous decisions.

As the Court's prestige grew, so did its surroundings, moving from a dingy basement in the Capitol to more exalted quarters with a buttressed ceiling.

Madison's appointment of Joseph Story as an Associate Justice in 1811, heralded fifteen years of a remarkable partnership in writing a host of landmark decisions. A higher power must have known that the death of John Marshall needed to be noted in history. For on the day of his funeral, the Liberty Bell in Philadelphia cracked as it tolled to mark the day.

ANDREW JACKSON AND THE TANEY COURT

Appointing the next Chief Justice would fall to Andrew Jackson. This was ironic in the sense that Jackson had been the one president to defy the Marshall Court in not upholding its decision in the Cherokee Nation case. A defiant Jackson had famously said, 'Marshall has made his decision, now let him enforce it!'.

Instead, the President decided that to protect the Cherokee Nation, they must be move to a more secure location in Oklahoma, thousands of miles away, leading to that tragic 'Trail of Tears'.

Jackson was already in his last year in office when he appointed Roger Taney as Chief Justice. Once again, it would be a highly political choice. For Taney had been a loyal political soldier in the

Jackson hierarchy, making many of the arrangements as Treasury Secretary leading up to the President's momentous decision to close down the Bank of the U.S. (BUS).

Taney would preside as Chief Justice for the next twenty-eight years, governed by a continuing belief in heightened federal authority over that of the states. The most important case by far that was decided by his Court had nothing to do with federal authority. Instead, it was a momentous decision intended to clear up decades of indecision as to the issue of slavery.

Dred Scott was a landmark case in terms of its horrendous effect in the lead-up to the Civil War. Where the Constitution's three-fifth's clause had designated a slave as only a portion of a man, this case eliminated any humanity, calling him nothing more than 'property', and as such, able to be taken anywhere in the Union by his master.

This decision was now supposed to finally end the discussion as to whether slavery could spread beyond the area where it had been sanctioned under the Constitution. Instead, it hardened attitudes North and South as both sides poured into various territories to determine its fate under state constitutions.

To make matters worse, Chief Justice Taney had been seen deep in conversation at the inaugural ceremony with then President Buchanan. It was widely assumed they had been discussing the case and the decision that was rendered only days later. If so, this would represent collusion between two branches, or what was being called, 'The Slave Conspiracy'. In the process, the Supreme Court lost much of its prestige as an impartial arbiter of the Constitution.

LINCOLN AND THE GILDED AGE

The next appointment of a Chief Justice would take place in December of 1864, a mere four months before Lincoln's assassination at the hands of John Wilkes Booth. Lincoln had already named four Associate Justices in his brief four years. One had been David

Davis, his best friend back in Springfield when both were riding circuit as fellow attorneys on the Illinois prairie.

He named Salmon P. Chase as Chief Justice, his political rival for the presidency, who had served as his very able Treasury Secretary. It had taken numerous behind-the-scene insults by Chase to finally have Lincoln accept his resignation. As always, Lincoln was a forgiving soul where he saw competence and the possibility of redemption.

Chase would serve for the next eight years, into the later years of the Grant presidency, as the South constructed the myth of 'The Lost Cause'. This claimed that the Civil War had been about preserving the noble cause of 'states rights', rather than slavery. In the process, the South rebuilt a new form of indentured servitude under a series of state laws that stripped away protections under the 13th, 14th and 15th Amendments. It was to be known as the era of 'Jim Crow'.

Fortunately, the next president, Andrew Johnson did not have the opportunity to appoint anyone to the Supreme Court when he stepped in to complete Lincoln's second term. If he had, he would undoubtedly have appointed a southern sympathizer as he continued to veto every congressional act to fulfill the Lincoln legacy.

President Grant's choice as the next Chief Justice was Morrison Waite, a name that we hardly recognize. For he would serve for the next fourteen years, well into what was known as 'The Gilded Age'. It was a time when business, rather than the government, ran the country and the titans of industry began their accumulation of great wealth.

He would be followed by Melville Fuller, appointed by President Grover Cleveland in 1888, who would serve as Chief Justice for twenty-one years.

The first twelve years would be a continuation of the Gilded Age as growing income inequality continued to grow. The Court was happy to rule in favor of business as it dealt with growing labor unrest. Incidents like The Haymarket in Chicago had federal troops called in to stem the violence with a significant number of deaths on both sides. A strike at Andrew Carnegie's U.S. Steel ended with fewer workers' rights and a fear of the consequences of future strikes.

Perhaps the most prominent decision of the Fuller Court was another that echoed the times as to our racial divide. This one sanctioned the policies of segregation in the South under <u>Plessy v. Ferguson</u>, again satisfying the South's way of dealing with the Negro issue. It approved the policy of 'separate but equal', claiming that 'equal facilities' justified the policy of segregation under federal law.

THE PROGRESSIVE ERA

Although Theodore Roosevelt would not have the opportunity to appoint a Chief Justice during his tenure, extending from 1901-1908, his larger-than-life footprint was stamped on both the presidency and the Court.

He appointed three stellar Associate Justices, most notably Oliver Wendell Holmes Jr. in 1903. Holmes would serve for the next twenty-nine years, retiring in 1932, at the height of the Great Depression and shortly before FDR would win the presidency. His judicial brilliance would dominate the Court for much of that time, even in dissenting opinions. For the most part, Roosevelt's actions to end the Gilded Age went unopposed by the Court. This included expanding workers' rights and diminishing the power of business through legislation, including a re-energized Sherman Anti-Trust Act.

Ironically, it would be Roosevelt's successor as president, William Howard Taft, who would have the unusual opportunity to continue transforming the Court, naming six justices, including elevating Associate Justice Edward Douglass White to Chief Justice. For that would have been Roosevelt's second term in office, if he had not announced that he would not run again in 1908, having considered his first term in succeeding President McKinley as a full term.

Because Roosevelt ultimately regretted that decision, he challenged Taft for the Republican nomination in 1912. When he lost that battle, he formed the Bull Moose Party and ran as a third party candidate, allowing Democrat Woodrow Wilson to slip into the presidency and continue the progressive era, begun under Roosevelt, with three appointments of Associate Justices. This included Louis Brandeis, who would serve on the Court for the next twenty-two years, ruling on much of the New Deal legislation enacted under FDR.

THE JAZZ AGE OF THE '20's
William Howard Taft, who was never comfortable succeeding the feisty Teddy Roosevelt as president, found his calling when Warren Harding selected him as Chief Justice in 1921. That decade, known as the Roaring 20's, was once again one of heightened business interests. The Taft Court was happy to mirror those values of 'laissez faire' unfettered capitalism. For once, the average citizen participated in the riches of a booming stock market.

Herbert Hoover was perhaps the individual with the best resume to assume the presidency in 1928, with the expectation that the economy would continue to boom under his stewardship. Within the first year and a half of his term, those dreams were shattered with the crash of the stock market in October of 1929.

A man with a rigid code of economic beliefs, Hoover was unable or unwilling to attack the Great Depression with a new economic policy. He did however, make some notable appointments to the Court, including Charles Evans Hughes as Chief Justice and Benjamin Cardozo as an Associate Justice. Both men were highly qualified and accomplished and would play a major role shortly in evaluating the legislation of the New Deal.

FDR AND THE NEW DEAL
The era of the presidency of Franklin D. Roosevelt, spanning four terms in office and extending from 1932 to 1945, would be one of

great change, including in the Judiciary. FDR would appoint a record nine justices in that time, including elevating Harlan F. Stone as Chief Justice. This was also the time when we entered World War ll with the Japanese attack in Pearl Harbor.

The Associate Justices appointed by FDR were particularly notable. All were possessed of great judicial talent and held strong beliefs as to the role of the Court in superseding congressional authority. These included Hugo Black, Felix Frankfurter, William O. Douglas and Robert Jackson. They would form various liberal coalitions over the next decade, debating when and where the Court might be intruding on matters that belonged to the Legislature.

Throughout the 1930's, many of them would have to deal conservative Chief Justice, Charles Evans Hughes. He had been an ally of Teddy Roosevelt in his early years in politics in taking on vested interests in New York State. He then served as a highly competent reformist Governor before serving on the Supreme Court as an Associate Justice.

After supporting much of the early New Deal legislation, Hughes began to draw a line in the sand by the mid-30's. His decision in the <u>Schechter Poultry Case</u> deemed the National Industrial Recovery Act too intrusive in the dealings of a business that did not engage in interstate commerce. Obviously, even the Liberal wing of the Court must have agreed as they joined Hughes in a unanimous decision. Individual entrepreneurship on a small scale was still safe from government oversight.

FDR, watching too much legislation being declared unconstitutional, decided to fight back with a plan to increase the number of justices on the court and thwart the opposition. In truth, this move was grounded in precedent, with the number of justices having varied over the life of the Court. However, this represented the first attempt to negate or ignore rulings by the Court since the time of Andrew Jackson. The public reacted accordingly, seeing this as overreach by the Chief Executive in poll after poll.

Ultimately, FDR lost the battle, but won the war. Hughes was fore-warned of the possible consequences, and the Court once again began to favorably consider further legislation as constitutional. This included the Wagner Act, creating the National Labor Relations Board as well as various provisions of the Social Security Act.

After Hughes' retirement, Chief Justice Stone, along with Justices Brandeis and Cardozo, formed the liberal bloc, known as the 'Three Musketeers'. It is therefore instructive to note that even a liberal court could write a decision like that in the Karematsu case. This upheld the constitutionality of placing citizens of Japanese origin in internment camps during World War II.

TRUMAN AND THE VINSON COURT

The death of FDR in April of 1945 was not totally unexpected, given the President's obvious rapidly declining health. Still, a huge sense of responsibility was thrust on the shoulders of Vice President Harry Truman. He had appointed Fred Vinson, a loyal political ally, as his Treasury Secretary. When Chief Justice Stone died suddenly in 1946, Truman named Vinson as his replacement, the last Democratic Chief Justice to serve in that position up to the current day.

Vinson was one of the few to dissent in the <u>Youngstown Steel Case</u>, when the Court ruled against Truman's seizure of the nation's steel mills during the Korean War as executive overreach. He can also be credited with patching up dissension on the Court with one liberal wing led by Associate Justice Hugo Black, and the other by Felix Frankfurter.

An additional decision to note as symptomatic of the times was his decision not to review the death sentence of Julius and Ethel Rosenberg for aiding the Russians in developing the atomic bomb.

THE WARREN COURT

By the time Vinson died a year and a half into the Eisenhower Administration, the President had already promised the next appointment on the Court to former California Governor Earl Warren. Eisenhower, an avowed centrist, was not prepared for the Warren Court, as it famously earned a reputation for groundbreaking decisions. He would later be quoted as saying that Warren's appointment as Chief Justice was 'the biggest damn-fool mistake I ever made'.

Warren acted in the mode of John Marshall, slowly gaining the support of all the justices, despite their differing views as to the role of the Judiciary. Frankfurter and Jackson insisted on judicial restraint and deference to the powers of the other two branches. Justices Black and Douglas, on the other hand, favored a more activist role in matters related to the Constitution's guarantee of natural rights and individual liberties.

Warren's great strength was again one he shared with the formidable John Marshall...putting coalitions together and cajoling members of the Court to lead them toward his writing unanimous decisions on important cases. Such was the case in the landmark decision in <u>Brown v. Board of Education</u>, eliminating segregation in public schools as unconstitutional under the 14th Amendment and trashing the standard of 'separate but equal'.

The decision would ultimately create a constitutional crisis of sorts as Governor Faubus of Arkansas brought in local police to prevent integration in Little Rock's schools. Eisenhower, to his credit, stood behind the Court's decision despite his reservations, sending in the National Guard and forcing Faubus to step aside.

Additional unanimous decisions would follow on the subject of integration, including a lower court decision labeling segregated buses as unconstitutional as well as prohibiting segregation in public accommodations.

Other landmark decisions would be written by the Warren Court to transform legal procedures in criminal cases. These included <u>Gideon v. Wainwright</u>, establishing the right to an attorney in criminal cases and <u>Miranda v. Arizona</u>, requiring arresting officers to advise defendants of constitutional protections. Pushback on the Right would ultimately label these decisions as 'handcuffing the police'.

Decisions reinforcing the policy and principle of 'one man, one vote' under the Constitution's 'equal protection clause' were calculated to thwart redistricting plans designed to disenfranchise African Americans. Still, the Court proceeded cautiously, lest it be caught in a 'political thicket' without clear measurable guidelines... an issue that would continue to challenge the Court right up to this day,

A BACKLASH FROM THE RIGHT
Many of the cases before the Warren Court, including one prohibiting mandatory prayer in public schools, eventually provoked a backlash from Far Right organizations such as the John Birch Society. This would represent the beginning of an assault on the Court that would dramatically alter public perceptions. It would also herald the march of the entire Republican Party further to the Right. Nevertheless, to this day, many of those Court's decisions have remained established law.

A Supreme Court appointment to take note of during the presidency of Lyndon Baines Johnson was the appointment of Thurgood Marshall in 1967 as the first black member of the Court. Marshall's appointment reflected his years in promoting black rights and most importantly, his role in assembling the persuasive case that determined the outcome in <u>Brown v. Board of Education</u>. He would remain an important voice on the Court over the next twenty-four years.

However, this ends an era of expanding the rights and protections for the average Americans. With the Nixon presidency, the Court will to move to the Right, promising to end what it calls 'judicial activism'. Ironically, it will be replaced with other judicial theories, known as 'textualism' or 'originalism'.

According to many, these will be nothing more than another 'judicial activism clothed in the false garb of modesty'. It is intended to prevent jurists from following the traditions, begun in the founding era by John Marshall, of viewing the Constitution as a fluid document to be interpreted with a respect for precedent and an understanding of the current needs of a changing society.

That is another story that deserves a telling of its own.

APPOINTING JUSTICES IN A CONTENTIOUS ERA

As stated previously, the importance of the appointment of a Supreme Court Justice by a sitting president remains one of the most overlooked and underestimated achievements in his or her tenure.

Gerald Ford wrote a very telling note to his only Court appointment, John Paul Stevens, when he completed Nixon's second term. The vastly underestimated Ford, who was much more than a place-holder in serving for two brief years, wrote that if he were recognized for nothing else, his appointment of the esteemed, and brilliant jurist from the Midwest was perhaps his most notable achievement.

Stevens would be needed more than ever from the Nixon era on, with the increasing intrusion of politics under the Senate's constitutional role in confirming presidential appointments to the Court.

THE END OF BIPARTISANSHIP
Lyndon Johnson was still President in 1968, when Chief Justice Warren announced his intention to retire. The President immediately nominated his long time friend, Abe Fortas, who was already serving on the Court as an Associate Justice. A Senate filibuster ended the confirmation process. Warren remained in office until June of 1969, giving Richard Nixon his first opportunity to reshape the Court.

Nixon, always clever in his use of the words to imply fealty to Republican dogma, had already noted his intention to nominate only 'strict constructionists' to the Court. That was not surprising, considering his campaign had already implemented the 'Southern Strategy' to put the region in the Republican column.

THE BURGER COURT

Nixon's selection of Warren Burger as Chief Justice seemed in line with the expected shift to the Right. Burger had climbed through the Republican ranks before being appointed to the D.C. Court of Appeals, a traditional gateway to the Supreme Court. However, contrary to expectations, the Court delivered a number of ground-breaking liberal decisions, most notably <u>Roe v. Wade</u> in 1973, recognizing the right to privacy in prohibiting states from banning abortions and abortion clinics.

Nixon, always understanding the need to betray party dogma at certain points, had by then appointed a number of highly qualified, independent-minded Associate Justices to the Court. These included Harry Blackmun, Lewis Powell and William Rehnquist, who now joined previous appointees to craft a highly controversial opinion.

<u>Roe v. Wade</u> was based in part on the theory that the Bill of Rights included what were called 'penumbras', or logical extensions, around the Due Process clause, including what was termed the 'right to privacy'.

In retrospect, the decision may have had better grounding in constitutional law if it had been based on the more widely accepted theory of 'substantive due process' under the Fourteenth Amendment. This clause had already been interpreted to expand the right beyond procedural protections to include substantive rights, such as freedom of personal choice in matters of marriage and family.

The blowback on the Right was significant. A large segment of the public, already alarmed with the decisions of the Warren Court, now found a Republican led Court going even further in attacking core values of the religious community.

Opposition to this decision is still with us today and is in large measure responsible for building the Evangelical movement that is such an important a part of the current Republican Party.

WATERGATE & BEYOND

By the summer of 1974, Congressional hearings on a break-in at Democratic headquarters, in a condominium known as the Watergate, were heating up. The President's Chief-of-Staff had re-signed in disgrace and was facing criminal charges, leaving Nixon more vulnerable. At that moment, Alexander Butterfield, a White House aide, made a stunning revelation in his testimony before Congress regarding the President recording conversations in the Oval Office, with a system originally installed by his predecessor.

The very existence of tapes that might include highly sensitive conversations on any number of subjects, including those burglaries at the Watergate, naturally led to Congress' demanding that the White House immediately turn over those tapes.

When Nixon denied the request, claiming executive privilege, the case quickly moved to the Court. Chief Justice Burger wrote the unanimous decision in <u>United States v. Nixon</u>, denying the President's claims and instructing that he turn over the tapes. Considering the composition of the Court, with many justices be-holden to Nixon for their appointment, this was a stunning display of judicial independence.

Burger's tenure came to an end in 1986. By then, President Ford, filling out the balance of Nixon's term in office, had appointed John Paul Stevens to replace William O. Douglass, the long-standing liberal icon from the New Deal era. It was a fitting replacement in terms of judicial brilliance and a somewhat playful personality. Stevens would go on to serve with distinction for the next thirty-four years, retiring in 2010, during the Obama presidency.

It should be noted in passing that Jimmy Carter was one of the very few, or perhaps the only president not to have the opportunity to make an appointment to the Supreme Court during his presidency.

THE REAGAN ERA

Ronald Reagan was already seen as a President who would govern from the Right, supposedly reducing the role of government. That definitely did not include the Court, whose decisions were important in expediting the process. It was therefore not surprising that his first appointment was William Rehnquist, a social conservative and constitutional scholar whom Reagan elevated to Chief Justice.

Rehnquist had long auditioned for the position as anchor for the Court's conservative minority, polishing its arguments to include the new judicial philosophy of 'originalism', as well as other contentious subjects, including abortion rights and religious liberty. Reagan then replaced Rehnquist with Antonin (Nino) Scalia, a man with a brilliant mind who used that brilliance to gain enough allies to trash longstanding precedents with abandon.

The President also appointed Sandra Day O'Connor, the first woman to reach the Court, in addition to Anthony Kennedy. Both were seen as solid additions to the Court's conservative ranks to give due deference to states' rights and judicial restraint.

The expectation was that the Court would no longer view the Constitution as a living document, evolving to suit the times, in the manner of a John Marshall. This had long been disdained by a growing chorus of Right wing think tanks, accusing liberals of corrupting the judiciary. The Court would now replace this with 'originalism' and 'textualism', theories that preferred to plumb the intent of those writing the Constitution in 1789 ... a new judicial activism of another sort.

When Lewis Powell retired from the Court, Reagan nominated Robert Bork to replace him. Democrats, already feeling besieged, were not at all happy with Bork's ambiguity as to preserving <u>Roe v.</u>

<u>Wade</u>. They rejected the appointment based on his politics rather than his judicial ability and set a precedent for the future. Judges would now be selected on the basis of a loyalty oath to one particular form of jurisprudence, rather than as impartial guardians of the rule of law.

AN EVOLVING JUDICIARY

If <u>Roe v. Wade</u> upset the Right, a host of dissenting decisions began to shape future decisions on such issues as campaign finance and gun control that would have the same effect on the Left.

In a case that prohibited the spending of corporate funds to support or oppose a candidate for state office, Justices Scalia and Kennedy wrote a dissenting opinion that would be a precursor for the Citizens United decision twenty years later.

Another case discussed the origins of the Second Amendment, laying out in great detail how the Amendment had been intended to protect a state's 'well regulated Militia' against the intrusions by the Federal Government. It even described the type of weaponry in great detail. However, this would be ignored in a future decision that transformed the Amendment into one protecting individual rights rather than states rights.

Other contentious issues of this era concerned the rights of defendants in capital punishment cases, especially when new DNA tests were overturning prior decisions. This spurred a further discussion as to the breadth and meaning of "cruel and unusual punishment' under the Eighth Amendment as it applied to the death penalty when a defendant was severely mentally diminished.

Throughout the Reagan years, the Court's tactics regarding abortion rights under <u>Roe v. Wade</u> was to focus on imposing greater legal restrictions, while upholding the fundamental decision as established law.

GEORGE HW BUSH

The presidency of George HW Bush saw the nomination of two Associate Justices. David Souter would be the first to face a battery of cameras in coming before the Senate Judiciary Committee. This process would now introduce the American public, for better or worse, to an element of congressional grandstanding in their hearings.

This same issue played out in a larger than life manner in the hearings to confirm President Bush's choice of Clarence Thomas to replace the retiring 'lion for black rights', Thurgood Marshall. As Thomas was also black, there was an element of acknowledging that this seat would be given to a minority candidate.

With televised hearings a pro forma event in the Senate approval process, the American public would view the accusations of Anita Hill regarding sexual harassment by Thomas. For the first time, this raised an issue going to character rather than judicial qualifications. This would play out once again in the recent hearings for Brett Kavanaugh, as both sides focused on the nominee's 'character issues' that might be considered as a window into so-called 'judicial temperament'.

THE CLINTON ERA

In 1993, a Democratic President entered their Oval Office, after twelve years of a march toward the Right. Clinton selected a second woman, Ruth Bader Ginsburg, who had already earned a reputation paving the way for women's rights under the banner of 'gender-based discrimination'.

Clinton's next appointment was Stephen Breyer, who would deliver strong dissenting opinions in cases involving gun ownership and its questionable use in areas surrounding schools. When the Court invalidated the congressional Gun-Free Zones Act of 1990 on the grounds that the facts did not involve the 'commerce clause', Justice Breyer ably rejected this claim on the basis that a quality education was a vital element in maintaining national and international commerce.

Justice John Paul Stevens, the elder statesman on the Court, gave further credence to Breyer's claims, saying that guns are articles of commerce and also articles that can be used to restrain commerce, giving Congress the power to regulate the possession of firearms.

This judicial era also represented an increasing focus on issues that resonated as part of the 'culture wars' between Right and Left. For the first time since the Nixon era, the court ruled on a case involving the personal behavior of the President. However this time, in the Paula Jones case, the 'crimes' had no connection to the performance of presidential duties. Yet, the Court determined that President Clinton was not immune from liability for any unlawful conduct that may have occurred prior to the he presidency.

GROWING CORPORATE POWER

By now, the legacy of the Reagan's trickledown economics had created growing economic inequality and corporate wealth. It would only be a matter of time before a new Gilded Age had those corporations demanding their due, with a Court more than willing to comply.

The first hint of this transformative moment appeared in 1999 in cases questioning the standard in <u>Buckley v. Valero</u>, which imposed limits on contributions to political candidates. Tellingly, those questioning this standard were Thomas, Scalia, and Kennedy.

For the moment, Justice Stevens had the last word, saying 'Money is property. It is not speech. Treatment of campaign contributions as a form of speech misleadingly enhances the appeal of the argument'. For now, the Court continued to bar corporations from making political contributions, including those from not-for-profit advocacy corporations.

Another major case before the Court at this time was <u>Bush v. Gore</u>, deciding the outcome of the presidential election of 2000 that was currently in dispute. The Court denied a recount on the basis that there was no acceptable standard and went on to decide the election for George W. Bush.

Although the Constitution and precedent clearly mandated the House to manage the proceedings when the election results were in doubt, the Court stepped in, with a decision that can only be described as the height of 'judicial activism'.

THE ROBERTS COURT

In the Fall of 2005, more major changes in the composition of the Court took place when Sandra Day O'Connor retired and Chief Justice Rehnquist died, thus leaving two openings on the Court.

President Bush 43 then appointed Associate Justice John Roberts as Chief Justice and had Samuel Alito replacing O'Connor. Roberts was well qualified, having served on the prestigious Court of Appeals and in the Justice Departments of the Reagan and Bush Administrations. During his confirmation hearings, he tried his best to sound non-partisan in an era of heightened partisanship, describing his job as 'calling balls and strikes, and not to pitch or bat.'

He also stated his respect for 'stare decisis' and established precedent, contrary to Justice Scalia, who dominated the conservative wing at the moment. However, he affirmed that he would have no trouble overturning a so-called wrong decision, as 'Brown' did with 'Plessy'.

The Court continued to move further Right in the <u>McCutcheon Case</u>, now declaring that there would be no 'aggregate limits' on campaign contributions, based on the First Amendment's guarantee of free speech. The Court went even further in limiting restrictions on corporations from using funds in their treasury to finance 'express advocacy', narrowing that term of art to a point that negated the standard.

The liberal wing was now the one that would have to make its voice heard in numerous dissents. Justice Ginsburg, the formidable

RBG, chastised the Court for upholding a ban on the procedure known as 'a partial birth abortion', without an exception regarding concern for the mother's life. Justice Ginsburg also dissented in another case, where Justice Alito wrote for the majority, basing dismissal of pay discrimination on a questionable technicality. In the end, Congress agreed with Justice Ginsburg's dissent, calling this blatant pay discrimination on the basis of sex and acting to correct this with the Lilly Ledbetter Fair Pay Act.

Concerns over global warming now surfaced in cases before the Court, when it determined that Massachusetts had legal standing, based on threats to its coastline, to challenge the EPA's claim of lack of statutory authority to issue mandatory guidelines on global warming.

It was the issue of gun ownership, however, that most echoed the radicalization of the reading of the Constitution by the Court. United States v. Miller had already set the precedent regarding 'the right to bear arms'. District of Columbia v. Heller of 2008, written by Justice Scalia in a 5-4 decision, now completely disregarded the history behind the Amendment, which was to guard against a national standing army threatening the rights of a state militia.

Instead, this Amendment was now transformed from protecting states from the intrusion by the federal government into one elevating individual rights when it came to gun ownership. Justice Stevens in his dissent called this 'the worst self-inflicted wound in the Court's history', citing the role of Congress in this area versus the very 'judicial activism' that the Right has scorned.

The history of escalating gun violence since the Heller decision speaks to the accuracy Justice Stevens' remark. Congress, which has the constitutional authority to correct the situation, remained powerless under Republicans who were more inclined to pander to a vital source of strategic votes.

THE OBAMA COURT
The election in 2008 of Barak Obama, our first black President, looked like an opportunity to alter the conservative nature of Court decisions. Justice David Souter retired and Obama made an audacious choice, selecting a woman of Hispanic heritage, Sonia Sotomayor.

The tilt to the Right by the Court continued when a non-profit corporation named <u>Citizens United</u> put out a documentary critical of Hillary Clinton. The narrow question was whether this constituted an ad, subject to regulation under current law? A sweeping decision now discarded all precedent, including established law such as the Taft Hartley Act and the Federal Election Campaign Act of 1971.

The decision, giving the right of free speech to corporations, eliminated in one fell swoop all prior precedent restricting speech for the purpose of preventing the voices of the few from driving out the voices of the many. The consequences are with us today. Corporations have been permitted to create further imbalance in our national dialogue. A conservative Court has now elevated money as the ultimate authority under a policy of rampant Social Darwinism.

A FITTING CODA
In 2010, Associate Justice Stevens retired at 94, after serving thirty-four years on the Court. President Obama appointed Elena Kagan, then Solicitor General as his replacement. In his last cases, Stevens wrote of his opposition to the Court's current 'strict textualists' and its tendency to ignore legislative history as well as important precedent. He quoted John Marshall when he said, 'where the mind labors to discover the design of the legislature, it seizes everything from which aid can be derived'.

Justice Scalia died in early 2016 after serving twenty-nine years on the Court. With the parties now engaged in an on-going culture war, Republican Majority Leader McConnell took the unprecedented action of refusing to allow Obama's designated appointee, Merrick Garland, to come before the Senate for confirmation. He claimed, without any precedent and contrary to congressional norms, that an election year appointment must be delayed until after the election.

THE TRUMP ERA

President Donald Trump further elevated the script of the Right Wing by turning to the Federalist Society to recommend jurists such as Neil Gorsuch to fill the Scalia vacancy in 2017. This was followed a year later with the appointment of Brett Kavanaugh to replace the retiring Anthony Kennedy.

Although there is now a supposed 5-4 conservative majority on the Court, a long-term goal of the Federalist Society and other right wing organizations, it appears that Chief Justice Roberts has started to move toward the center on a number of cases. These include decisions upholding the constitutionality of Obamacare under the taxing power as well as decisions rejecting state laws to limit Medicare funding for Planned Parenthood and access to abortion clinics.

Despite its current conservative bent, the Court has in general followed public opinion in its sudden embrace of gay rights, making those on the Right increasingly uncomfortable. Perhaps this lack of cohesion as to a particular judicial point of view may also represent an attempt by the Court to distance itself from President Trump and his disputes with the decisions of so-called 'Obama judges'. The Chief Justice notably criticized this remark when he responded: 'We do not have Obama judges or Trump judges. What we have is and extraordinary group of dedicated judges doing their level best to do equal right to those appearing before them'.

The end of this story is yet to be determined, perhaps with the upcoming elections in November and the possibility of a president who will once again harken to constitutional norms.

Nevertheless, we may have to be prepared for a showdown with a court that has increasingly moved to the Right over the past several decades, and perhaps shaped the direction of American society more than either of other two branches of government. Will a president address this by expanding the number of justices on the Court, as FDR threatened to do in the 1930's or will lifetime tenure on the Court be modified in some way?

With Congress abdicating its role in crafting legislation to meet the evolving needs of the people, the Courts have become the major player in legislating in its own way and setting the guidelines for social and economic policy. This is a role never foreseen under the Constitution, and one that may require a new set of 'checks and balances', given the Judiciary's excessive power among the three branches of government.

THOSE FIRST LADIES

While we are discussing various appointments that are critical to a successful administration for any president, it is appropriate to review the history of another member of the team who is neither appointed nor a member of the Cabinet. That would be those First Ladies.

These women have rarely been mere adornments, married to a high-powered individual in most cases. They have often been politically savvy in their own right, serving as advisors of sorts in nurturing a husband's political career. At the very least, they have provided the comfort of a shoulder to lean on in critical times to escape the burdens of office. They have also served as intermediaries in family matters, some of them more shocking than others.

THE FOUNDING ERA
Our very first, First Lady, Martha Washington, was the wealthiest widow in Virginia when the courtly Washington married her. One might have thought it was for her wealth that attracted him, as she was rather plain looking and stout. But the marriage endured and Martha proved herself to be a loyal helpmate. During the darkest days of the Revolution, when the troops were at winter quarters at Valley Forge, Martha was there as well, attending to the soldiers who were facing frostbite, dysentery and worse.

The couple had no children, probably due to Washington's being sterile from a case of smallpox, contracted in his youth. Nevertheless, he treated her two children from a prior marriage as his own.

When he reluctantly accepted the presidency as the only man who could fill the position mandated under a new Constitution, Martha was an adept hostess, conducting weekly levees for the wives of government officials with her charming down-to- earth manner that put all at ease.

The next First Lady was a total opposite. Not that Abigail Adams could not be charming as well, but her keen intelligence and literary skills set her apart from other women of the times. Even Thomas Jefferson was smitten by her formidable presence during their to-gether time in Paris at the height of the Revolution.

What her husband John lacked in tact and charm, she possessed in spades. He relied constantly on her advice and counsel, particu-larly during his presidency, when he lacked the political skills to get much accomplished. That in part is one of the reasons that Adams spent so much of his presidency back in Quincy, where Abigail preferred to spend her time.

The marriage was also a true love-match, as their letters attest to, when both were separated by a vast ocean. That passionate rela-tionship endured many months of separation, with Adams abroad in search of funds to sustain the Revolution.

Being an Adams was never easy, a truism their children learned only too well. For both husband and wife were stern taskmasters. Only their golden child, John Quincy, rose to their level of expec-tations as a future president. Their other two sons died early of alcoholism.

Thomas Jefferson's wife, Martha, died young of too many dif-ficult childbirths. Consequently, he spent his years abroad right through his presidency as a bachelor. His lifestyle would never have survived the media scrutiny of today.

For it was the African Venus, Sally Hemings, who shared his bed for much of that time and bore him several children, beginning when he was serving as our ambassador to France and continuing through his years as president.

What is lesser known is that Sally was his wife's half sister, both sharing the same father. Jefferson had promised his wife on her deathbed that he would never remarry. He kept that promise. However, it did not mean that he could not be attracted to that one woman who bore an uncanny resemblance to his wife.

The diminutive James Madison, a brilliant scholar and our fourth president, was a bachelor until his early forties. Then he met the beautiful young widow, Dolley Paine. She was everything he was not ... vivacious, outgoing, and charming. She was also an incredibly effective helpmate in promoting his career and turning the White House into that special place where all the rich and powerful in Washington yearned to be invited.

When the British were about to invade the White House during the Battle of 1812, it was said that the formidable Dolley loaded up a wagon full of valuable possessions at the very last minute, including a valuable Gilbert Stuart portrait of Washington. However, it turns out that the painting of Washington was only a copy.

Dolley, much younger than her husband, outlived him by decades, still presiding over the Capitol as its unofficial hostess. By her side was her best friend, Eliza Schuyler Hamilton, who lived well into her ninety's, dedicated to keeping alive the memory of her famous husband.

It would be decades before another formidable First Lady appeared on the scene. No doubt, Andrew Jackson's wife, Rachel Donelson, would have been one. A pipe-smoking, independent frontier woman, she married Jackson after suffering through an abusive relationship.

Apparently the paperwork ending that first marriage had not been properly executed. In the campaign of 1828, the Republicans were sure to accuse the Jacksons of a bigamous relationship, enough so that Rachel died before her husband entered the White House, supposedly of a broken heart.

The next decades marked the lead up to the Civil War. There was more than enough angry rhetoric in Washington's political life to drown out the voice of reason, including that of a First Lady.

Mary Todd Lincoln was determined to leave her mark on history as much as her husband, no matter what the cost. Born into an affluent, politically connected family in Lexington Kentucky, she aspired to marry a man who would be president. However, she had not calculated the cost of doing so.

Originally she had been her husband's superior in breeding and political savvy, helping Lincoln make his way up the political ladder. But she soon found his exceptional talents exceeding her own, which heightened her insecurities. Once in the White House, she was determined to set the standard for Washington society as the hostess supreme. When this did not work out, Mary took her anger out on her husband.

It was the death of Willie Lincoln, their golden child, of yellow fever that hastened her descent into madness. Through it all, Lincoln was a tender, understanding soul, knowing that he in part had been responsible for much of his wife's erratic behavior.

The years following the death of Lincoln, known as the Gilded Age, were more about making money than governing the country. Aside from the presidency of General Grant, these years were filled with mediocre men and their fairly mediocre wives.

THE MODERN ERA

It was only with the dawn of the Twentieth Century and the accidental presidency of Teddy Roosevelt that things started to change. TR was a veritable force of nature. His wife, Edith Carow, had been the love of his life since childhood. Only a brief, impulsive, marriage to a Boston debutante in his youth had intervened.

Her death, while delivering their first child, Alice, was a constant reminder for Edith that she had not been his first choice. Young Alice was sure to remind her stepmother of that. Even after marrying the Speaker of the House, Nicholas Longworth, Alice created lots of gossip in the Capitol, carrying on a long line of affairs that shocked the public.

Edith was her husband's intellectual equal, well read and often taming her husband's manic ways. However, it was actually TR's older sister, Bamie Roosevelt, who acted as the family prime advisor. Her home, near the Executive Mansion, was known as Little White House, where ambassadors and other dignitaries were likely to congregate.

Woodrow Wilson's second wife, Edith Bolling, whom he married in the White House upon the death of his first wife, was exceptional in ways never anticipated before or after. In 1919, her husband, having just returned from Europe and already ill, decided to travel across the country to 'sell' his League of Nations' to the American public.

The physically exhausted President suffered a severe stroke in the process, returning to the White House as a permanent invalid. This would remain hidden from the public for the duration of his term. With the assistance of White House aides and an easily deceived press, Edith Bolling Wilson assumed the role of 'president' for the next eighteen months. This ultimately led to a constitutional Amendment to cover that situation, although its terms are rather complicated and leave an appropriate solution still in doubt.

The Roaring Twenties were another decade of great wealth and hedonism, with Prohibition providing a false sense of moral authority. Warren G. Harding, the President to follow Wilson, typified the times as a congenial type who promised the country 'normalcy'. His wife Lorena, better known as 'The Duchess', was emblematic of the times. She was best known for mixing drinks, despite Prohibition, for those cronies who visited the White House for a nighttime game of poker. She would then end the evening, serving her special scrambled eggs.

The Depression ended those so-called 'good times'. In 1932, Franklin Delano Roosevelt was elected to set things right with a new approach. And with that, the image of a First Lady was altered for good by his wife, Eleanor Roosevelt.

FDR knew full well that he had married an exceptional woman. In fact, it was those qualities that attracted him when they had met. They were both Roosevelt's, distant cousins, born into great wealth. As a young adult, Eleanor was more interested in working at the Settlement House and helping the children of immigrants acclimate to a new life then she was in playing at being a debutante. That passion to help the disenfranchised and the forgotten became a lifetime mission, sometimes driving her husband to the point of great frustration as she badgered him to do more.

It was a complicated marriage, lacking the physical intimacy, which FDR found elsewhere in his long-term relationship with Lucy Mercer. Nevertheless, they made a great team. While he attended to the daunting issues facing the nation, both at home and overseas, Eleanor was actively involved in seeking justice for the working class and civil rights for the black community.

When we entered the war against Nazi tyranny, requiring that we gear up production as the 'arsenal of democracy', Eleanor made sure that workers were fairly compensated and that the black community received its fair share of the jobs.

At the end of the war, she performed the same task, this time having returning veterans receive a free college education and fair housing for their young families. With FDR's death, she went on to serve as our first ambassador to the UN, an organization her husband had nurtured at every opportunity in planning for a postwar era that would require U.S. leadership.

It was not until 1960 that another First Lady appeared, who would again bring a unique quality to her role in the White House. The marriage of John F. Kennedy and Jacqueline Bouvier was another complicated affair. Nevertheless, JFK's election brought refreshing youth and vigor to the White House after the Eisenhower years of great competence, but little style. In this age of television, all of the various family activities from Hyannisport to Washington, were watched by millions.

The First Lady in particular possessed exceptional elegance and beauty that set the nation swooning. Her clothes, her hairstyle elevated fashion in the U.S. and around the world as never before, emulated by every women to the best of her ability. The arts flourished as well, thanks to the First Lady's educated eye, including having musicians like Pablo Casals play at the White House.

The Kennedy's added another novelty, two adorable young children, Caroline and 'John John', to enthrall the public. All of this was cut short with that assassination in Dallas, another event vividly documented on television.

The nation mourned with the widow and her two small children during the heartbreaking funeral services. The nation continued the passion of 'Jackie-watching' even when she moved on, marrying Aristotle Onassis and then becoming an important editor in the publishing industry.

It would be difficult for the next few First Ladies to match this type of star power.

Lady Bird Johnson, a smart and charming Texan, had her program to beautify the landscape, while keeping her larger-than-life husband from making inappropriate remarks.

Pat Nixon was a study in rigid self-discipline, never revealing her feelings except in that heart-wrenching scene when she stood stoically by her husband's side as he resigned, rather than face impeachment.

Betty Ford's brief tenure was actually quite impactful for American women, a First Lady who preceded 'women's lib', yet also believed in being honest with the public. She was totally at ease in revealing her battle with breast cancer, her depression as well as a drinking problem. The country loved and admired her transparency.

The next rather unique First Lady was Nancy Reagan. A product of Hollywood, she projected glamour, though not quite at the level of Jackie Kennedy. Unfortunately, in a time when 'trickle down' economics began to savage the middle class, her extravagance smacked of Marie Antoinette's 'let them eat cake' moment.

Where Nancy Reagan really shone, however, was as her husband's pre-eminent advisor. Possibly only Abigail Adams surpassed her in this role. It was all done in the privacy of the bedroom. Otherwise, she made sure to gazed adoringly at her 'Ronnie' whenever he made a speech.

We would certainly have to credit Nancy Reagan for firing aides who were not sufficiently loyal to her husband. She was also possibly responsible for eliminating Reagan's talk of an 'Evil Empire' script, so that he could reach out to Mikhail Gorbachev to end the Cold War...no small feat.

The Administration of George HW Bush had the outspoken Barbara Bush speaking common sense to the American public and pushing childhood literacy, a worthy cause.

The next impressive and groundbreaking First Lady was Hillary Rodman Clinton. Possibly the most highly educated First Lady, she entered the White House with a Yale Law School degree and an impressive career in government, including participating in the Watergate hearings.

The Clintons were sold as a two-for-one package, which was not exactly what the public was looking for. Hillary's obvious abilities continued to meet with public resistance as many women seemed more threatened by her skills than prepared to embrace them. She seemed to lack an ability to connect, especially when defending her life choices and saying that she was not about to 'stay home and bake cookies'.

Both Clinton's got off to a rather rocky start, with a series of scandals lingering from their Arkansas years, mostly her husband's, a factor that would haunt her years later in her bid for the presidency.

It was actually after the White House years, as the U.S. Senator from New York, that she finally hit her stride as an effective legislator. That served to launch a drive in 2008 for the presidency, only to lose to Barack Obama in a close primary and settle for an appointment as Secretary of State in the Obama Administration.

Laura Bush was the antithesis of Hillary Clinton, a former librarian who was happy to stay home and bake cookies. Her role was primarily in tempering her husband's tendency for braggadocio, as when he declared 'Mission Accomplished' early in the disastrous war with Iraq.

Michelle Obama, the first black First Lady, was already setting records when she entered the White House, a structure built by slave labor in 1800. Like many others, the public would view her with suspicion, based on some statements made during the campaign. However, she soon proved as adept as her husband in messaging to the public and clearly stating that her first priority was her two young daughters.

Nevertheless, her outgoing charm and common sense advice made a hugely favorable impression, including planting a vegetable garden on the White House lawn and advocating healthy choices for children in particular. This ultimately had an effect on the food served in schools and through government programs.

There could not be a greater disparity between Michelle Obama and the next First Lady, Melania Trump. Setting aside her husband's performance, her role in the White House has been minimal. Ironically, she has espoused the dangers of 'childhood bullying' as her stated mission, a quality at which her husband seems to excel. It is also ironic that she is an immigrant from Slovenia considering her husband speaks so frequently of the ills of immigration.

And so we come to the end of our discussion of our First Ladies. Often, they mirrored those times, but occasionally they blazed a path for the future, in their finest moments. Many would probably confess that they were not always happy with the 'fish bowl' atmosphere they were forced to endure. However, few would not have been proud to represent the country at home and abroad for those few precious years and leave their mark on the nation's history as more than just the wife of a President.

AFTERWORD: RENEWING THE AMERICAN DREAM

This phrase represents the task that awaits every president when he or she takes office and gives that inaugural address. Those words must be uplifting, for it should always be his or her goal to lead us toward that more perfect Union, perhaps the most important phrase in our Constitution. For America will always be, for better or worse, an experiment in the ability of mankind to govern himself, or in Lincoln's words, to reach for our 'better angels'.

From the start, this nation drew millions to its shores who were escaping so-called 'hopelessness', and seeking 'hopefulness' in a better life for themselves and their loved ones.

That 'hopefulness', in Jefferson's words, was defined as 'life, liberty and the pursuit of happiness'...or more succinctly, 'the promise of America'.

Lincoln took that phrase from the Declaration of Independence and used it to define the plight of slaves who were deprived of the fruits of their labor. FDR expanded the meaning of that phrase as granting both 'freedom to' and 'freedom from'. His genius was in balancing the rights that keep government from interfering in our daily lives, while at the same time committing government to ensure each individual a life of dignity and self worth.

The Founding Fathers in 1787 would have agreed that the term 'a more perfect Union' implied the need for the Constitution to be interpreted by the Court to suit the times and keep alive the promise of America. Chief Justice John Marshall certainly recognized this point, using certain important phrases in the Constitution that gave it the elasticity necessary to meet the needs of future generations.

Balance is at the heart of the American experiment in democracy. It is what our Constitution is all about...that Madisonian finely tuned machinery of checks and balances that was achieved during that steamy summer of 1787 in the State House in Philadelphia. It was only through difficult moments of compromise during those five months, from May through September, that fifty-five founding fathers finally completed their work.

No one left Philadelphia entirely satisfied with the results. Certainly not Madison and not even that eternally optimistic bon vivant, Doctor Franklin, who famously explained the outcome of months of debate to a passerby, saying, 'A Republic, madam...if you can keep it!'

Some thought the Constitutional Convention an abject failure, while others were relieved that we had at least written a document that was far better than the abysmal Articles of Confederation it was to replace. Yet, it has turned out that the very flaws, ambiguities and omissions in this document represent its ultimate strength. For it is a work in progress...continually guiding us toward that 'more perfect Union', while providing a roadmap of procedures to maintain the guardrails of democracy.

Today we face a host of questions that are central to renewing the promise of America. Once again, we can look to our history and see how this task was handled in prior generations.

Jefferson's Republican Party was formed to address what was perceived to be a tilt toward monarchical ways by the Federalists, under Washington, the most revered man of the times. In retrospect, Hamilton's vision was more prescient, foreseeing a credit-worthy nation with institutions to gain the respect of the rest of the world community. If giants of history such as Jefferson could fail to see the future with clarity of vision, one must confess that this will not be an easy task for future generations.

Renewing the American dream will require re-establishing a constructive dialogue between our two parties and dimming the voices of those who feel otherwise. That may very well be the first step in the process.

If these musings can provide the reader with the proper context to better understand these issues and put our citizenship to good use, then this journey will have been worthwhile.

CITATIONS & ATTRIBUTIONS

CONSTITUTIONAL ISSUES

- **Prelude to the Constitution**
  - Chernow, Ron. *Washington*. New York: Penguin Press, 2010.

- **Conceived in Racism**
  - Blight, David W. *Frederick Douglass: Prophet of Freedom*. New York: Simon & Schuster, 2018.

  - Foner, Eric. *Reconstruction America's Unfinished Revolution, 1863-1877*. New York: HarperCollins, 2014.

- **An Era of Redemption**
  - Goodwin, Doris Kearns. *Leadership In Turbulent Times*. New York: Simon & Schuster, 2018.

- **Vital Phrases in the Constitution**
  - Smith, Jean Edward. *John Marshall: Definer of a Nation*. New York: Henry Holt and Company, 1996.

- **The Saving Grace of Liberalism**
  - ○ Lepore, Jill. "In Every Dark Hour." *The New Yorker*, February 3, 2020.

- **The Future of Impeachment**
  - – Rohde, David. "Sword and Shield." *The New Yorker*, January 20, 2020.

  - – "Timeline: Every Big Move in the Mueller Investigation." *Axios*, February 16, 2018. https://www.axios.com/mueller-russia-investigation-timeline-indictments-70433acd-9ef7-424d-aa01-b962ae5c9647.html.

UNIQUELY AMERICAN ISSUES

- **Benjamin Franklin: The First American**
  - – Isaacson, Walter. *Benjamin Franklin An American Life*. New York: Simon & Schuster, 2003.

- **Stymied By Myths**
  - – Saletan, William. "The Trump Pandemic: A blow-by-blow account of how the president killed thousands of Americans." *Slate*, August 9, 2020. https://slate.com/news-and-politics/2020/08/trump-coronavirus-deaths-timeline.html.

- **Balancing Fiction and Reality**
  - – Albright, Madeleine. *Fascism*. New York: HarperCollins, 2018.

  - – Rees, Laurence. *Hitler's Charisma*. New York: Pantheon Books, 2012.

COMPONENTS OF PRESIDENTIAL GREATNESS

- **Presidents Who Mirror the Times**
  - Brands, H. W. *T.R.* New York: Basic Books, 1997.

  - McCullough, David. *Mornings on Horseback.* New York: Simon & Schuster, 1982.

- **A New Birth of Freedom**
  - Smith, Jean Edward. *Eisenhower in War and Peace.* New York: Random House, 2012.

- **Presidential Messaging**
  - Holzer, Harold. *Lincoln at Cooper Union.* New York: Simon & Schuster, 2004.

  - Wills, Garry. *Lincoln at Gettysburg.* New York: Simon & Schuster, 1992.

- **Presidential Swagger**
  - Meacham, Jon. *American Lion.* New York: Random House, 2008.

- **Addressing Mob Rule**
  - McCullough, David. *John Adams.* New York: Simon & Schuster, 2001.

- **A President's Untold Story**
  - McCullough, David. *Truman.* New York: Simon & Schuster, 1993.

- **The Fox and the Hedgehog**
  - Chernow, Ron. *Alexander Hamilton.* New York: Penguin Press, 2004.

- Gaddis, John Lewis. *On Grand Strategy*. Penguin Press, 2018.

- **The Hallmarks of Democracy**
  - Sandburg, Carl. *Abraham Lincoln The Prairie Years and The War Years*. New York: Houghton Mifflin Harcourt, 1954.

- **Wartime Presidents**
  - Brands, H. W. *Traitor to His Class*. New York: Anchor Books, 2009.

  - O'Toole, Patricia. *The Moralist*. New York: Simon & Schuster, 2018.

CHANGING POLITICS

- **Party Politics: Addressing Polarization**
  - Tomasky, Michael. *If We Can Keep It*. New York: W.W. Norton, 2019.

- **Politics and Religion**
  - Haberman, Clyde. "Religion and Right-Wing Politics: How Evangelicals Reshaped Elections." *The New York Times*, October 28, 2018.

- **Reinventing The New Normal**
  - "Coronavirus Will Change the World Permanently. Here's How." POLITICO, March 19, 2020. https://www.politico.com/news/magazine/2020/03/19/coronavirus-effect-economy-life-society-analysis-covid-135579.

- **Leadership in Unexpected Places**
  - Balz, Dan. "As Washington Stumbled, Governors Stepped to the Forefront." *The Washington Post*, May 3, 2020.

- **Fundraising: A Full Time Job**
  - Goldmacher, Shane. "Biden Pours Millions Into Facebook Ads, Blowing Past Trump's Record." *The New York Times,* June 8, 2020.

  - Ellis, Joseph J. *American Sphinx.* New York: Vintage Books, 1998.

  - Marantz, Andrew. "#Winning." *The New Yorker,* March 9, 2020.

- **A Changing Political Landscape**
  - Brands, H.W. *Reagan.* New York: Anchor Books, 2016.

  - Komlos, John. "Column: How Reaganomics, Deregulation and Bailouts Led to the Rise of Trump." *PBS,* April 25, 2016. https://www.pbs.org/newshour/economy/column-how-reaganomics-deregulation-and-bailouts-led-to-the-rise-of-trump.

- **Trump's War Against The Government**
  - Christie, Chris. *Let Me Finish.* New York: Hachette Books, 2019.

  - Drutman, Lee. "America Is Now the Divided Republic the Framers Feared." *The Atlantic,* January 2020.

  - Lewis, Michael. *The Fifth Risk.* New York: W. W. Norton & Company, 2018.

TROUBLING TRENDS

- **White Nationalism**
  - Parker, Ashley, and Felicia Sonmez. "As Trump Stands by Charlottesville Remarks, Rise of White-nationalist Violence Becomes an Issue in 2020 Presidential Race." *The Washington Post,* April 29, 2019.

  - Serwer, Adam. "White Nationalism's Deep American Roots." *The Atlantic,* April 2019.

- **Isolationism versus Globalism**
  - MacMillan, Margaret. "Why the U.S. Has Spent 200 Years Flip-Flopping Between Isolationism and Engagement." History.com, March 16, 2018. https://www.history.com/news/american-isolationism.

- **The History of Income Inequality**
  - Koebler, Jason. "How Elon Musk Is Like a 19th Century Railroad Baron." *Vice,* January 29, 2015. https://www.vice.com/en_us/article/wnj78z/how-elon-musk-is-like-a-19th-century-robber-baron.

  - Walsh, Toby. "Facebook and Google Are Run by Today's Robber Barons. Break Them Up." *The Guardian,* October 23, 2018.https://www.theguardian.com/technology/2018/oct/23/facebook-and-google-are-run-by-todays-robber-barons-break-them-up.

- **Military Spending and National Priorities**
  - Matthews, Jessica T. "The New Nuclear Threat." *The New York Review of Books,* August 20, 2020.

- Smithberger, Mandy. "Why Are We Still Prioritizing Military Spending?" *The Nation*, May 4, 2020.

- **The Non-Growth Economy of the Future**
  - Cassidy, John. "Steady State." *The New Yorker*, February 10, 2020.

  - Remnick, David. 2011. *The Bridge*. New York: Vintage Books.

  - Semuels, Alana. "Does the Economy Really Need to Keep Growing Quite So Much?" *The Atlantic*, November 2016.

MAKING THE RIGHT APPOINTMENTS

- **Selecting The Right Chief-of-Staff**
  - Whipple, Chris. *The Gatekeepers*. New York: Broadway Books, 2018.

- **The Evolving Role of the Secretary of State**
  - Baker III, James A., and Thomas M. DeFrank. *The Politics of Diplomacy*. New York: G.P. Putnam's Sons, 1995.

- **Appointing Justices in a Contentious Era**
  - Stevens, John Paul. *The Making of a Justice*. New York: Little, Brown and Company, 2019.